MEDUSA'S MIRROR

MEDUSA'S MIRROR

Studies in German Literature

By

AUGUST CLOSS

LONDON
THE CRESSET PRESS
MCMLVII

Printed in Great Britain by
The Camelot Press Ltd., London and Southampton

PREFACE

'A man in print . . . shall stand, like the old weathercock over Paul's steeple, to be beaten with all storms': Thomas Dekker, *The Wonderful Year 1603*.

I cherish the hope that this collection of essays and pieces will find a place not only among students of German but also among lovers of literature in general.

The chapters of the present collection are not forced into a unity. But under the title 'Medusa's Mirror' I have gathered several of my short literary compositions in which directly or indirectly the theme of Reality and Poetic Symbol is dealt with. Analysis and interpretation are, I trust, kept in balance. There is also an outer connecting link of the subject matter to be found, since almost all sections of this book, heterogeneous as they may appear to be, are dedicated to the study of German literature. Some have been revised, others are entirely new. Occasional repetition is unavoidable in order to retain the unity of each chapter. Most important and difficult German quotations have been translated into English or paraphrased.

In a planned sequel to this volume I hope to be able to dedicate myself to the great essayists and prose writers: F. Kafka, Thomas Mann, H. Hesse, H. von Hofmannsthal, Ernst Jünger, H. Broch, and others.

I am grateful to all those Publishers and Editors who have generously allowed me to reprint in revised form articles of mine which have appeared in journals and book editions: the *Modern Language Quarterly*, University of Washington Seattle; the *Fédération Internationale des Langues et Littératures Modernes* (Proceedings of the fifth and sixth Triennial Congresses, Florence and Oxford); *German Life and Letters*, Oxford; The Phoenix Press, London; Fred Marnau's *New Road 4, Directions in European Art and Letters*, Grey Walls Press, London; Basil Blackwell's *German Texts*, Oxford; The *Contemporary Review*, London. I am also grateful to Messrs. John Lane, The Bodley Head Ltd. who have allowed me to reprint extracts from G. Dunlop's translation of *The Plays of G. Büchner*.

No attempt has been made to offer a comprehensive bibliography, and only such publications are mentioned as are immediately related to my argument.

The book is introduced by a *Prelude* and concluded by an *Epilogue* which is by no means exhaustive but simply intended as an indication of some powerful new literary trends appearing simultaneously in England, in the U.S.A. and on the Continent.

Above all, I wish to acknowledge my sincere thanks to those friends without whose encouragement the publication of the present book would not have been possible, and to my daughter Elizabeth for helping to correct the proofs and compile the Index. My profoundest debt is to her to whose memory this book is dedicated.

Contents

Prelude: INTUITION AND INTELLECT   I

I SUBSTANCE AND SYMBOL IN POETRY   8

II MINNESANG AND ITS SPIRITUAL BACKGROUND   43

III TRISTAN UND ÎSOLT: Gottfried von Strassburg   57

IV AUSTRIA'S PLACE IN GERMAN LITERATURE   83

V GOETHE AND KIERKEGAARD   96

VI FRIEDRICH HÖLDERLIN   113

VII NOVALIS: 'Hymns to the Night'   134

VIII NIHILISM AND MODERN GERMAN DRAMA: Grabbe and Büchner   147

IX GEORG TRAKL: An Austrian Poet   164

X RAINER MARIA RILKE'S POETIC VISION   169

XI STEFAN GEORGE'S 'THIRD HUMANISM'   185

XII GERHART HAUPTMANN: L'ultimo dei giganti   202

XIII GERMAN POETRY AFTER 1945   213

XIV RECONCILIATION: Bernt von Heiseler's 'Versöhnung'   222

Epilogue

I THE EUROPEAN SCENE: Some Trends in Present Day Literary Criticism   225

II THE POET AND HIS AGE: Man's Mortal Cleavage: The Mass Age   252

Index   259

PRELUDE

Intuition and Intellect

THE ORIGIN OF all poetry is shrouded in mystery and has for centuries gripped the imagination of distinguished writers and critics. To mention only one outstanding example, Jacques Maritain's *Creative Intuition in Art and Poetry*, its rich material, with and without comment, bears testimony to the fascination which that subject has for us since the days of Nietzsche and particularly nowadays, when the belief in the divine origin of poetry is challenged.

The ancient Muses we know cherished poetry and music. We hear of Hermes, that he played on the strings of a tortoise-shell, singing his songs. The Icelandic *Elder Edda* also deals with the divine origin of poetry, for example the *Hóvamól*, in which the youthful Odin hangs on the Weltesche Yggdrasil, like Christ on the Cross, for nine whole nights, wounded by a spear. He has dedicated himself to the sacrifice. He falls to the ground but the magic runes and the mead refresh him, and he thus grows and thrives:

> I ween that I hung on the windy tree,
>   Hung there for nights full nine;
> With the spear I was wounded, and offered I was
> To Odhin, myself to myself,
> On the tree that none may ever know
>   What root beneath it runs.[1]

In this poem, full of rules for prudence and pieces of prover-bial advice, the famous lines on the gaining of the potion of inspiration are also inserted.

Odin's mead is the magic potion Odrerir which a giant's beautiful daughter Gunnlod guards in the mountains, and which Odin then cunningly wins from her in a love adventure. The Kwasir saga in the *Bragaroedur* of the *Snorra Edda* tells us

---

[1] *Hóvamól* 139, trans. H. A. Bellows, *The Poetic Edda*, New York, 1923.

about it. The basis is a saga about mountain maidens who entice the hero into their realm. The above tale of the magic potion which inspires man to poetry is connected with it, and with that of the origin of Kwasir: the Asen and the Wanen make peace, they spit into a vessel, and from the spittle they make Kwasir, a wise man. But two dwarfs kill him; they mix his blood with honey and prepare mead from it which turns human beings into poets and wise men. A giant gains possession of this magic potion, and his daughter Gunnlod protects it in the mountains. Odin slithers in the form of a snake through a hole in the mountain and steals the potion and then carries it off to Valhalla in the disguise of an eagle. Pursued by the giant, Odin loses some of his precious booty; the eagle's droppings are the poet's divine share. Similarly, Zeus's eagle takes the nectar from a mountain, and Indra fetches his precious Soma.

Lady Gregory in her *Gods and Fighting Men. The Story of the Thuatha Danaan* tells us of another secret source of poetic inspiration:

> And they had a well below the sea where the nine hazels of wisdom were growing; that is, the hazels of inspiration and of the knowledge of poetry. And their leaves and their blossoms would break out in the same hour, and would fall on the well in a shower that raised the purple wave. And then the five salmon that were waiting there would eat the nuts, and their colour would come out in the red spots of their skin, and any person that would eat one of those salmon would know all wisdom and all poetry. And there were seven streams of wisdom that sprang from that well and turned back to it again; and the people of many arts have all drank from that well. . . .[1]

We are here reminded of Shelley's *Defence of Poetry* where the poetic song is called the image of life, expressed in wisdom and eternal truth.

It is a Christian-Platonic-Aristotelean philosophy of art which suggests that 'the potentiality of the raw material was predestined to receive the informing act, which was modelled on the plan or intention of the Eternal Mind'.[2] This confirms Michelangelo's belief in an inherently necessary expression, cf. his Sonnet, translated by Longfellow:

[1] P. 2.   [2] Robert Sencourt, *The Consecration of Genius*, pp. 178-9.

2

Non ha l'ottimo artista alcun concetto
Ch'un marmo solo in se non circonscriva
Col suo soverchio, e solo a quello arriva
La man che obbidisce all' intelletto.

Nothing the greatest artist can conceive
That every marble block doth not confine
Within itself, and only its design
The hand that follows intellect can achieve.

Similarly, in poetry word and mind, style and spirit are
essentially a unity—a unity which in the sacred hours of poetic
inspiration reaches into the depths of the unconscious.

From the fourth part, sixteenth Book, of *Dichtung und
Wahrheit* we learn that Goethe's inspiration poured forth not
capriciously but rather against his will: Goethe ran to his desk,
did not even give himself time to set right his writing-pad, but
wrote down his poem 'from beginning to end, without moving
from the spot', as if in a fever: 'von Anfang bis zu Ende,
ohne mich von der Stelle zu rühren.'

We hear also of similar occurrences of nocturnal inspiration
in the life of Petrarch. Goethe experienced times when he
could produce a printed page with ease daily.[1] As in the case
of Goethe or Hölderlin, and indeed of all true poets, creation
begins unconsciously. T. Vischer's words could certainly be
applied here: 'Everything that lies in the light of the mind,
was there at first in the veiled form of instinct.'[2] In this connexion we also think of Schiller's lines in *Die Künstler*:

Was wir als Schönheit hier empfunden,
Wird einst als Wahrheit uns entgegengehn.

Schiller himself needed a musical mood before his creative
activity, cf. his letter of 18 March 1796 to Goethe: 'I find that
at the beginning there is feeling without a decided or clear
object; this is only formed later. A certain musical frame of
mind precedes, and only then the poetic idea follows on this.'
We must not forget that poets and singers were originally
identical. Schiller's letter of 27 March 1801 to Goethe is also
significant: 'In experience the poet too begins only with the
unconscious. . . . Without such a dark and mighty totality of
idea, which precedes all technicalities, no poetic work can arise.'

[1] Cf. 235, III Eckermann.   [2] *Das Schöne und die Kunst.*

3

Lyrical poetry is, according to Hölderlin, 'the metaphor of a feeling'. Goethe, for whom learning did not necessarily mean good judgement (Eckermann II) and who often regarded scholars' problems sceptically as merely problems of bare existence, was no friend of explanations of poems. He, more than any other, understood the mysterious power of form in poetry; he also knew, as did Rilke later, that a deep intimacy with things is very necessary in order to create a poem (Eckermann II) and that he 'who, like Claude Lorrain, has not the whole world at his command, will seldom produce anything good, even with the best use of ideas'.

Friedrich Schlegel expressed a similar opinion in his letters to Wilhelm (8 May 1793 and 28 August 1793). Hebbel calls the often all-too-foggy and fruitless discussion on lyrical poetry an 'etymologisches Becherspiel'. H. von Kleist reaches the heart of the matter when he says: 'We do not know, but it is a certain condition of ours that knows.'

Penetrating light is thrown on the depth of poetical experience and formation out of Dionysiac chaos by Nietzsche's *Birth of Tragedy from the Spirit of Music*, in which he says that the lyrical poet forms all the passionate emotions from the whispering of affection to the raging of madness. In as far as he creates music in images, he himself rests in 'the calm sea of Apolline contemplation', although everything which he sees through the medium of music is 'in urgent, seeking movement. . . .'

Nietzsche calls lyric poetry an 'effulguration of music in pictures and concepts. . . .' Music cannot be will, because as such it would have to be wholly banished from the domain of art, for the will, in Schopenhauer's sense of the word, is the unaesthetic-in-itself. 'Yet music appears as will. For in order to express the phenomenon of music in pictures, the lyrist requires all the stirrings of passion, from the whispering of infant desire to the roaring of madness. Under the impulse to speak of music in Apollonian symbols, he conceives of all nature, and himself therein, only as the eternally willing, desiring, longing existence. But in so far as he interprets music by means of pictures, he himself rests in the quiet calm of Apollonian contemplation, however much all around him which he beholds through the

4

medium of music is in a state of confused and violent motion. . . .' 'The sphere of poetry does not lie outside the world like some fantastic impossibility of a poet's imagination: it seeks to be the very opposite, the unvarnished expression of truth. . . . The Dionysiac Greek seeks truth and nature in their most potent form: he sees himself metamorphosed into the satyr.'[1]

While, as we heard, Schiller sought inspiration through a musical atmosphere, in the case of Richard Wagner a 'hallucination' preceded the creative construction, to which he added the music of words. That exalted feeling, an especial 'psychic state of ecstasy', as for example Otto Ludwig called it, is the basic necessity of all poetic creation and corresponds to the Christian belief of St. Augustine in love and grace. Indeed one could consider the praise of Christian love in the thirteenth chapter of the *First Epistle to the Corinthians* from the Apostle Paul as a paraphrase for genius:

> Though I speak with the tongues of men and of angels, and have not love I am become as a sounding brass or a tinkling cymbal.

The secret of inspiration itself was enticing as a subject for poetic representation in the modern lyric, as for example in Paul Valéry's *La Pythie* where the contrast between passive contemplation and active life or creative conception and spiritual transformation of the passionate inspiration is poetically symbolized in the virginal priestess who is overcome and made pregnant by an external power. Only in surrender does La Pythie gain the inner victory and compromise between body and mind: 'Mes deux natures vont s'unir.'

The difficult conflict is carried on in the borderland between the spiritual and sensual spheres, in which the limits of personality are ultimately lifted. Poetry is, according to Paul Valéry's conception in *Les Pas*, not only the vessel of God, but also created from equally important contrasts of mastery and devotion, a seeking and a finding: 'Douceur d'être et de n'être pas.'[2]

True lyric poets such as Goethe, Hölderlin, Shelley, Mörike

[1] *The Birth of Tragedy or Hellenism and Pessimism*, trans. by W. A. Haussmann, ed. by Oscar Levy.
[2] Cf. C. M. Bowra, *The Heritage of Symbolism*, 1943, pp. 30ff.

5

and others have recognized the depths of such a conflict when they look to the poet as the truest and noblest of mankind. 'Poets are the creators and creation of their times', says Shelley in the preface to *Prometheus Unbound*, and in his *Defence of Poetry* he calls creative capacity the basis of all knowledge:

> Poetry . . . is at once the centre and circumference of knowledge . . . but when composition begins, inspiration is already on the decline, and the most glorious poetry that has ever been communicated to the world is probably a feeble shadow of the original conceptions of the poet. I appeal to the greatest poets of the present day, whether it is not an error to assert that the finest passages of poetry are produced by labour and study. . . . Milton conceived the *Paradise Lost* as a whole before he executed it in portions. . . .

In the face of such poetry, Paul Valéry's verse appears to be the fruit of years of difficult struggling. The amazing thing in Valéry's work is that this very weight of production could nevertheless ripen to poetic inspiration and still more, that this inner struggle itself became the object of his lyrical mood. Valéry writes about poetry itself and about its creative origin. His poetry is analytical autobiography. Such a lyrical flight cannot in the very end be made intellectually clear. The motivation of it is often the most unlikely happening, a waiting full of foreboding before the decision, above all, however, a purely physical feeling. The deeper meaning of *La Pythie* is just that *in* the body and *through* the body, the decisive conflict is and must be fought out.

Genius, as Schopenhauer says, is objective introspection. By this, the world as a 'Creation of Reason' is distinguished from that of an arbitrary, instinctive compulsion. Reason and self-knowledge dominate the genius's will, hence the ultimate optimism of a Goethe or the contemplation of a Jean Paul, or an effect as sombre as the rainbow over a storm-tossed abyss.

Art and Nature must merge into each other; cf. Horace's *Ingenium et studium*:

> . . . ego nec studium sine divite vena,
> nec rude quid prosit video ingenium; alterius sic
> altera poscit opem res, et conjurat amice. . . .

In Klopstock's *Die Lerche und die Nachtigall* (1796), Nature

(Lark) and Art (Nightingale) become the leit-motif of the poem:

> Wer den Gesang der Nachtigall und Bardalens vereinet,
> Singet schöner als sie,

and Goethe's *Natur und Kunst* (1802):

> Kunst und Natur, sie scheinen sich zu fliehen
> Und haben sich, eh' man es denkt, gefunden.

In poetry the union and merging of these counter-striving forces is fulfilled. Thus Stefan George's maxim is true: 'Let there be nothing where the word for it is lacking':

> Kein ding sei wo das wort gebricht.

For Hölderlin, poetic utterance is a sign emanating from divine powers.

Formal verse seems to be the only means of establishing one's inmost poetic vision coherently. Yet the mere outward division of lines is in itself not as essential as is so often imagined; it does, however, serve as a reflected word-picture of the *inner* character of a poem, which can become very important, especially where so-called 'free verse' is concerned. In every line there is 'ethos' which, on the threshold of our century, has led Arno Holz, etc., away into experimental channels.

The unifying rhythmic beat of waves, the swaying up and down in the life of the poem, is the last incontestable measure for grasping free rhythmic movement.

Apart from its rhythmic movement and imagery, the essence of a poetic expression also rests in the musical power of a word or sentence or paragraph or syntactic period, for the poem, we believe, does not derive its origin only from the intellect; although reflection, as for instance in C. F. Meyer's poems *Der tote Achill* and *Pentheus*, can become the direct impulse of a song, the main spring of the rhythmically expressed sound-form lies in layers deeper than those of the intellectual powers of a poet.

I

Substance and Symbol in Poetry

To Generalize is to be an Idiot.
To Particularize is the Alone Distinction of Merit. . . .

The sun's light, when he unfolds it,
Depends on the organ which beholds it.

W. BLAKE.

IN LYRICAL POETRY what secret underlies the limitless flux and the process of its condensation of which Goethe speaks in the poem *Lied und Gebilde*:[1] 'Schöpft des Dichters reine Hand, Wasser wird sich ballen'? According to Novalis, poetry is translation; our very existence is a metaphor of the spirit, a universal trope: 'Am Ende ist alle Poesie Übersetzung. Unser Dasein ein Universaltropus des Geistes.' We ask ourselves: Where can one find the clue to solve the mystery of poetic form? Is there an absolute standard? How often do we meet with intriguing opinions on the subject in scholarly researches, which, according to Eckermann's *Gespräche mit Goethe*, cannot yet be regarded as displaying real judgement. How differently, for example, antithesis is employed by different poets and in different ages, particularly in the Baroque, or by Schiller, Heine, Nietzsche among others! A fair judgement can certainly be formed only from a knowledge of the central point in a work of art; the inherent rhythm and symbolic language and ethos of a poet.

To this one must add the individual claim and demand which the material makes on the creator and the character of a work of art. Michelangelo, for example, seeks to apprehend the latent form potentially inherent in material such as stone, and he points out in his fifteenth sonnet that the form is already predestined in the unhewn block of marble.

The old conception that enthusiasm is the source of poetic

<hr>

[1] *West-Östlicher Divan.*

inspiration is incontestable, yet modern (particularly contemporary) poets and critics (e.g. Paul Valéry, R. M. Rilke,
and Louis MacNeice in his personal essay on *Modern Poetry*)
strongly challenge the foggy notion of a purely spontaneous
creative force in life. A. E. Housman calls poetry 'a secretion:
whether a natural secretion like turpentine in the fir, or a
morbid secretion, like the pearl in the oyster'. This is no new
idea. In *Timon of Athens* Shakespeare makes the poet say:
'Our poetry is as a gum, which oozes From whence it is nour-
ished; the fire i' the flint Shows not till it be struck. . . .'[1]
But Gottfried Benn (1886-1956) goes much further and contrasts the power of the intellect with that of 'worthless joy in
existence': cf. *Sils-Maria*:

> Doch wer die Stunden denkt:
> ihre Welle, ihr Spiel, ihr Wesen,
> der hat die Stunden gelenkt. . . .

Benn's poem *Wer allein ist* is a rejection of Goethe's 'Die and be
re-born':

> Nicht mehr Stirb und nicht mehr Werde:
> Formstill sieht ihn die Vollendung an.

Benn seeks 'Entwicklungsfremdheit' in his *Statische Gedichte*.
Form alone is to him 'Glaube und Tat', belief and action; life
is a 'niederer Wahn', petty illusion. In his 'Marburger Rede',
Probleme der Lyrik (1951), he advocates the so-called 'absolute
poem' in place of the poem of lyrical mood. The absolute poem
is a product of artistry. It is the supreme endeavour on the part
of the intellectual and isolated artist to experience his own Ego
as essential content in a world of perishing values; cf. also
F. R. Leavis's *New Bearings in English Poetry* (1932): 'English
poetry in future must develop (if at all) along some other line
than that running from the Romantics through Tennyson,
Swinburne, *A Shropshire Lad* and Rupert Brooke', i.e. the new
direction is to come from T. S. Eliot, W. H. Auden, etc. The
absolute poem, according to G. Benn, is that which is left of a
poem when through a process of distillation the artist has
purified and cleared it of all dregs such as mood—atmosphere—
'profundity'. This is the antithesis to Shelley's view: 'When

[1] Act I, Scene I.

composition begins, inspiration is already on the decline.'
According to G. Benn's fashionable diagnosis of style the
following four symptoms betray an outworn mood or mode of
poetry: Andichten, Wie, Farbenskala, seraphischer Ton:

1. The Romantic address to Nature can be an integral part
of some perfect poems such as Eichendorff's *Sehnsucht* or Goethe's
An den Mond, but 'their form as expression is more than a
hundred years old.'

2. The excessive use of similes introduced with 'as' and 'like',
is said to weaken (through epic and journalistic elements) the
creative tension of a poem. No doubt Rilke seems to be an
exception, cf. particularly Rilke's poem: *Geburt der Venus* and
its many similes prefaced by *wie*: wie ein junges grünes Blatt,
wie Monde, wie eine junge Frucht, wie ein Springbrunnen,
wie ein Blumenstiel, wie Hälse von Schwänen, wie Morgen-
wind, wie Segel, von der Ferne voll, wie aus Umarmung, and
above all the precious and startling simile:

> wie ein Bestand von Birken im April,
> warm, leer und unverborgen lag die Scham.
>
> *lay, like a group of silver birch in April,*
> *warm, empty, all unhidden, the vagina.*[1]

3. G. Benn condemns the vague application of colour or the
traffic in words which once sounded new and which wear off all
too quickly (e.g. 'steilen': to rise perpendicularly).

4. The seraphic tone all too often at the very start of a
poem, propels the reader into 'heavenly spheres'. Instead of
this, many a present-day poet hammers into the reader slang,
jazz and cant expressions of his time. But he does not direct
his verse 'to humanity'. Although he demands actuality, not
l'art pour l'art ('Man muß dicht am Stier kämpfen': one
must fight close to the bull), he yet seeks to master the 'absolute
poem', i.e. a poem *without* belief, a poem *without* hope, and a
poem which is addressed to *nobody*—but which claims to be
metaphysical. Its relentless law is static expression and clarity
of style. It is not a matter of private, subjective concern, but of
highest intellectual achievement.

Specialization seems to G. Benn to be the only anchor in the

---

[1] '*Selected Poems*. Rainer Maria Rilke', trans. by J. B. Leishman, The Hogarth
Press, London.

absence of a spiritual centre or of a 'Gesamtkunstwerk' in our twentieth century.

The search for pure style and absolute form is in certain ways a welcome purifying reaction against the chaotically eclectic blending of styles in the time of our grandparents and parents and indeed even in the present day; cf. H. Sedlmayr's *Verlust der Mitte* (1948, 1951[2]), where the fine arts of the nineteenth and twentieth centuries are pointed out as symptoms and symbols of our spiritual situation. In this age of glass, concrete and iron structures, the machine becomes the ruler of the masses and of form values, cf. our streets with their super-garages, our cinemas, offices, and factories. Churches of concrete, so-called 'soul-garages', sports-stadiums, and sky-scrapers stand side by side with pseudo-Gothic and pseudo-Greek buildings. Boarding houses, students' unions, etc., adorn their façades with Corinthian columns; railway stations have Gothic steeples, or they look like Swiss chalets. Gigantic insurance palaces of steel and cement with their dazzling light-effects and skylons are cool witnesses of the triumph of the engineer over the architect.

In the most recent period of the rejection of Baroque orna-ment and of the turning towards total standardisation and geometrical, anti-human and inorganic style (cf. the works by Henry Moore, Franz Marc, Picasso; Cubism, Surrealism, etc.), the European becomes more than ever susceptible to the dark forces of existence, for which there is no Goethean counter-balance: see, e.g., F. Werfel's *Stern der Ungeborenen* (which has a strong resemblance to the art of Hieronymus Bosch and Brueghel), the satirical pictures of G. Grosz, also Thomas Mann's *Doktor Faustus* or E. Langgässer's *Das Unauslöschliche Siegel* or Walt Disney's phantasies, etc.

At the same time, specialization in art and business is ever increasing; it claims absolute mastery over its own particular subject. But this striving after 'pure style' is the death of the so-called 'Gesamtkunstwerk', which through the Church was possible in the Middle Ages, and, for the last time in the history of European culture, in the aesthetic world through Richard Wagner's Bayreuth Festivals.

Now, however, life, religion, science, and art are split up into specialized compartments, a fact which is already most uncannily reflected in the speech of the 'Low' and 'High Brows'. Later, we shall see how T. S. Eliot, W. H. Auden, and others, are attempting to win back again the lost sense of a unity of existence. But the real trouble lies deeper: if we are not to wither we need a new spiritual bed-rock for the survival of our European cultural life.

Pure seeing has already been advocated by Cézanne; instead of lines, he painted spots of colour; the subject-matter (whether human or an inanimate thing) is of secondary concern. *Pure 'garden art'* also tends to become autonomous and to renounce sculpture as well as architecture. *Pure architecture* scorns the ornament (cf. Le Corbusier, A. Loos, etc.). *Pure sculpture* avoids the 'painterly' style and any bombast of expression; its effect, alas, is often 'as dead as plaster'; compare Bernini with modern sculptures.

Poetry, too, is falling a victim to the purge through its 'professional' specialists; its radical and fashionable representative is Gottfried Benn. His interpretation of the modern poet is, in spite of obvious differences, clearly if not consciously, rooted in Nietzsche's aesthetic concept of the artist in his *Birth of Tragedy*:

> The artist has already surrendered his subjectivity in the Dionysian process; the picture which now shows to him his oneness with the heart of the world, is a dream-scene, which embodies the primordial contradiction and primordial pain, together with the primordial joy of appearance. The 'I' of the lyrist sounds therefore from the abyss of being: its 'subjectivity' in the sense of the modern aesthetes, is a fiction . . . the pictures of the lyrist are nothing but *his very* self and, as it were, only different projections of himself, on account of which he as the moving centre of this world is entitled to say 'I': only of course this self is not the same as that of the waking, empirically real man, but the only verily existent and self-resting at the basis of things, by means of the images whereof the lyric genius sees through even to this basis of things. . . . Hence all our knowledge of art is at bottom quite illusory, because, as knowing persons we are not one and identical with the Being who, as the sole author and spectator of this comedy of art, prepares a perpetual entertainment for himself. Only in so far as the genius in the act of artistic production coalesces with this primordial artist of the world, does he get a glimpse of the eternal essence of art, for in this state he is, in a marvellous

manner, like the weird picture of the fairy tale which can at will turn its eyes and behold itself; he is now at once subject and object, at once poet, actor and spectator (l.c.).

Thus, according to Nietzsche as well as to Benn, only as an aesthetic phenomenon is existence justified.

The story of the poet's life and trials is, however not altogether irrelevant, although the work of art must in itself be more important than everything else. We must, naturally, also take into account what the poet inherits, i.e. literary concepts and forms, the tradition of imagery and particularly language. What is possible for a Klopstock, was not yet possible for a Christian Günther. But, of course, the poet's own biography can have a decisive influence on his expression, too. If we know, for example, that H. Leuthold's split personality drove him to madness but his verse to formal perfection, then it is just this contrast between Leuthold's tragic fate and pure command of form that has immense meaning for us: cf. *Der Waldsee*:

Wie bist du schön, du tiefer blauer See! . . .

Einst kannt' ich eine Seele, ernst, voll Ruh,
die sich der Welt verschloß mit sieben Siegeln,
die, rein und tief, geschaffen schien wie du,
nur um den Himmel in sich abzuspiegeln.

We do not want to speak, however, in generalizing terms and say that genius is always a form of madness, as, on the other hand, the pathological state of mind is by no means identical with genius, but F. Grillparzer is in a certain way right when he says: 'Ich glaube, daß das Genie nichts geben kann, als was es selbst in sich gefunden und daß es nie eine Leidenschaft oder Gesinnung schildern wird, als die es selbst als Mensch in seinem Busen trägt. . . .'

The concept of superior strength as inseparable from disability or moral defect is the subject of Edmund Wilson's brilliant study, *The Wound and the Bow* (1929). The author traces his theme back to Sophocles's tragedy *Philoctetes* in which the hero is equipped with an invincible bow and is suffering from an incurable wound. There are plenty of other examples in literature and legend: from *Wayland the Smith* to Th. Mann's *Dr. Faustus* in which the hero consciously

13

contracts a terrible disease in order to release in himself creative forces, or to Dickens's two Scrooges, etc. The bow (the creative activity) and the wound (the physical or psychological injury) mysteriously belong to each other.[1]

If, therefore, O. Walzel in his *Kunstwerk* claims that the poet's life story can contribute nothing to his poetry 'Was es nicht selbst enthält', then that remark cannot stand the test, especially when we think of Goethe's *Harzreise im Winter*, a poem that does not make the question concerning its creator at all superfluous; we can again refer to the above-mentioned Heinrich Leuthold or to Ricarda Huch's bold metaphor: 'Edler Schaft, du Marmorsäule, schlanke . . .' where the most extreme self-revelation is expressed in the love of woman to man; cf. also Rilke's Sonnet XVI, part 1: 'Du mein Freund, bist einsam . . .' about which Rilke wrote to his wife Clara:[2] 'One must know or guess—that Sonnet XVI is addressed to a dog', or cf. Rilke's late poem:

> Vom Zeichner dringend hingeballter Schatten
> Hinter das nur noch scheinende Gesicht:
> So kommt die Nacht dem reinen Stern zustatten.
>
> Da ist ein Ding, das alles unterbricht,
> Wozu die Dinge sich verstanden hatten;
> Denn, da es wurde, siehe, war es nicht.
>
> O langer Weg zum schuldlosen Verzicht,
> O Mühe zum ermächtigten Ermatten.

> *That ball of shadow sketched with such insistence*
> *behind the new only apparent face:*
> *thus night will come to the pure star's assistance.*
>
> *Here is a thing that's ventured to displace*
> *all the conventions of a thing's existence,*
> *for when it started it has run its race.*
>
> *O long road to retreat without disgrace,*
> *O travail to that authorized desistence!*[3]

Without a knowledge of a picture to which the eminent Rilke and Hölderlin translator, J. B. Leishman, has very kindly drawn my attention, the above poem cannot possibly be

---

[1] Cf. here also p. 228.   [2] *Briefe aus Muzot*, No. 64.
[3] J. B. Leishman's translation.

understood. It is Joseph Severn's *Keats on his death-bed*. The original is to be found in the Keats-Shelley Memorial House in Rome. According to E. Zinn, it was André Gide who, on 27 January 1914, showed Rilke a reproduction of that picture.

On the other hand, in Goethe's case, for example, nothing is more devastating for modern literary criticism than his misunderstood remark about poetry being a confession of his life: 'Alle meine Werke sind Bruchstücke einer großen Konfession.' Often the slightest stimulus satisfies the poet, and a city like Venice (cf. Nietzsche's poem of the same name) rises up before our eyes:

> An der Brücke stand
> jüngst ich in brauner Nacht.
> Fernher kam Gesang:
> goldener Tropfen quolls
> über die zitternde Fläche weg.
> Gondeln, Lichter, Musik. . . .

or the song of a nightingale in a Hampstead garden impels Keats to write his great ode or a glance into a dictionary inspires a ballad, as for example in the case of Eduard Mörike who in the year 1868 wrote to Moritz von Schwind how once, thirty years previously, he had by chance come upon an old German woman's name, 'Rohtraut', in a lexicon and Mörike added: 'it lit my soul as if in a roselike glow—and already the king's daughter was there. . . .'

There is no doubt that a cause (so often unpoetical in itself) can occasionally play a part in the interpretation of the poem and here and there even in a decisive way. On the other hand, it is wrong to demand: 'Literary criticism should *always* be partly biographical'.[1] There still remains to us, as the primary source of knowledge, the poetic word.

The Word can fulfil several functions from the abstract to the most tender expression of feeling: (1) it is meaning, communication, abstract comprehension; (2) it carries associations with it; (3) it sounds; (4) it underlies the poet's expressive arrangement and choice; (5) it creates an image, it becomes a symbol. All these functions and possibilities are inherent in the poet's language:

[1] MacNeice: *Modern Poetry*, p. 75.

1. The Word denotes something abstract as a direct communication, but a poem such as Goethe's *Auf dem See* can apparently almost completely hide its direct and abstract meaning from the reader and yet, through poetic imagery and landscape-description, vividly convey the inner conflict in the poet's heart:

> Auf der Welle blinken
> Tausend schwebende Sterne,
> Weiche Nebel trinken
> Rings die türmende Ferne,
> Morgenwind umflügelt
> Die beschattete Bucht,
> Und im See bespiegelt
> Sich die reifende Frucht.

On the waters a thousand hovering stars twinkle, soft mists drink up the towering distance, the morning breeze wings round the shady bay, and the ripening fruit mirrors itself in the lake.

An inner change lies before us here in the poem which is not expressed directly by word. The process is deprived of its epic quality. Instead of thought, sensuous images of nature speak to us and utter a poetic reality, not a philosophical truth. We remind ourselves here of the words in Keats's *Ode on a Grecian Urn*:

> Beauty is truth, truth beauty—that is all
> Ye know on earth, and all ye need to know.

There can be no question of fixed prescriptions for the artist. Any attempt (on the part of the critics) to set up a system of philosophical abstractions, stale patterns and a priori doctrines fights shy of solving the most vital problem of *inner* form. Poetic visions are not philosophical ideas.

Moreover, any preoccupation to the exclusion of other values with secondary (though important) features such as content, political issues, etc., of necessity often leads one away from the secret of poetic expression. But a study of social conditions can reveal much, as is shown by F. W. Bateson's statement in his book, *English Poetry* (1950), about Gray's *Elegy written in a Country Churchyard* (1751) which is interpreted as a 'tract for the times. It was a plea for decentralization, recalling the over-urbanized ruling class to its roots in a rural

16

society, based upon the benevolent despotism of the manor house'.

According to F. W. Bateson the content of poetry is 'human nature in its social relations', i.e. 'all poems are therefore in the last analysis public poems'. Romantic poetry expresses the 'Plutocracy of Big Business, modern poetry the Managerial State'. F. W. Bateson's arguments are persuasive, cf. here p. 231ff. Obviously the thoughts are not alien to poetry, but both must not be separable. They should, as John Middleton Murry, in *Countries of the Mind* (1931), puts it, 'be an intrinsic part of an emotional field in the poet's mind' . . . or as Keats says—'What the Imagination seizes as Beauty must be Truth'.

The fact, however, cannot be challenged that the so-called 'magic' in modern poetry is all too often nothing but an intellectual though fascinating game of conflicting elements, cf. also Aristotles's perception of the 'similarity in dissimilars'.[1]

Poetic truth is not abstract or philosophic truth inorganically plastered on, embroidered and elaborated, or wrapt in rhythm, rhyme and other sound values. The poetic word has its own setting, it own organic unity; it is expression, not communication.

2. The word conjures up associations, for example words such as Roland's Dark Tower—forest—moon—sea—tree, etc., call up a subjective response, which is varied according to the character, experiences, literary reminiscences, and emotion of poet and reader; cf. Edith Sitwell's poetic fantasies or the Baroque exuberance of imagery in the modern poem, *Mond*:

> Beinerner Diskus, der zum Zenit emporschwirrt,
> Gold der Azteken, Münze, mit der ich
> Charon entlohnen werde für seinen Fährdienst,
> türkische Klinge, wie sie den Himmel verwundet . . .[2]

In *The Philosophy of Rhetoric* (1936), I. A. Richards investigated the working and interanimation of words. These must not be judged in isolation and must not be put together like bricks: 'Bricks, for all practical purposes, hardly mind what other things they are put with. Meanings mind intensely—more indeed than any other sorts of things.' . . . 'Gross uses of *beautiful* might make the word itself a thing suited only to gross

[1] *Poetics, XXII.*   [2] H. Piontek, *Die Furt*, 1952.

uses.' . . . 'The mere putting together of two things to see what will happen—is a contemporary fashionable aberration, which takes an extreme case as the norm. This is André Breton, the leader of the French Super-Realists.' . . . 'Mr. Breton sees no need to consider what should be put with what—provided they are sufficiently remote from one another. . . .'

The many indecisions as to what a word or expression means, are analysed in William Empson's *Seven Types of Ambiguity* (1930): 'a word in a speech which falls outside the expected vocabulary, will cause an uneasy stir in all but the soundest sleepers; many sermons rely with a painful frankness upon this.' This study of double meaning (e.g. 'dark night' in Synge's *Deirdre of the Sorrows*), opposite meanings (e.g. 'Macbeth is ripe for shaking . . .'), and exquisite contrasts ('take but bring again [the kisses]')—('take those lips away')[1] is followed by Empson's *The Structure of Complex Words*, which will occupy our attention in the section on imagery and so-called poetic key-words.

The above associations are relatively easy to recognize. But the atlas-load of our past appears to be too great when learned annotations are necessary, as in the case of T. S. Eliot, the modern master of free associations, who maintains that 'poets in our civilization, as it is at present, *must* be difficult', because our life has become too complex. . . . Those workings of association become strengthened when the word, e.g. rose, tree, moon and so on, enters into relationship with the other words of the poem, e.g. William Blake's *O rose thou art sick*—the rose = symbol of womanhood attacked by the cerebral male principle (the worm), or the rose being earthly love corrupted by possessive instinct. According to Empson, the rose in general suggests a 'sort of grandeur in the state of culture'. As to the rose in the epitaph on Rilke's tombstone: 'Rose, o reiner Widerspruch, Lust, Niemandes Schlaf zu sein unter so viel Lidern' (Rose, O pure contradiction, joy to be no man's sleep under so many lids.), H. E. Holthusen writes: 'the rose stands here as a symbol for the pure, incomprehensibly reconciled contradiction between the tormenting secret of the death he had to die and the blissful secret of the beautiful to which all who read him must succumb.'[2] Not only the rose, but also the

---

[1] *Troilus and Cressida* and *Measure for Measure.*   [2] Translated by J. P. Stern.

tree, etc., calls up infinite possibilities of association. Blake hit the nail on the head when he said: 'A fool sees not the same tree that a wise man sees.' To the mystic the tree is often the tree of love; for Rilke it is an image of pure existence, or of God Himself, for example his *Book of the Hours*:

> The branch from the tree of God, which reaches over Italy
> Has already bloomed.

Thus the magic of words arouses limitless associations, particularly when the poet wishes to grasp and form the mysterious state of hovering between consciousness and foreboding, or light and darkness, e.g. Mörike in the poem about the down-like time of dawn, *An einem Wintermorgen, vor Sonnenaufgang*:

> O flaumenleichte Zeit der dunkeln Frühe . . . .
>
> Einem Krystall gleicht meine Seele nun,
> Den noch kein falscher Strahl des Lichts getroffen. . . .

or Hölderlin in his *Rhein* hymn:

> Im dunkeln Epheu saß ich, an der Pforte
> Des Waldes, eben, da der goldene Mittag,
> Den Quell besuchend, herunterkam
> Von den Treppen des Alpengebirgs. . . .
>
> *I sat among sombre ivy at the gate of*
> *The forest, just as the golden noontide,*
> *Visiting the spring, descended thither*
> *From the steps of the Alpine chain.*[1]

Thus lyrical poetry, like the single poetical word, is balanced between two worlds: Soul and scenery, depth and surface, image and reality.

3. In the word above all lies the *evocative* power of tone. R. de Souza, in *un Débat sur la Poésie*, singles out six essential notions:

1. Every poem owes its essentially poetical character to the presence of a mysterious and unifying reality.

2. To read a poem poetically, it does not suffice, and even is not always necessary, to seize the sense. There is an obscure enchantment independent of the sense.

3. Poetry cannot be reduced to rational discourse; it is a mode of expression which surpasses the normal forms of discourse.

[1] Translated by J. B. Leishman in his *Selected Poems of Friedrich Hölderlin*.

4. Poetry is a certain kind of music, but not merely music, for it acts as the conductor of a current which transmits the intimate nature of the soul.

5. It is an incantation that gives unconscious expression to the state of soul in which the poet exists before he expresses himself in ideas or sentiments. We relive in the poem that confused experience, which is inaccessible to distinct consciousness. The words of prose excite, stimulate, cap our ordinary activities; the words of poetry appease them, tend to suspend them.

6. Poetry is a mystic magic allied to prayer.[1]

But it would be a futile method to hunt after the specific, *isolated* function and quality of each vowel and consonant (as the philosopher does in Molière's *Bourgeois Gentilhomme*) without listening to the sound-pattern (Klangform and-leib) and sound-gesture of a work of art; cf. Eichendorff's moonlit, penumbral fluidity, M. Claudius's natural sincerity, George's disciplined solemnity; Schiller's melodic curve often rises violently and falls in a single line, particularly in his *Rütlischwur*. The external sound-values must clearly express the inmost emotion, as in Goethe's refrain:

> Meine Ruh ist hin, mein Herz
> ist schwer . . .

or in Gottfried's inversion of the two names:

> Tristan Isôt
> Isôt Tristan . . .

The very inversion and juxtaposition of the two names symbolize the two lovers' tragic and inseparable oneness. Moreover, many poems have been written to a special musical pattern. If we know nothing of Elizabethan music, we shall almost certainly have misread the poetry of the Elizabethans, and after hearing an Elizabethan madrigal or motet we read *L'Allegro* as a new poem.[2]

4. The expressive word, moreover, depends on the poet's arrangement and choice. Naturally here we are not concerned with simple counting-out rhymes, e.g.:

[1] See H. Read, *Phases of English Poetry*, 1950.
[2] K. Wilson, *Sound and Meaning in English Poetry*, 1930.

20

Wer geht mit nach Engelland?
Engelland ist zugeschlossen
Und der Schlüssel abgebrochen.
Zehn Pferd an einem Wagen,
Muß man mit der Peitsche schlagen.
Bauer, bind' den Pudel an,
Daß er mich nicht beissen kann!
Beißt er mich, so straf' ich dich
Un en Taler dreissig.

or with old German mock rhymings:

Wie der Acker sind die Ruben,
Wie die Vater sind die Buben,
Wie die Ähren sind die Kearnl,
Wie die Mutter sind die Dearndln.

or with nursery rhymes:

Es ist ein Mann in Brunn gefalln,
Hab ihn hören plumpen;
Wär der Kerl nicht nein gefalln,
Wär er nicht ertrunken.

Although the lyrical poet need not discard the means of logical word-formation, his primary task is the creation of his emotion, experience or vision through a poetic image and sequence of words: e.g. Goethe's *Der du von dem Himmel bist*, where the pent-up longing for peace and rest is suggested by the position of the key-word 'Friede' almost at the end of the poem.

As to choice, there is now more than ever a justifiable tendency to introduce into lyrical poetry current idiomatic expressions and jargon of our civilization, because 'if the poetry and the intelligence of the age lose touch with each other, poetry will cease to matter much'.[1] But science can go rapidly out of date: e.g. Heinrich Lersch's

Eisen, du vor allem geliebter Stoff! Werk-Same!
Aus den glühenden Leibern der Hochöfen fließt du in
die Gebärmütter gewaltiger Bessemer-Birnen,
fließt durch Kranpfannen in die ewig bereiten Formen,
    und findest über Walzwerke,
hydraulische Pressen, Ziehbänken, auch den Weg zu mir! ...

[1] F. R. Leavis, *New Bearings in English Poetry*, London, 1942.

21

Who is familiar with the compounds and the technical terms
in the line: 'Auf Stopfbüchse, Ventilsitz, Hanschlitz, Dampf
will mit Gewalt hervor'? ... Such lines of dead catalogues have
but a short life, whilst for instance those in John Clare's
Shepherd's Calendar about the crane 'cranking' a jarring
melancholy cry:

> through the wild journey of the cheerless sky

are extraordinarily expressive—not only for the age in which
they were written. They will live on because of their creative,
vivid imagery. The hoarse cry of the crane startles one; it
calls up a landscape of never-ending marshes and a dull and
heavy sea.

Now, up-to-date expressions become popular. Out of dis-
inclination for the rhetorical and mellifluous 'tapestry diction'
and for pontifical oratory (bound to idealized form) the most
recent lyrical poetry purposely seeks to depoetize and widen
its scope by methods of shock and it seeks to venture boldly
into the diction of provocative, or colloquial speech by way of
sensation or surprise, e.g. the following extract from *The Age
of Anxiety* by W. H. Auden (1948):

> Emble asked Rosetta to dance. The others sat watching.
> Quant waved his cigar in time to the music and sang a verse
> from an old prospector's ballad.
>
> > When Laura lay on her ledger side
> > And nicely threw her north cheek up,
> > How pleasing the plight of her promising grove
> > And how rich the random I reached with a rise.
>
> > ... but fairer there, with
> > An early Madonna's oval face
> > And lissom limbs, delighting that whole
> > Degraded glen, the Goddess herself
> > Presided smiling; a saucy wind,
> > Plucking from her thigh her pink wrapper
> > Of crêpe-de-chine, disclosed a very
> > Indolent ulcer. . . .

and T. S. Eliot's *The Hollow Men* and *The Wasteland* with the
theme of decay and death in the middle of the springtide of the
earth. The monotony of jazz and modern commonplaceness
can be heard in the conscious repetition of sound and thought.

The rhythm clearly drowns the melody. The poetic image is thus often shot with a strange mixture of *sublime and banal* or acridly *topical elements*: psychoanalysis (particularly in W. H. Auden's work), social problems, clinical apparatuses, etc., unless it is corroded to the core by the vitriol of morbid cynicism or by an irresponsible use of 'collage' and film technique. Apparently unconnected images are deliberately forced into an obscure unity. But the once *Unexpected*, as MacNeice admits in his *Modern Poetry*, does not wear well, cf. Lautreamont's 'chance meeting, on a dissecting table, of a sewing-machine and an umbrella'—the cliché of Surrealism which is so stale now. In contrast to that sensational trick we think of Keats's 'plot of beechen green and shadows numberless' in his *Ode to a Nightingale*—also an unexpected image which, however, still moves us profoundly not only because of, or better, in spite of, its bold juxtaposition of the word 'plot' and the poetical shadows followed by the adjective 'numberless', but also because of the musical enchantment I spoke of in connexion with the sound-values of the words.

If verse is to be brutalized before it can be readable and 'human' again, it does not follow that verse is great because it is crude or sentimental. It is perhaps *popular*. But Herbert Read in *Phases of English Poetry* (1948) rightly says: 'There is no poetry in *Tipperary* and *Keep the Home Fires Burning*—there is only sentimentality. But it is just a possibility—and no more than a possibility—that the music-hall song and its allied forms —music-hall pattern and revue libretto—contain the germ of a new popular poetry.' T. S. Eliot and W. H. Auden must instinctively have felt this when they tried to bridge the gap between a hypercivilized, fastidious intelligence and the claims of the populace in a music-hall.

5. Several times we have already touched upon the question of reality and imagery. This leads us to the fifth and most important function of the word: the poetical image and symbol. In the interplay of sound and symbol, body and soul, a poem's most inward movement is crystallized, for instance in Trakl's *Grodek*:

> ... umfängt die Nacht
> Sterbende Krieger, die wilde Klage
> Ihrer zerbrochenen Münder. . . .

or Shakespeare's *Winter's Tale*:

> ... daffodils
> That come before the swallow dares
> And take the winds of March with beauty.

In the image lies the power of revealing a poetic experience, visual or other. I do not propose to classify all kinds of images in this connexion. Burke once wisely said: 'Though no man can draw a stroke between the confines of night and day, yet light and darkness are upon the whole tolerably distinguishable. . . .'

The same applies to the poetic image. Through it the lyrical word transmutes the object: it is body, soul and spirit. As an individual picture it reaches at the same time into the depth of universal significance. It remains personal while so doing. Therefore Gundolf is in the wrong when he plays George against Wolfram and considers *the* vigil, *the* courage of the templars, *the* Parzival-mood as such as archetypal images of the powers of medieval life, whilst he maintains that throughout the verses of Walther, Gottfried, and Wolfram 'nowhere' did a primal tone occur. George's images[1] are often self-sufficient, timeless, and unconnected abstractions devoid of all fullness of history. But the song must always be personal, even as a worker's song, a dance-song or a marching song. It throws out wide circles just as does a stone, which in the water sends out circle after circle from one centre.

The image is the central point, die Urzelle, in the organism of a work of art, and is not to be divorced from its context or the life of a poem, e.g. Hölderlin's image *Chaos* (meaning 'das Offene'), or the image of the *bucket* and the *untended garden* in Shakespeare's *Richard II*, or the image of the clothed (hypocritical) dagger and the naked babe in *Macbeth*, the 'uncontrollable mystery on the bestial floor'.

One year after the appearance of Caroline Spurgeon's book on *Shakespeare's Imagery and what it tells us* (1935), in which most extensive statistics concerning Shakespeare's likes and dislikes, his acquaintance with nature, animals, etc., are displayed before our eyes, W. H. Clemen published his important study of

---

[1] Stefan George, *Sagen und Sänge*.

Shakespeares Bilder,[1] which strikes to the root of the whole problem of imagery. W. H. Clemen shows how Shakespeare in his maturer plays uses imagery as a *centre*, an *organic* part of his creative work: 'every image, every metaphor gains full life and significance only from its context . . . it appears as a cell in the organism of the play.'

Doubtless, the language of poetic imagery is difficult to analyse. The critic's often all too mechanical method of searching for the various grammatical categories and tricks of the trade does not reach the central point and must remain on the periphery of the assessment of values, however carefully he endeavours to register all possible details of grammar, nouns, adjectives, the use of the second and first persons, repetitions, accumulations, in the impressionistic or expressionistic style, antithesis, the neutral pronoun, nuances, and so on, as, e.g., in Johannes Schlaf's impressionistic *Dingsda* and *Frühling*.

Moreover, this one fact must be considered. Not only the imagery of each single poem but also each literary genre (the sonnet, stanza, and so on) has its own fate and mirrors its own laws of form in the spiritual movement of the time and of the specific country or poet. We clearly recognize in Platen's sonnets a victory which is won only through struggle, whilst in the polemic sonnets of the nineteenth century that nobility of form and pure balance of contrasts, which A. W. Schlegel praises in his *Sonnett*:

> Hoheit, Füll' in engern Grenzen
> und reines Ebenmaß der Gegensätze. . . .

deteriorates or goes to rack and ruin.

The study of the poetic genres and particularly the notorious, mechanical analyses of metre are doomed to failure if a Beckmesser who counts all the beats out, as in R. Wagner's *Meistersinger*, is the judge. It need hardly be mentioned in this connexion that metre and rhythm are not identical. Metre is purely mechanical, soul-less, unless metre and mood merge into an organic unity. The mere registration of iambic or trochaic metre, for instance, like the registration of vowel sounds, does

---

[1] Translated into English under the title: *The Development of Shakespeare's Imagery*, 1951.

not count for much in itself, as poems written in the same
metre may differ from each other as rock from water, e.g.
Schiller's iambic *Die Kraniche des Ibykus* and Uhland's *Des
Knaben Berglied*, or the trochaic verse-form in Goethe's *Zauber-
lehrling* and in Lenau's *Sonnenuntergang*:

> Seine Wort und Werke
> merkt ich und den Brauch. . . .

> Sonnenuntergang:
> Schwarze Wolken ziehn,
> O wie schwül und bang
> Alle Winde fliehn!

Therefore the over-emphasis on stressed and unstressed
syllables and on sound values can easily deteriorate into an
inane preoccupation with surface matter, an occupation as
senseless as the sieve of the Danaides, particularly if meagre
results remain isolated and are confined to a dabbling in
shallow waters, e.g. acoustic and optic effects, onomatopoeia,
word melody, etc. All this can be important, but, alas, it fails
to touch the core of the matter.

This lies in the secret of inner form which is symbolically
reflected in the relationship between content and expression.
We want to know how natural rhythm and metrical beat and
imagery are adjusted to the subject-matter. This inner form is
peculiar to each work of art and expresses the poet's vision
which through word and rhythm is condensed into poetic
images. The length of poetry is no criterion of form, for Hölderlin's vision of Hellas, *Archipelagus*, is as great as Goethe's lyrical
jewel, *Auf dem See*.

The poetical picture must not be mistaken for the idea.
Goethe warns us here with reference to his *Faust*, that it must
not be strung on the 'meagre' thread of a single idea.[1] Similarly
Goethe contrasts the personal concept of Tasso: 'Bein von
meinem Bein und Fleisch von meinem Fleisch',[2] sharply with
the general idea of Tasso. Shelley in *A defence of Poetry* mocks
at the 'owl-winged faculty of calculation'.

The question of ethics is by no means ruled out, particularly
in view of the *Psalms*, Dante's *Divina Comedia* or Hölderlin's

---

[1] Cf. Eckermann 6. V. 1827.   [2] Eckermann 6. V. 1827.

Archipelagus, or in other great hymns and odes; cf. MacNeice in *Modern Poetry*: 'The good poet has a definite attitude to life; most good poets . . . have beliefs.' This is a view very different from that of Oscar Wilde, who divorces the art of words from ethics and who cannot accept criticism of style in terms of life and morality.

Poetic truth is, as already mentioned above, not abstract or philosophic truth; it is the sublimation of our emotions or experiences to a powerfully formed vision which can claim permanence in a transient world. Ultimately, however, the poet stands as much *above* life as he is rooted *in* life.

The more revealing a poet's language, the more significant his intensity, the more original his imagery is, the deeper is our response to his poetic symbol and quality of incantation. The subject does count; but the poet does not express a dogma. He can choose creative work as his subject, but enshrine it in the image of a clasp or a lamp: cf. Stefan George's *Spange*: 'I planned it as an iron band':

> Ich wollte sie aus kühlem eisen
> Und wie ein glatter fester streif. . . .

or Mörike's *Auf eine Lampe*, a genuine work of art:

> Wie reizend alles! lachend, und ein sanfter Geist
> des Ernstes doch ergossen um die ganze Form—
> Ein Kunstgebild der echten Art. Wer achtet sein?

Cf. also Rodin's so-called *Cathédrale*; a torso, two simple hands erected upwards become symbol of the cathedral. Thus a poet or artist in general can take up an apparently irrelevant image or a trite thing, yet produce a profounder poem or work of art than one who writes *about* human relationship to God. Of course, there *is* a difference between a cauliflower and the head of Apollo; but it all depends on the *creative* (not informative or philosophical) relationship to the things of this world in the fullest sense of the word. The poet's force is that of a transformer and a 'second maker' in Shaftesbury's sense.

In the passionate outpourings of poetic visions, for instance by Hölderlin, lies an *inwardly* necessary form which envelops each turn of phrase, each metaphor, indeed each gesture of language. Image and original, depth and surface are one. We cannot arrive at any valuable interpretation of the poem by means of the merely analytical method, which views the form outwardly: for the *inner form* is not abstract, nor arbitrary, but is at once content and spirit revealed through imagery. As Schiller says in his *Briefe über die ästhetische Erziehung des Menschen* (1793), published in the *Horen* in 1795, the true creation of the artist lies in the fact that he 'extinguishes' matter by transmuting it into form. Likewise he maintains that in a truly beautiful work of art, it is not the content but the form which produces the effect: for the form essentially affects the whole being of an artist whilst the content, however noble and all-embracing it might be, has always a confining effect upon the spirit, and only if the form is real, can aesthetic freedom be expected. Here lies the true secret of the art of the master. *He extinguishes and transforms his material through the form*: and the more imposing, the more arrogant, the more seductive the very material itself is, the more independently it pushes forward with its own effect, or the more the observer inclines to involve himself directly with the material, so much more triumphant is the art, which controls him and asserts dominion over matter. . . . Naturally, there is a beautiful art of passion, but a beautiful *and* passionate art is a paradox, for the eternal result of beauty is freedom from passion. No less paradoxical according to Schiller is the conception of a beautiful *and* didactic or moralising art, for nothing is more at variance with the conception of beauty than a wish to convey a certain opinion.[1]

In the Introduction to the *Hausbuch aus deutschen Dichtern* Th. Storm, too, defines the limits of what he considers the pure lyric, to which he refuses to admit political and merely reflective lyrical poetry. He maintains that poetry should appeal to us not through thoughts but through *images* and not through an a priori determined metrical pattern but through a form that is a *vital* expression of human life. That Storm did not remain absolutely true to his theory goes without saying. His theory of the *absolute lyric* represents only the final scientific conclusion of his ideas.

The trilogy—intellect, fancy, emotion, or thought, image, feeling—should, according to Storm, be considered as a *unity*

[1] Schiller's 22nd letter: *On the aesthetic education of man.*

and expressed as such. The idea is not ruled out, but must be experienced as part of the poet's imagery and vision.

This leads us to a closer definition of metaphor, the poetic image and its original, to the 'Körperlichkeit der Poesie' as F. Grillparzer calls it.

The change of objects through form (as Schiller puts it) must, of course, be accompanied by concentrated feeling, in order to be able to reach from the surface into the depths. For *a double* reflects itself in every object. The object is more than it shows itself to ordinary sight. And the object seems to be something, which in truth it is not. Every poet (not only the Classical and Romantic writer) reveals himself in his attitude to truth and reality. . . . W. Blake is said to have confessed of himself: 'Natural objects always did and now do weaken, deaden and obliterate imagination in me.'

Rex Warner points to the symbolic speech of a world of 'double meanings' in his Introduction to Herman Melville's *Billy Budd and Other Stories*, e.g. the *tortoises*: 'they seemed newly crawled forth beneath the foundations of the world' (*The Enchantadas of Enchanted Isles*), or the *bird*: 'the bright, inspiring chanticleer of ocean', or the faces of *maidens* in *Tartarus of Maids* in which old and young looks fuse; moreover, there is a characteristic *juxtaposition* of civilized society and original nature reflected in the tragic fate of Billy Budd.

W. H. Auden dedicates a whole work, *The Enchanted Flood*, to the study of this conflict. In this book a bundle of traditional associations is subject-matter of a 'Romantic Iconography of the Sea'; the world of double-meanings is shown: (*a*) the *sea* is to him symbol for the state of living barbarism and the primordial undifferentiated flux . . . the *desert*=lifeless, mechanized decadence: (*b*) the *shell*=symbol of imagination and poetic truth, truth of feeling: the *stone*=abstract geometry, truth of reason; in the latter lies the peril of sterile abstraction, in the former that of chaotic anarchy: (*c*) the conflict in the *double-natured* hero (the Flying Dutchman and Don Quixote).

Each group of the above examples is rooted in a double existence. Above all, Melville's *Moby Dick*, though describing the whale-hunting, at the same time symbolically offers a picture of human passions and existence.

In the book, *El tema de nuestro tiempo* (1923) (*Die Aufgabe unserer Zeit*, 1928), José Ortega y Gasset speaks about *metaphoric expression* as the most effective means of depersonalization: 'Enthumanisierung'. He calls poetry the 'higher algebra of metaphor'.

Neither autobiography, nor psychology, but the poetic image is the most important thing, because the art of metaphor can *purify* man's personal feeling and sublimate it to an objective vision which is the touchstone of real culture. Uncultured life is barbarism; devitalized culture leads to Byzantinism. But Ortega y Gasset is not right when he calls Wagner's *Tristan* an autobiography, as if Richard Wagner projected his adultery with Wesendonck into music so that for us nothing else is left but to become for a few hours an adulterer! The story of *Tristan* is, however, rooted in a primordial image, cf. here pp. 57ff. and 43.

Maud Bodkin in her work, *Archetypal Patterns in Poetry* (1934), surveys a wide field of archetypal motifs: Orestes, Prometheus, Hamlet, King Lear, Milton's Satan, Faust, etc., and unfolds before us a number of primordial images ('urtümliche Bilder') derived from the great myths of world literature. Although with R. Wagner's *Götterdämmerung* the twilight seems to have set in as regards the creation of new myths, the old images and symbols still possess the power of rejuvenation and change; cf. Hölderlin's memorable line in *Andenken*: 'Was bleibet aber, stiften die Dichter.'

There is no doubt that the study of poetic imagery unfolds to us some of the most important features of lyrical expression, see, e.g., L. A. Willoughby's *Unity and Continuity in Goethe* (1947), where the themes: change—polarity—continuity—unity are illustrated in the analysis of a lovable ghazal: 'In tausend Formen magst du dich verstecken, Doch Allerliebste, gleich erkenn' ich dich.' There is for us in Goethe's lyrics an unsurpassed treasure of poetic imagery. In symbolic pictures such as mirror, charioteer-wanderer (both representing the two poles of self-realization, self-limitation), weavings, etc., his lyrical power shines forth, and in them he not only lays himself open as a person, but enters at once into every human soul. For example, who does not respond to the self-revealing rapture of

the Earth-spirit in *Faust*: 'In Lebensfluten, in Tatensturm. . . .'?
We need very careful preliminary researches on a poet's
individual language and imagery, forms of speech and symbolism. Much is still to be done in this field.

It is only from the poets' *complete* conception of the world that
the full symbolic content is resolved for us in a single poem.
So it is with Goethe. He recognizes and accepts the world of
appearance in which he sees mirrored, however, a higher
reality.

This idealistic concept of existence decides the symbolic
interpretation of Goethe's creations. Like Kant in his *Kritik der
Urteilskraft*, Goethe also guards against any *non*-aesthetic
didacticism in the work of art. The latter must be autonomous;
it should neither instruct nor try to improve or transform morally, although—in spite of its artistic self-sufficiency and
completeness—no really great work of art must and can
clash with moral law, because both are expressions of the
highest human power of reason=Vernunft (not intellect, or
Verstand).

Over and over again Goethe stresses the *inner* and *organic*
law of each work of art which he compares with Nature. The
former is not an imitation of Nature, but a 'second', 'higher'
Nature; cf. his *Campagne in Frankreich*, Trier, 25 October 1792.
He does not accept the abstract norm. Rather, the mysterious
law of Nature in ceaseless activity is reflected in the work of
art, which has its own rules, and, as in Goethe's own life, causes
the outer form to unfold from within. Even the choice of subject
betrays in the works of Goethe an inner necessity: cf. his
Faust, Hermann und Dorothea, Römische Elegien, etc., for in the
material lie ready the form and the substance, hidden like a
bud.

The fact that every artistic expression cannot be fitted on to
a poem is shown in his own notes on the 'outer' form of his
Roman Elegies.

Behind all change, for Goethe there is an organic, inner
development controlling artistic creation as in Nature itself.
He is for ever pointing to the common root in his scientific
studies and aesthetic criticisms and indeed all nature; cf.
Die Metamorphose der Pflanzen (1798):

31

Einfach schlief in dem Samen die Kraft: ein beginnendes Vorbild
Lag verschlossen in sich, unter die Hülle gebeugt,
Blatt und Wurzel und Keim, nur halb geformet und farblos;
Trocken erhält so der Kern ruhiges Leben bewahrt. . . .
. . . Jede Pflanze verkündet dir nun die ew'gen Gesetze,
Jede Blume, sie spricht lauter und lauter mit dir. . . .

Simply slumber'd the force in the seed; a germ of the future,
Peacefully lock'd in itself, 'neath the integument lay,
Leaf and root, and bud, still void of colour, and shapeless;
Thus doth the kernel, while dry, cover that motionless life. . . .
. . . *Every plant unto thee proclaimeth the laws everlasting.*
Every floweret speaks louder and louder to thee.[1]

and the same is true of the *Metamorphose der Tiere* (1795 probably), in which, too, the poet recognizes the law of freedom in an
organic development, and the secret of fullness and limitation:

Doch im Innern befindet die Kraft der edlern Geschöpfe
Sich im heiligen Kreise lebendiger Bildung beschlossen.
Diese Grenzen erweitert kein Gott, es ehrt die Natur sie. . . .

The whole is more than its parts. The whole stands at the
beginning of creation, it is *not* made up by its parts; centre and
periphery are one; cf. *Epirrhema*:

Müsset im Naturbetrachten
Immer eins wie alles achten;
Nichts ist drinnen, nichts ist draussen;
Denn was innen, das ist aussen. . . .

and *Typus* (printed 1827, written 1820), where again the unity
of the biological and artistic laws is emphasized. Nothing is
without, which is not within. Nothing is arbitrary:

Es ist nichts in der Haut,
Was nicht im Knochen ist . . .
Was freut denn jeden? Blühen zu sehn,
Das von innen schon gut gestaltet:
Aussen mag's in Glätte, mag in Farben gehn:
Es ist ihm schon voran gewaltet.

And finally Goethe's sonnet *Natur und Kunst* (1802):

Natur und Kunst, sie scheinen sich zu fliehen,
Und haben sich, eh man es denkt, gefunden; . . .
In der Beschränkung zeigt sich erst der Meister,
Und das Gesetz nur kann uns Freiheit geben.

[1] E. A. Bowring, *The Poems of Goethe*, London, 1853.

Nature and Art, it seems to us, diverge,
But soon, before we know it, are united. . . .
A master shows his powers in limitation,
And freedom follows only law's direction.

According to Goethe, the law of organic necessity of development is, as we have seen, applicable to Nature as well as Art. The latter, as mentioned already, does not aim at imitation of Nature, but a creative presentation of the world (that is of a 'Higher Nature') which is directed towards men, and whose inmost being is formed symbolically, thus having nothing to do with arbitrary events or chance. For the poet's picture is a primeval picture at the same time. It is infinite in the finite, or as Goethe says in his significant review of *Des Knaben Wunderhorn*: 'im kleinen Raum die ganze Welt'—the whole universe in a small compass, universal as well as individual.

The great secret behind the workings of Nature and Art is that *inner* evolution, that formation from *within*. As Goethe, the mature thinker, is anxious to shed all subjectivity in reviewing books and seeks to 'live himself' into the inner laws of a work of art, so he also tries to trace 'the inner consistency' of his own works: . . . 'geprägte Form, die sich entwickelt. . . .' (*Urworte. Orphisch*). His moral and aesthetic concepts are anchored in this belief in a single, pregnant form, which develops from within. He discards the a priori *Norm* which is inflexible and incapable of change. The artist is the mediator between object and subject, for his vision pervades 'things' and is at the same time persuaded by them. His creative activity is an interchange, inhaling and exhaling, taking and giving, in a natural equilibrium. Every creative work has its own law, even 'pure' art also bears the stamp of the author's personality; cf. D. S. Savage in *The Withered Branch* (1950): 'Art is personal, being rooted in the existence of a concrete and particular individual.'

When Dr. Heinroth in his *Anthropologie* called Goethe's power of thought 'gegenständlich' he understood the very core of Goethe's creative existence; cf. Goethe's essay *Bedeutende Fördernis durch ein einziges geistreiches Wort* (1823): 'Der Mensch kennt nur sich selbst, in sofern er die Welt kennt': 'Man only knows himself in as far as he knows the world,' . . . and 'Mein

Anschauen selbst ein Denken, mein Denken ein Anschauen':
'In observing I think, and in thinking I observe.'

All experience and all creation spring from a *central* source.
Therefore Goethe's inclination to 'Gelegenheitsgedichte', to
which the particular situation, 'Das Besondere irgend eines
Zustandes unwiderstehlich . . .', attracted him. Similarly,
observation and intuition (in his scientific research as well as
in his poetry) are mingled in equal balance. There is sensuous
and sensitive experience and at the same time the recognition
of a higher reality. Thus Goethe can truly demand: 'Daß du
schauest, nicht schwärmest.'

At present, new theories and themes or phrases are coming to
the fore: crowds, machines, town-life, the atomic age, etc.
But the ancient themes still preserve their symbolic value—
Nature is the inexhaustible fount of primordial figures: *storm and
calm*=symbols of the poet's state of inspiration, ecstasy and
exhaustion (cf. Hölderlin); the *fountain*=symbol of the life-
giving force; *hortus inclusus*=the garden of paradise; *light*=
symbol of perfection (cf. the archangels' hymns in *Faust*); the
serpent=symbol of rejuvenation and of Christ ('And as Moses
lifted up the serpent in the wilderness, even so must the Son of
Man be lifted up . . .');[1] above all the *moon*, the *mountains* and
the *flowers*, especially the *rose*.[2] In all these cases the essential
question is; *how* a thing (not *what*) has been expressed in poetry,
cf. Rilke's image of the *tree* (symbol of pure existence) in his
first sonnet to Orpheus, or his Christian symbol of the *heart*
as the wine-press.[3]

In *Eckermanns Gespräche* (1824) Goethe speaks of the inner
law of form. According to his statement, which is most illuminating, the context of his *Römische Elegien* would in fact sound
'really wicked' ('ganz verrucht') if one wanted to put them into
the verse-form of Byron's *Don Juan*.

Yet the neurasthenic endeavour of some most recent lyrical
writers towards *revitalizing and renovating worn-out metaphors* by
means of surprise technique and shock-method is short-lived.
These primordial symbols with their constant wear and tear
have little or nothing to do with the literary tricks which after a
brief spell of popularity wander into the junk-room of incidental

---

[1] John iii. 14.   [2] Cf. J. J. Stoudt, *Pennsylvania-Folk-Art*, 1948.   [3] VIII Son.

collections of tropes and figures of speech. Who does not shudder at the thought of the *old prosodies* and of their neatly arranged categories? 'Metaphor'=the combination of two conceptions because of their similarity (the corn sways) (the sky laughs); the Synecdoche=the combination of two conceptions because of their outward affinity ('greyhead'), pars pro toto; Metonymy =the combination of two conceptions because of their inner affinity (cause and effect), etc. Moreover, there are the familiar varieties: personification, hyperbole, euphemism, paraphrase, etc., and the innumerable figures of sounds: assonance, alliteration ('und hohler und hohler hört man's heulen . . .'); onomatopaeia; finally the many repetitions, anaphora, epiphora, accumulations, etc.

This step to Parnassus does not replace originality. The Anacreontic genre and Baroque verse are rich sources of such abstract figures of speech. The whole field of metaphoric expression is exciting and full of surprises. We hardly realize that many a seemingly original image or comparison is not at all original but derivative, borrowed, e.g. see Graf Rudolf von Fenis, who took from Folquet of Marseilles the image 'mir ist al dem der ûf den boum da stîget . . .'[1] or Novalis's IV *Hymn to the Night*, where the 'kristallene Woge' is reminiscent of Jacob Böhme's comparison in *Psychologia Vera* (40, 4) and above all of the crystal sea in the *Apocalypse* (4, 6).

Other metaphors set out to startle the reader, cf. Hugo von Montfort's brainwave:

> Da strich man ûss das mer
> mit einem besen. . . .

Or the metaphors can either heighten or narrow the sphere of experience: cf. Ferdinand von Saar's *Drahtklänge*, which are compared to an 'Äolsharfe dieser Welt', and E. Young's *Night-thoughts*:

> My soul which flies to thee, her trust, her treasure,
> As misers to their gold. . . .

and E. Sitwell's 'The light is braying like an ass . . .' or T. S. Eliot's image which narrows down, breaks up and debunks the subject-matter cleverly:

[1] *MSF* F. Vogt, 354.

35

> When the evening's spread out against the sky
> Like a patient etherized upon a table. . . .

This is the technique of discontinuous images in a dying world which has lost its tradition and its life centre: 'Son of Man . . . you know only a heap of broken images, where the sun beats' (T. S. Eliot). The great poet reveals to us the *wholeness* of human experience in a mysterious existence.

Only a genius such as Shakespeare is master of metaphoric language, e.g. in *Cymbeline*, where the sudden turn from tragedy to intimate wistfulness creates a unique mood of serenity:

> Fear no more the heat o' the sun,
> Nor the furious winter's rages:
> Thou thy worldly task hast done,
> Home art gone, and ta'en thy wages:
> Golden lads and girls all must,
> As chimney-sweepers, come to dust. . . .

If, however, the image is struck by the all too harsh ray of intellect, it shrinks, or it is etherealized as in Rilke's *Brief aus Muzot* (No. 10). Pappeln='Rufzeichen des Raums', cf. in contrast to that, Keats' *Hyperion*=(tall oaks) 'those green robed senators of mighty woods'; or it loses in depth but gains in intellectual oddness: 'The moon is like a disk of candle-grease', or Gascoyne's startling line, 'the sun above them [the lovers] is a bag of nails . . .', or D. von Liliencron's playful comparison:

> Da fand ich deinen kleinen Mund,
> die rote Perlenküste. . . .

What a difference between this and Mörike's 'Purpurlippe' in his profoundly symbolic verses, *An einem Wintermorgen vor Sonnenaufgang*, which do *not* appeal merely to an intellectual curiosity. In a similar way also Droste's 'Seidentüchlein' is symbolically convincing in her *Lerche*; or Hebbel's 'zwei Tropfen' on the lily in his poem *Ich und Du*. These images arise organically from the centre of the poem; they are not isolated decorations but deeply rooted in the poetic context.

In conclusion, the two following detailed analyses will, perhaps, confirm and elucidate preceding arguments:

Ans Haff nun fliegt die Möwe
und Dämmrung bricht herein:
über die feuchten Watten
spiegelt der Abendschein.

Graues Geflügel huschet
neben dem Wasser her:
wie Träume liegen die Inseln
im Nebel auf dem Meer.

Ich höre des gärenden Schlammes
geheimnisvollen Ton,
einsames Vogelrufen—
so war es immer schon.

Noch einmal schauert leise
und schweiget dann der Wind:
vernehmlich werden die Stimmen,
die über der Tiefe sind.[1]

In *Dichter und Dichtung* A. Schaeffer compares and contrasts
this poem with the poetry of Stefan George. It is quite true,
that, in contrast to George's rigid verse-form, Storm's lines
flow past like the countryside in the gathering twilight. But
Storm's portrayal of nature has an inner form, which gives
forceful unity to the four verses.

Strangely enough the country scene is only the more strengthened in symbolic and visual power by the *abstract* comparison:

Wie Träume liegen die Inseln
im Nebel auf dem Meer. . . .

and by this means, it forces its way the more vividly into the
imagination of the reader. Thus the poem is not merely
descriptive, as an outward analysis might suggest.

The *concrete* outlines form a clear picture in our minds; the
dike (the bay cut off from the sea by a tongue of land), the
shoals or mudflats (the marshy part of the sea, which is laid
bare at low tide and cut off by a chain of islands), twilight falls:
the sea-gull flies to the dike: the damp shoals gleam in the
evening glow.

The external features intensify the impression: 'Grey wings'
come whispering towards us, near the water. The single
adjective 'grey' brings colour into the countryside: the other

[1] Storm, *Meeresstrand.*

37

two, 'bubbling' and 'mysterious', convey the mood but are colourless.

In addition to this there is the *acoustic* impression upon the senses in the two last verses as when the mud increases secretly, and then the gentle wind, until everything is silent and the voices over the deep become audible.

The *abstract* mentioned above is extraordinarily active, for through it the peculiar atmosphere of the landscape is formed as a wavering and dying away of the surrounding objects in the fog. There is no will-less surrender to Nature, but the poet stands *in* her. The objects surrounding seem to dissolve at a glance, the ear perceives now only the puzzling voices from the ground. Although Th. Storm usually shapes the lyrical subjective mood into the objective, but here encroaches upon the opposite path, this is only apparently so, and mingling of his concrete lines with the inner world leads to no romantic disintegration of substance.

Thus this song is woven with the softest touches and sounds. Mood and reality intermingle and imprison us in a strangely closed and at the same time hovering feeling of the incomprehensible depth of our existence.

Storm's personal fate, his nostalgia amidst the Danish-German conflict was doubtless the stimulus, but not the core of this poem. It is a picture of memories, which has been formed as a natural experience (Storm sent it to his father as an answer to the latter's exhortation to master his nostalgia). It broadens out to have a universal appeal, because it summons up that mood of longing which touches us all.

As to outward form-devices, the complete lack of verbosity and the metrical arrangement in four verses with rising verse-rhythm and tone-depicting stressed lifts ('einsamen') are significant. The contents is expressed through natural phenomena: (*a*) evening dusk; (*b*) dream-atmosphere and the quietness of the wind; (*c*) awakening of the subterranean powers. Thus, the song rises above the private fate of the poet into a symbol of the mysterious unity of all being.

On a level with Storm's almost purely lyrical poetry can be placed a poem of C. F. Meyer, *Die sterbende Meduse*, a portrait full of artistry but also symbolic depth.

The Greek myth of Perseus is well-known, but in the hands of so true an artist as C. F. Meyer the material becomes a new reality and at the same time a compelling symbol. Eros weaves magic threads between the sleeping Medusa and the resolute hero Perseus who watches Medusa in the mirror. Perseus sees her sweet tired head and the breathing form of her young being. Shortly before her death Medusa (once the beautiful sweetheart of men) is no longer the terrifying Gorgon. The gruesomeness has changed into a serene mood. For a moment all fate seems reconciled:

> Begonnen hat der Seele Feierzeit.
> Der Dämmer herrscht. . . .

She feels that she is released. Her death brings, in a moment of remembrance of perfect happiness, the long-sought-for rest. Medusa hears the flutes of the shepherd blow once more. The fateful end is not brought before our eyes; only three short verbs in three short sentences, tell the end with abrupt precision:

> Sie zuckt. Sie windet sich. Sie ruht. . . .

No abstract overstatement, no moralizing reference to our own existence disturbs the poem which has universal meaning: (a) the happy and pure years of youth; following which (b) the hardening of the heart; (c) the healing power of Eros; (d) finally death, but death not as horror or act of revenge but as releasing liberation. The unspoken feelings of passion which are called up in Medusa, unaware of Perseus's approach, receive depth through that undercurrent of *universal* fate. In addition to that symbolic meaning, C. F. Meyer's poetry, has, however, another significance—it unfolds to us the author's own mystery of poetic creation. *Perseus's shield, is, after all, symbol of the image into which the poet imprisons a terrible reality and through which alone he is able to save himself from destruction.* Thus Storm's nature poem almost steeped in lyric mood and C. F. Meyer's carefully deliberated work of art stand face to face with one another as equals.

An experience is used as the poetic symbol in both poems. Neither of them is simply statement, or description, or a picture; they both have symbolic value without pointing directly to this, but we are aware of it in both poems, whose material (in the one an object of *art*, in the other *nature*) is not chosen at random, but organically integrated in the poet's creative work.

Each poem has its own language and its own rhythm, just as each poet is imbued with his own language and his own rhythm. The length of a poem is of no importance here. Yet it must be created from one feeling, one vision, from one organic centre. Therefore the hunt for similar subject-matter and similar themes has often but little to say about the poem, for the same theme or motif can be expressed in basically different ways, cf. Handel's *Largo* with Chopin's *Largo*, or compare the motif of falling in Weinheber's 'Löst sich ein Stein und fällt und fällt . . .' with the precipitous jerky plunge of the eagle in Nietzsche's *Dionysos-Dithyramben* ('*Nur Narr! Nur Dichter*') and with Dante's *Inferno*: 'e caddi come corpo morte cade . . .' (and fell, as a dead body falls) . . . (Dante is overcome with pity at the sight of Francesca and her lover Paolo, and falls to the ground, as if dead, when he has heard their painful story . . .), cf. also Milton's description of Mulciber's fall: 'from morn To noon he fell, from noon to dewy eve', or the numerous parallels and similar motifs in Goethe's *Götz*, *Stella*, *Wahlverwandtschaften* and in lyrical poetry in general: cf. the many *Augengedichte* in Baroque and nineteenth-century poetry, the *Abendlieder*: (Gryphius: *An die Sternen*, Günther: *Abendlied*, Claudius: *Die Sterne*, Eichendorff: *Die Nacht*, Lenau: *Bitte*, Hebbel: *Weihe der Nacht*, Geibel: *Nun die Schatten dunkeln*, etc.), the *Naturlieder* (Spee: *Der trübe Winter ist vorbei*, the Volkslied: *Ich hört' ein Sichlein rauschen*, Goethe: *Frühzeitiger Frühling*, Uhland: *Frühlingsglaube*, C. F. Meyer: *Frühling, der die Welt umblaut*, Eichendorff: *Sehnsucht*, Liliencron: *Schöne Junitage*, etc.).

Both C. F. Meyer and Gottfried Benn wrote a poem called *Karyatide*: In C. F. Meyer's work serene plasticity of form and inner torment wage war against each other:

> Im Hof des Louvre trägt ein Weib
> Die Zinne mit dem Marmorhaupt,
> Mit einem allerliebsten Haupt.
> Als Meister Goujon sie geformt

Zu seinen Linien, überschlank
Und stehend auf dem Baugerüst
Die letzte Locke meißelte,
Erschoß den Meister hinterrücks
(Am Tag der Saint-Barthelemy),
Ein überzeugter Katholik,
Vorstürzend überflutet' er
Den seinen Busen ganz mit Blut,
Dann sank er rücklings in den Hof.
Die Marmormagd entschlummerte
Und schlief dreihundert Jahre lang,
Ein Feuerschein erwärmte sie
(Am Tag, da die Kommüne focht.)
Sie gähnt, und blickte rings sich um:
Wo bin ich denn? In welcher Stadt?
Sie morden sich. Es ist Paris.

Compare this poem with Gottfried Benn's *Karyatide* (in *Trunkene Flut*), who rather surprisingly, in view of his scorn of Goethe's 'Stirb und Werde', uses expressionistic and ecstatic imagery (derived from the Baroque bombast and from the Sturm und Drang), through which he demands the complete liberation of the Karyatide from the stone's slavery. Each of these songs is subject to its own laws of form, quite apart from their purely external and easily detectable peculiarities.

The individual image must not in itself remain self-sufficient or endeavour to appeal to the intellectual curiosity of the reader but it must originally emerge from the poem's own life. The poem itself—as in the case of C. F. Meyer's *Karyatide* and *Die sterbende Meduse* or Hölderlin's *Hälfte des Lebens* or Goethe's *Wandrers Nachtlied II* (Über allen Gipfeln ist Ruh)—becomes a symbolic image. In Goethe's poem, for instance, the peace of the world is also a promise of his own peace.

But we must be honest: we cannot and shall not ever fully fathom the depth of a work of art. The truly great poet creates from the centre of his being. His work of art is blossom *and* fruit; it is like Rilke's *Füllhorn*, immeasurable or in Goethe's sense 'inkommensurabel', brimming over with superabundance but formed:

Horn a goddess carries on her shoulder
soaring pattern of divine excess;

41

grown too mighty for a human holder,
blown by human longing none the less. . . .

I should like to conclude these reflexions with Novalis's warning in *Fragmente*: 'Tadle nichts Menschliches. Alles ist gut, nur nicht überall, nur nicht immer, nur nicht für alle. So mit der Kritik . . . Jedes Gedicht hat . . . seine eigene Umgebung, seine eigene Welt, seinen eigenen Gott.'

II

Minnesang and its Spiritual Background

> Every utterance or word lives and has its home in a particular environment. The word in the family is different from the word in business or in public. The word which has come to live in the warmth of a personal relationship is frozen to death in the cold air of public existence.
>
> D. BONHOEFFER, *Ethics*

LOVE AND LOGOS

IN MOMENTS OF great decisions, freewill gives man worth and dignity—even when his physical existence is tragically doomed. Man's strongest instincts: the aggressive, self-assertive will to *live* and the destructive, self-effacing will to *die* or (in Freud's terminology) the 'Lebensinstinkt' and the 'Todesinstinkt', have profoundly shaped the face of our civilization. These instinctive impulses are perpetuated in poetic symbols, most intensely perhaps in the images of *Prometheus* and *Tristan*. The latter may certainly only in part be considered an illustration of the ideas of courtly love. *Prometheus* is a symbol of man's passionate, predatory self-realization. *Tristan* is a symbol of man's urge towards self-extinction; it is a death-yearning, drowned in the Wagnerian music of the 'Liebestod' and the twilight of the Gods. Similar destructive and self-assertive impulses are also revealed in animal existence, for instance in the life of the worker bees, who, when autumn approaches, ruthlessly slaughter their own drone bees in order to be able to avert famine in the winter months; or there are the lemmings—rodents of the north, who, facing starvation through over-production, commit suicide in enormous masses in the water.

Mass hysteria seems at least *one* reasonable explanation of the apocalyptic catastrophe which befell Europe in the struggle of 1939-45. The holy right to *exist* is the one and last human

43

value violently claimed by modern man, e.g. in F. Werfel's *Troerinnen*. But the voice of instinct, whether it tends towards life or death, clashes with that of the intellect. In Werfel's tragedy *Juarez und Maximilian* these two irreconcilable contrasts, instinct and intellect, or sense and spirit, are strikingly formulated as the antithesis between the beast avid only of selfish gain, and the "ascete of power": 'die zweckgeile Bestie und der Asket der Macht'.

Each of us has to face that conflict and make his choice: either to shut oneself off from the irrational forces of human existence and harden one's all too sensitive skin against brutal shocks, or to surrender in self-annihilation. Kant, like other deep thinkers, advocated the irrevocable dignity of man against the market-price of things. Poets like Schiller, Goethe, Hölderlin; and H. von Kleist were the undaunted singers of personal, outer and inner freedom in Germany; cf. here p. 101.

This eternal war between mind and body, intellect and instinct is particularly, often quite unconsciously, stressed in the works of old and modern writers. Those are the most sensitive reactions as to what is going on in our souls. There is, for instance, the naturalistic concept of our existence, which is interpreted as the product of milieu, sex, and hunger. Such a Marxian view is violently opposed by Stefan George's vision, or by the lust for self-extinction in Neo-Romanticism, or by the call for 'transformation' in Rainer Maria Rilke's *Duino Elegies*. Whilst passion must not be formless, the poetic pattern itself is not self-sufficient; cf. the preceding chapter here and the recent controversies against and in defence of Shelley, and T. S. Eliot's call for the impersonal pattern in his Introduction to *The Serpent* by Paul Valéry: 'Not our feelings, but the pattern which we may make of our feelings is the centre of value.'

In the course of our Western civilization, this dualism of intellect and life-instinct seems to undergo an unending cycle of variations. Only in rare, sacred moments of human development are these contrasts harmonized, as, for instance, in the fifth century of Greece, or in Germany in the twelfth and thirteenth centuries: e.g. in the portrait-sculptures of Bamberg (The Rider, Elisabeth, Adam and Eve, the Synagogue, etc.) and of Naumburg (Ekkehard and Uta, Hermann

and Reglindis, Timo, Dietrich, Wilhelm, etc.), in the Minnesang of Walther and H. von Morungen, the great medieval
romances, *Tristan* and *Parzival,* moreover in the Weimar
classicism and particularly in Goethe's own life and poetry.

We see how again and again the artist's work enshrines the
conflicts and mysteries of logos and love. My theme here must
of necessity remain limited to *one* aspect, i.e. to the poetic
expression in the medieval Austrian and German Minnesang.
It is fascinating to trace its own inherent form as well as its
ethos, and at the same time to lay bare its literary heritage.

Courtly Love

Although the minnesingers themselves have not worked out a
systematic doctrine of courtly love, it can nevertheless to a
certain extent be deduced from their songs. Some characteristic
features stand out clearly: the beauty and nobility of the beloved lady are elevated above the limit of any mortal being.
Fulfilment of the heart's yearning is denied to a lover, but the
power of minne ennobles him and makes him virtuous. When
speaking here of courtly love, we cannot enter into the intricate
problem of Eros and Agape, earthly and heavenly love, nor do
we follow those who, blindly basing their views on Freud's
theories, emphasize sex at the cost of all other expression of our
existence, nor those who, basing themselves on Adler's, see will-
power as the source of everything. The Austrian and German
minnesang arose out of a complex of values which had grown up
under special social, political, and regional conditions and
which shaped themselves to a unique though short-lived
literary epoch, a so-called 'Sonderkultur' which reaches back
into the mysterious resources of our mind and body and
exercises its influence far beyond its boundaries on to Dante,
Shakespeare, the Baroque caprices, and further on to Richard
Wagner's *Tristan und Isolde,* and our present age.

Surveying the whole field, scholars often too readily fall
victims to overstressing the problem of origin, influences,
parallel developments, etc., at the cost of the inherent expression of minnesang which has also a life of its own, and which
grew out of its own culture and creators and public of which

45

were nearly all recruited from the ordo equestris. The songs of Heinrich von Morungen, Walther von der Vogelweide, Wolfram von Eschenbach, etc., could ultimately grow only from the roots of their own creative resources.

The cosmopolitan chivalric society provides its background. It reflects the attitude of the *vassal to his liege-lord*. Courtly love (minne) is described as a service ('dienest'). Just as the vassal is loyal to his liege-lord, so the lover to his 'frouwe', who is 'aller wîbe ein krône': the most perfect of all women. He is her subject and in her service, 'holt', 'eigen', and 'undertân'. Minne is secret ('tougen'). 'Rüemen'—boasting—is fatal because the spies ('huote') jealously wait for their revenge. Whilst a religious ethos underlies the concept of the 'miles Christianus', in the Minnesang the stress lies rather on aesthetic values. The courtly lover aspires a wish-fantasy of physical and spiritual harmony, a *'kalokagathos' ideal*, the glory of the spiritualized, beautiful body, as represented in the noble beauty of the statues at Bamberg and Naumburg, and in the description of Îsolt in Gottfried's *Tristan*.

Hannah Closs in *Art and Life* (1936) compares the character-study in stone of Uta at Naumburg with Gottfried's description of Îsolt and offers a striking translation of Gottfried's verses:

> Her dress clung intimately to her, it moulded itself to her body, it did not stand away anywhere, it sought it everywhere from top to bottom; it fell into folds at her feet just as much as any of you would desire. . . . Instead of the clasp which should have been there, was fastened a little string of pearls. Into it the beautiful maiden had thrust the thumb of the left hand; the right she held low down, you know well where one should close a cloak, and held it close in courtly manner with her two fingers. . . .[1]

Grace in movement and behaviour, tact and restraint provide a welcome balance to the rugged defiance of medieval knighthood. Its representatives not only enjoyed but also practised the art of the minnesang. Whether the socially exclusive 'Minnedienst' (service of knight to his lady) is part of the professional duty of a medieval ministerialis or not cannot be proved, as its established tradition lacks a legally binding

[1] 10,913ff.

formula. Public and poets and composers of the music were identical. Dancing, harping, and making or composing poetry were part of the education of a knight. He learned how to behave correctly and converse with the ladies: 'wol gebâren und wider die frouwen sprechen'. It was the duty of the poet to serve his society: 'der werlde vröude mêren', to increase the world's joy, to soothe the sad hour: 'swaere stunde senfter machen', and to serve God. The medieval knight had to be magnanimous, ingenious, largifluous, egregious, strenuous—a real Miles dei. Here lies the root of Baldasarre Castiglione's *Cortegiano*, printed 1528, but completed in 1516 (the year of Thomas More's *Utopia* and Ariosto's *Orlando Furioso*), and of the modern Gentleman ideal.

In the fourth book of the *Cortegiano*, we read:

> Dalla *temperanzia* nascono molte altre virtú; ché quando un animo è concorde di questa *armonia*, per mezzo della ragione poi facilmente receve la vera fortezza, la quale lo fa intrepido e sicuro da ogni periculo, e quasi sopra le passioni umane; no meno la *giustizia*, vergine incorrotta, amica della *modestia* e del *bene*, regina di tutte l'altre virtú . . . La *magnanimitá* ancora succede a queste . . . la *prudenzia* . . . ed in tal felice catena ancora sono colligate la *liberalitá* . . . la *mansuetudine*, la *piacevolezza*, la *affabilità*, e molte altre che or non è tempo di dire.[1]

Medieval German literature (*Parzival*, *Tristan*, the *Nibelungen*, Walther's and Heinrich von Morungen's minnesongs, etc.) reflects the code of chivalric society. A sense of balance punctuates all forms of expression of life in which courtesy, manners, and above all integrity of spirit became a unity. This balanced outlook on life achieved a golden mean, called 'tugent' (inner virtue).[2] It seems as if Plato's 'andreia', 'sofia', 'dikaiosyne', 'sofrosyne', and Marcus Tullius Cicero's four virtues: fortitudo, temperantia, iustitia, prudentia, were now interpreted in terms of chivalry; Cicero's ethical terms: utile, honestum, summum bonum, apparently attained a new valuation. He who was 'höfisch' had to possess self-control, moderation; due measure: 'maze', generosity: 'milte'; faithfulness: 'triuwe' towards others

[1] Chapter XVIII.

[2] As to the system of the chivalric virtues and Ehrismann's representation, see E. R. Curtius's virile criticism in his *European Literature and the Latin Middle Ages*, 1953, pp. 519ff.

and faithfulness or constancy 'staete' towards himself; good manners: 'zuht' and propriety, social grace: 'vuoge'. To be a stay-at-home: 'sich verligen' was considered shameful. Such a conception of a knight's duties (his 'schildes ambet', his 'arebeit') betrayed a very high moral standard. This social and ethic code sought perfection in its aspiration towards God. Walther clearly points to it when in his poem, *Ich saz ûf eime steine*, he aims at a harmony of summum bonum=God's grace ('gotes hulde'), honestum ('êre'), and utile ('varnde guot'); cf. also Hartmann's dialogue between Heart and Body in his so-called *Büchlein* and the important Latin *Dialogus Inter Corpus et Animam* by Fulbertus.

CATHARISM

But in the foreground of our argument stands the problem of *fin' amors* (*fin*=pure, chaste), or *reine Liebe*. The question of origin remains even today still unsolved, although many striking parallels can be brought to evidence, e.g. between the ethos of Minne (*Minne-ethos*) and Catharism. In the latter the above dualism between instinct and intellect, is sharply pronounced. We need only refer to the following essential points which, however, have not and will not perhaps for some time be accepted by orthodox literary critics. We do not go so far as to claim that the Provençal troubadors and German minnesingers are directly dependent on Cathar ideas. But it does seem more than possible that religious and cultural influences which permeated the atmosphere of the time, and for which, moreover, thousands ultimately were ready to die, have tinted, if not definitely coloured, the aesthetic expression of the period of the region, from which a stream of vital influences went to Germany. Here are some important points: the Cathars founded their church on a female principle; they condemned marriage as an earthly bondage; they made use of a language of secret symbols; they longed for complete extinction or spiritualization of our material existence; finally, their one and only kiss at the consolamentum reminds one of the kiss which the minnesinger receives from his beloved.

The Cathars and Albigenses of the twelfth century, whose

fate was sealed by Simon de Montfort's cruel crusade of 1209 and at the disastrous Battle of Muret (1213), fervently believed that man's soul is imprisoned in the body, the evil principle of our life. Their ideas can clearly be traced back to *Manichaeism*, according to which light and dark are eternal, and from the beginning absolutely separate; only now light and dark became mixed, but in the future they will be separate again. The Manichaens were incidentally, like the Cathars, vegetarians; they did not seek to hold property, and were against killing and propagation. Moreover, like Mani (third century A.D.), the Cathars rejected the dogma of Christ's incarnation and believed in the dualism of spirit and matter, which is inextinguishable. They renounced marriage so that the soul may not be polluted by the temptation of the flesh and the bodily union, which to them is a Satanic act. Man is, according to Catharism, a fallen angel, who has forfeited his inner dignity. There is no room to refer to the other precursors of the Cathar creed—to the Priscillians in Spain (fourth century), to the Paulicians founded by a Syrian monk in the seventh century, to the Bogomiles in the twelfth century, and to the Waldenses, a Puritan sect founded in the twelfth century in the valleys of Piedmont, Dauphiné and Provence by Peter Waldo of Lyons, who were contemporaries of the Cathars, and whose doctrines show some remarkable affinity with theirs.[1]

The following five rites of Catharism can be singled out distinctively: the *Blessings of Bread;* the *melioramentum* (genuflexions at the end of each ceremony or meeting); the *apparelhamentum* or general public confession in set, formulated

---

[1] As to Catharism, the principle sources are the *registers of the Inquisition:*

(I) (a) No. 609 of the Municipal Library of Toulouse, which covers the years 1242-7 in that region.

(b) MSS. 25-8, Collection Doat, Bibliothèque Nationale in Paris, covering most particularly the years 1273-4 and 1285-90.

(c) The Manual of the Inquisition written by Bernard Gui, the inquisitor of Toulouse and in Italy from 1306-23. It is also a handbook as to how to treat or handle the heretics.

(II) In contrast to the above, there are the Cathars' own sources:

(a) A Ritual of the Consolamentum, written in Languedocian, published by Clédat in 1887, now in the library at Lyons.

(b) A Latin work, the book of John.

(c) The inscriptions in the caves of the Sabarthes the last refuge of the persecuted Cathars.

(d) The *Liber de duobus principiis*, at Florence, published by A. Dodaine in 1939.

prayers, once a month; the *Kiss of Peace* which the Cathars give each other after the ceremonies, but as the Cathars must not touch a woman, one woman first kisses the Gospel and then 'exchanges the kiss' to the other woman; finally the famous *consolamentum* or *Baptism of the Holy Spirit*, which entails a long probation, and which meant that the candidate had to leave his family and devote himself entirely to the Church of God in the Cathar congregation. He had to take a vow not to eat meat, nor eggs, nor cheese, nor fat, not to lie, not to swear, not to kill, he had to be 'pure', i.e. a Cathar. The 'Credentes' were the believers in contrast to the true Cathars, who were called 'Perfecti' or 'Parfaits' by the Catholics and 'Good Christians' or the 'Good Men' ('Bonshommes') by their own followers.

In his declaration, the courageous Cathar Bishop Guilhalbert of Castres gives us the essence of Catharist faith:

> I have left father, mother and children. I have given up everything the Gospel commands me to renounce. Gold and silver I no longer carry in my purse. I am satisfied with each day's food and am not anxious whether tomorrow I shall have the wherewithal to be clothed and fed. You behold in me the beatitudes which Jesus Christ preached and in which His Gospel consists. You see me poor, meek, peaceable, pure in heart; you see me in tears, suffering, hunger and thirst, persecution and the world's hatred for the sake of Righteousness.

As to the Cathars' concept of good and evil, see *Le Génie d'Oc: Le Problème du Mal* (D. Roché), *Les Cahiers du Sud:*

> Ce qui caractérise l'attitude de manichéens et des cathares, c'est qu'ils prennent le mal comme une réalité manifestée par les souffrances physiques et morales. A cette attitude s'est opposé Saint Augustin bien qu'il en ait toujours subi l'influence à certain égards, car il avait été pendant neuf ans auditeur manichéen. . . .[1]

We have stressed the tenets of the Cathars as they flourished within the over-ripe civilization of Languedoc, which, to our mind, could not help being stimulated either consciously or unconsciously by them. Montségur near Foix became the rocky castle of the heretics who, before their ultimate ruthless extermination, had fortified themselves behind its high and sombre walls. Béziers had long before been burned to the

---

[1] Cf. also R. Nelli's *Introduction à une dialectique du bien et du mal* and the *Textes manichéens et cathares*—especially the extracts from 'la cène secrète', etc. ibid.

ground, and the young Count Trencavel met with a tragic, treacherous end in the dungeons of his own fortress at Carcassonne.[1] With his iron fist Simon of Montfort swept away that Southern culture, which he considered the canker of Christianity, a pollution of our earth, and Satan's seed. Thus with a sudden onslaught the heart of a unique period in European development was broken; an epoch which had not only drunk in the tradition of Classic culture, but had also been fertilized by the neighbouring Hispano-Moorish civilization.

Hispano-Moorish Prototypes

As early as 1031 Cordoba had become a republic, and the Omayyad rule come to an end, but the Arabian chivalry, Arabian courtly love poetry and Arabian code of honour lived on amongst the conquerors through generations. Moreover, trade connexions, the Crusade, direct and indirect contacts of Provençal life with the Andalusian heritage created, in spite of language barriers, invaluable bridges between East and West. This was particularly the case with the Provence, the Pyrenees, and also Aragon. It can hardly be denied, and has been amply proved, that in Hispano-Andalusian court poetry are to be found many essential features of thought and form which reveal a close affinity with the German courtly love lyrics; i.e. the homage of the poet to his noble lady, the wooing and worship of his beloved, the part played by the married lady and by the spies, and the love-yearning, the secrecy and hopelessness of courting, etc. Even the dawn-song, through Provençal intermediaries, has its equivalent in Arabian poetry; the origin of the alba may, however, be the pseudo-Ovidian love letter of Leander to Hero. This story of Hero and Leander ultimately goes back to a Persian source.

As to the concept of 'pure love', important Arabian prototypes can be mentioned:

The theme of pure love was celebrated among the mythical Bedouin tribe of Odhrah. It was traditional among the Banou Odhrah that when lovers love, they die. . . . The Odhrah ideal was

[1] See also the 'Historic Notes' at the end of Hannah Closs's creative interpretation of the Albigensian Crusade in her last novel, *The Silent Tarn* (1955), and her preceding novels, *High are the Mountains, And Sombre the Valleys.*

51

Djamil, who died in this way for love of Buthania. Djamil . . . a
poet of the first century after the Hegira. He died in Egypt in 701.[1]

The influence of Platonic and Neo-Platonic ideas upon their
work is unmistakable, and also explicable, as Arabic philosophy
was stimulated by them through the translations by the Syrian
Christians in the seventh, eighth, and ninth centuries. These
Syrians not only brought wine and silk to Europe, but also
helped to spread Greek culture in Alexandria. But the Greek
literature rendered into Arabic by them was that of the
Alexandrian age, not the Classic Greek.

Ibn Sina-Avicenna (+1037), preceptor of a prince and
popular philosopher, was a younger contemporary of Firdausi
(+1020). In Avicenna's philosophy, the dualism of body and
soul is clearly marked; yet in contrast to the Cathars he believed
in a God-created world which is beautiful and which could not
be improved any more. There we distinctly hear an echo of
Plato's 'best possible' world. It is not certain whether Avicenna's
Treatise on Love definitely inspired the early troubadours
Guillaume IX (+1127) and Marcabru (about 1130-48), but
there is no doubt that Avicenna was much read and translated,
and it is most likely that amongst his works the *Treatise on Love*
played an important part.

> Guillaume IX, Marcabru, Cercamon, Bernart Marti, are just
> as idealistic in their attitude towards and conception of true love,
> i.e. Courtly Love, as are Jaufré Rudel and Bernart de Ventadour.
> For them all this love,—*fin' amors* . . .—is a love of pure desire
> and not of physical possession.[2]

Moreover, A. R. Nykl in his *Dove's Neck-Ring* holds that 'a
number of Marcabru's poems show a strong Andalusian influence, especially the two Estronell (zurzur?) songs, which excite
so much wonder in Pillet. In Marcabru's imitator, Peire
d'Alvernhe, and in Jaufré Rudel similar echoes are noticeable.'
A. R. Nykl is convinced that melody, rhythm, and rhyme of
Andalusian poetry influenced the autochthonous Provençal
song. Naturally it is difficult to speak of *direct* influences, as 'the
ultimate *source* of many of the conceits in both regions' (Spain

---

[1] Cf. A. J. Denomy: *Fin' Amors* (Medieval Studies, III, 1946). Cf. *Le Génie d'Oc
et l'homme méditerranèen* (*Les Cahiers du Sud*), as to the theory of l'âme-soeur in the
works of Ibn Dâwoûd and Ibn Hazm, p. 31.
[2] Denomy, l.c.

and the South of France) 'was Greece, through the sensually
realistic Ovid in Latin, and through the gentle spiritual Plato
in the Arabic of the Bagdad period: in Aquitania about
A.D. 1100 we can no longer speak of "origins", but rather a fusion
of these two streams and their blending in the lingua romana,
not as a miracle, but as a new offshoot, perfectly explicable by
geography, ethnology and history. It would be quite plausible
to assume as has been suggested by Pillet, Vossler, and Jeanroy
that the powerful personality of Guillaume IX has been "the
melting pot in which these ingredients were given new form".'

PLATO, OVID AND OTHER SOURCES

It was in the heyday of Arabic Spain under Al-Mansur
(+about 1002) that Ibn Hazm (born 994) lived. His love-
treatise, *Taug*, written in 1022, re-echoes Platonic ideas:
'Love . . . is a reunion of poets of the souls, separated in this
creation, within their original higher element.'[1] Noble love is
harmonious. 'Love . . . is a delightful condition and a disease
yearned for.' But in this work on the symptoms of love, on love
from afar, at first sight, through messengers, with eyes, with
speech, on faithfulness, secrecy, continence, and unfaithfulness,
etc., Ibn Hazm aims at the spiritualization of matter: 'Love is a
spiritual approval and a mutual commingling of souls.' True
love grows stronger—not weaker—through the removal of the
beloved object.

The peculiar mingling of passion and intellect is most
characteristic of the Minnesang as well as of *Taug*; cf., for
instance, the intellectual conceit in the following strange comparison in Ibn Hazm's work: 'I am turning my eye wherever
you go, precisely as if you were changing (denomination) like
in grammar a noun and its adjective.'

As another essential source of inspiration may be mentioned
Ibn Roshd-Averroes (+1198), who was a resolute thinker, a
preceptor of a prince, doctor of medicine, and interpreter of
Aristotle. Averroes saw life's evil in the necessity of matter.
In our human existence good and evil must mix. Love is,
according to him, the principle of all movement in life. Pure

[1] Nykl, l.c.

love ennobles the lovers. It seems as if the dualism of Catharism mentioned above could not possibly have anything to do with Averroes's philosophy, as the Cathar heretics considered the body a devilish temptation. But only the Perfecti were able to reach such an unearthly height whilst the dualism of good and evil and the rejection of marriage could easily carry away the lesser minds to ecstatic licentiousness and immorality. The least one can ask for in our proposed theme is, I feel, a definite recognition of a possible stream of influence from Cathar doctrines to their contemporary literary thought and expression and vice-versa. It is beyond doubt that a valuable stream of influence came into the idea of courtly love from the renowned treatise, *De Amore*, by Andreas Capellanus. This book (composed about 1184) manifests strong contacts with Arabian sources, probably with Avicenna.

According to the latter's *Treatise on Love*, the human mind is bound to the body, but not hopelessly imprisoned in it; the soul seeks to free itself from the loving embrace of matter. Pure love avoids therefore all vulgar sensuality—a sensuality which in literature was fanned by Ovid, the favourite Classic author of the Middle Ages. Ovid describes the lovers in Cupid's bondage; also Ovid's lovers yearn, they grow pale and sleepless, and are consumed with jealousy; they are conquered by Cupids: 'Palleat omnis amans: hic est color aptus amanti.'[1] Cf. also 'ducentur capti iuvenes captaeque puellae: haec tibi magnificus pompa triumphus erit'.[2]

Moreover, the ultimate source of the so-called 'Wechsel' in *Minnesangs Frühling* can justly be traced back to Ovid's *Heroides*. Heinrich von Morungen is, like many others, indebted to Ovid's *Amores* and *Metamorphoses*.

The real literary heirs of Ovid, however, were the Vagantes in the *Carmina Burana*, etc. The concept of pure love in the courtly minnesang goes back to deeper roots. Pure love does allow kiss, embrace, and bodily nearness, and yet it rises high above morality, because such nearness and touch (not the last physical consummation) must increase the desire and ennoble virtues. It is a love which rewards the faithful lovers by making the good ones better and the bad ones good.

[1] *Ars Amatoria*, I, 729.   [2] *Amores* (I, 2, 27-8).

This concept of 'fin' amors' is crystallized in Andreas Capellanus's system of love. Its main trend of argument is clear: 'love is not marital affection': cf. the seventh dialogue: 'Love can by no means exercise its functions between husband and wife,'; fifth dialogue: 'Pure love, in contrast to mixed love, allows kiss and embrace, but omits the final solace. . . .'

It seems likely that the author of *De Amore* had been under the influence of St. Bernard of Clairvaux (+1153), who speaks of the three degrees of love, carnal, rational, spiritual, and who strongly differentiates between the elite of the 'fins cuers leals' and the 'vileins'. The cleric Andreas Capellanus, in spite of his fatherly warning against Eve's temptation, betrays, however, a rather worldly heart, especially when he speaks of his lovesick nuns. J. J. Parry, in his Introduction to Capellanus, sees in *De Amore* a mirror of Queen Eleanor's court of love during the years 1170-4; the actual composition of *De Amore* most probably belongs to a later date.

Eleanor of Poitiers became the inspiration of many a poet. Uhland in *Rudello*, the first ballad of his cycle *Sängerliebe*, sings the praise of the Provence which to him is the cradle of Minnesong:

> In den Thalen der Provence
> ist der Minnesang entsprossen,
> Kind des Frühlings und der Minne,
> holder, inniger, Genossen. . . .

Excluding obviously autochthonous poems in the *Minnesangs Frühling* of the knightly lyric of the Danubian valley which provides lucid evidence of the difference between the 'trûtliet' of the old love lyric and the artificial courtly Minnesang, nobody can now seriously doubt the decisive stimulus coming from that sun-drenched south. But we have already pointed out several other equally weighty parallels (Catharism) and influences coming from the Arabic, Andalusian courts, from Plato and Ovid and the Roman Catholic Church. Here we must add the cult of the *Holy Virgin* who is 'mother of God' and intermediary between God and men (as the lady between lord and vassal), and the *Latin hymns*, e.g.

> Noctis tempus iam praeterit,
> Iam gallus canit viribus. . . .

and

> Lux clara surgens rutilat,
> Quae dulce festum nuntiat.[1]

Also the musical form of litany, hymn and sequence have left their imprint on the melody (*don, wîse*) and on the construction of courtly love poetry which was sung to the accompaniment of harp or fiddle.

Further, there is the epistolary literature in medieval Latin, written by Marbod from Angers, by Alderich from Bourgueil and Hildebert from Tours. From this eleventh-century circle literary threads lead to England. Hildebert, for instance, paid a glowing homage to Adela, daughter of William the Conqueror and wife of the Count of Blois, whom he calls 'prima dearum'; Mathilda, wife of Henry I of England and daughter of King Malcolm of Scotland, was also enthusiastically praised by him and by Marbod.

Having already referred to many other parallel themes in the Arabic code and in Catharism, etc., we can see that Classical, Christian, and heretical Arabic and Germanic elements are combined in the graduated system of ethical values which corresponds with the graduated system of medieval society. It was certainly difficult to reconcile the idea of Germanic heroism with that of Christian humility and the idea of pure love with that of reckless frivolity, but the synthesis was achieved at the height of medieval European chivalry.

Only if we see courtly love poetry as the expression of a unity of forces from without and within, can we do it justice. The hermit Trevrizent teaches the erring Parzival how to gain this unity of seemingly irreconcilable contrasts: tradition and originality, mind and body, intellect and instinct, of which we spoke at the beginning:

> The body's prize and yet the soul's paradise:

> Des lîbes prîs unt doch der sêle paradîs.

[1] *Analecta Hymnica.*

III

Tristan und Ìsolt

GOTTFRIED VON STRASSBURG

> Gottfried, not Walther, was the nightingale of perfect
> note. His romance of *Tristan* is as much song as story and
> has been rightly spoken of as a Hohelied der Minne, a
> high song of love.
>
> M. F. RICHEY, *The Medieval German Love Lyric*

> *Tristan* of Gottfried von Strassburg, which is, except for
> the *Canterbury Tales* and the *Divina Commedia*, the greatest
> poem of the Middle Ages.
>
> R. S. LOOMIS, *The Romance of Tristan and Ysolt*

COURTLY LIFE AT THE TIME OF ELEANOR OF POITOU, BRERI, CHRESTIEN

GOTTFRIED's *Tristan und Ìsolt* (about 1210) belongs to the immortal treasures of the world's literature. His lyrical epic still makes a direct appeal to us today, for it is at once personal and impersonal as every true work of art should be.

After more than seven hundred years *Tristan und Ìsolt* provides a mine of material for the student of comparative literature—a material rich in legends, fairy tales, mythological, Celtic and Classical motifs, whilst modern poets are still irresistibly drawn to the fierce and passionate tale that underlies the medieval romance. But indeed the very graceful form in Gottfried's work clothes a sensibility and ideas of unexpected profundity which verge on the metaphysical and make his poem appear almost as the gospel of a religious faith, the religion of *Minne*.

Many scholars are unjustifiably inclined to exalt the ethical values of Wolfram's *Parzival* at the expense of Gottfried's 'aestheticism'. Both poets in their own way created works of

57

artistic power and spiritual depth that make them rank worthily beside Dante. In Gottfried the spiritual meaning of things is conveyed to us to a great extent by the aesthetic form, which suggests rather than describes ideas.

Gottfried's *Tristan und Îsolt* belongs to the year in which his greatest rival, Wolfram von Eschenbach, finished his *Parzival*. Gottfried probably died before the completion of *Tristan und Îsolt*, which was composed about five years before the signing of Magna Carta, or five years before the coronation of Frederick II in 1215. While Gottfried was writing his work, Walther von der Vogelweide was engaged in the political strife raging between the Papacy and the Empire; Albrecht von Halberstadt began his *Metamorphosen* and Herbert von Fritzlar his *Lied von Troya*; Hartmann von Aue had already finished *Iwein* (before 1204).

Though the zenith of medieval German literature and art now is a thing of the past, the magic words 'courtly love' still call up a fascinating vision of knights and minstrels. Remote as that time may seem to us now, its poets and singers created works of permanent value, which, having survived for hundreds of years, touch us more deeply today than ever before. We are thinking not only of the passionate tragedy of Tristan, the hero and minstrel, but of the medieval world in all its aspects: the solemn mood of Parzival, the power of the Knights Templar, the vigil and accolade.

Today there is no doubt that Walther's political songs and love lyrics, Heinrich von Morungen's aubade *Owê, sol aber mir iemer mê/geliuhten dur die naht* and gay dancing measure *Ich hôrt ûf der heide/lûte stimme und süezen sanc* belong just as much as *Tristan und Îsolt* and *Parzival* not only to the highest achievements of courtly society, but also to the immortal heritage of all time. Nevertheless, like all great literature, Gottfried's *Tristan und Îsolt* bears traces of the age and society from which it sprang. In its allusions, emotions, ideals, motives, its very gestures it shows features peculiar to courtly culture. We may mention Tristan's upbringing and that of Îsolt, the ceremony at which Tristan is dubbed knight, and the May festival at Tintagel, Gottfried's praise of Tristan on horseback and the famous description of Îsolt, which remind us of the vigorous statue of the knight on horseback at Bamberg and the sculptured figures of the founders of Naumburg Cathedral. In this courtly world *minne* was regarded as the supreme moral virtue: *ez liebet liebe und edelt muot/ez staetet triuwe und tugendet leben.* Gottfried's *morâliteit* shows how personal renown, increase of material goods, the world and God may be reconciled. *Frau Minne* uplifts us by her magic power. It was this conception of courtly life based on love which led Gottfried to write his well-known polemic against his great adversary, Wolfram von Eschenbach.

Limitation of space prevents us from dealing here with the numerous Eastern and Western sources of the doctrine of courtly love to which regional, historical, and literary factors made important contributions. We cannot overestimate the part played by the vivacious Eleanor of Poitiers (born 1122) in the courtly culture, *hövescheit* and *cortezia*, of the age. Her grandfather, duke William IX of Aquitaine, was the first Provençal troubadour whose name we know; her father William X, died suddenly in 1137. The fifteen-year-old Eleanor was now the richest heiress in Europe and ruled over territory surpassing in size that of the King of France. The same year her marriage to Louis VII was celebrated. But Eleanor thought she had married 'a king not a monk', and during the adventurous crusade, in which she herself took part at the side of her royal husband, serious disputes arose between them. On their return the Pope was able to reconcile them, but only temporarily; when she was thirty years old she divorced Louis and offered her hand in marriage to Henry Plantagenet (later Henry II of England), her junior by eleven years. Henry was perhaps the most splendid prince of the age, and a generous patron of art and learning. The chronicler Wace, Marie de France and probably Robert de Borron were connected with the Anglo-Norman court of Westminster. Here, as before at the court of Poitou, Eleanor's wit soon kindled the flame of poetry and literary discourse. From December 1154 she was 'Queen of England, Lady of Ireland, Duchess of Normandy, Aquitaine, and Gascogne, Countess of Poitou, Saintonge, Angoumois, Limousin, Auvergne, Bordeaux, Agen, and of Anjou, Maine, and Touraine'. But her life with her powerful English husband was troubled; finally, she came to oppose him and stir up her sons against their father. It was especially in Richard I that her own personality was most strongly developed. She outlived Henry by many years. Mathilda, her daughter from her union with Henry II, married Henry the Lion and may well have been the patroness whom Eilhart von Oberge praised so highly. Henry the Lion spent some months in Normandy after Frederick Barbarossa had exiled him from Saxony in 1182. From there he travelled with Mathilda to the Anglo-Norman court of his father-in-law, and here she may have received much literary stimulus. Marie, Eleanor's daughter by Louis VII, married Henry I of Champagne. She was the patroness of Chrestien de Troyes and it was at her court too that Andreas Capellanus wrote his *Tractatus de amore*. The other daughter of Eleanor and Louis VII was Alix, wife of Thibaut V of Blois, at whose court Gautier of Arras composed *Eracles*. But the greatest literary centre was Eleanor's court at Poitiers. Here perhaps the original source called *Urtristan* was composed about 1150 by a poet whose name has unfortunately remained unknown to us. Soon after, Bernart de Ventadour sang in praise of Eleanor's mature beauty and likened himself to Tristan in his yearning for his beloved mistress, who journeyed to a distant land. This is probably the earliest reference to Tristan and Îsolt:

> Tan trac pena d'amor
> qu'a Tristan l'amador
> non avenc tan de dolor
> per Yzeut la blonda

although we can arrive at no definite conclusion as to the date of the so-called *Estoire* on account of the brevity of the allusion.

How did the story of Tristan reach Poitiers? For Tristan was, as we shall see from the etymology of the name, originally a Pictish hero of Scotland, and only later became a Breton. A certain conteur, Bledhericus (also called Bleri or Breri), is said to have introduced Cymric tales to the court of Eleanor's father. The Celtic elements of the Tristan saga may then have reached Provence through this Bledhericus. Thomas, too, mentions a Breri who knew the history of the British kings, that is Geoffrey's *Historia*. Breri was not, however, the only bearer of Cymric sagas, for there were many *conteurs bretons* at the court of William X. But we must not forget that it was the medieval custom to refer to a 'source', even if the author of a saga had himself introduced innovations.

Chrestien de Troyes was the first poet, whose name we know, to compose a version of Tristan.[1] References to *Tristan* and parallel passages in his other works prove that he knew the *Urtristan*. Unfortunately, his *Tristan* is lost, but in *Cligés* we have an important counterpart. In *Cligés* (as in *Tristan*) the story of the parents forms a prologue to the main work; here also we find the play on the words *la mer, amer, l'amer* which we know from Thomas's version; and here, too, is the conflicting love of the uncle, nephew, and the uncle's bride, but the adultery is avoided by means of magic and apparent death; here, too, we meet with a figure reminiscent of Brangaene. We have already indicated how Chrestien sets up *Cligés* as the ideal of unimpeachable knightly chastity in direct contrast to the unlawful love in *Tristan*. Whether Chrestien was influenced by Thomas or vice versa cannot be determined. The play on words mentioned above does, however, belong rather to Thomas's style than to that of Chrestien. It seems most probable that Chrestien composed *Tristan* in his youth, then later read Thomas and afterwards wrote *Cligés* in order to counter the passionate love-story.

Eleanor probably brought the *Urtristan* to England, and at her court we can well imagine that Thomas was inspired to write his version of *Tristan*. He introduced English names and allusions to the story.

BASIC ELEMENTS IN THE STORY OF *Tristan und Îsolt*

What was the original saga like? What is the nucleus of the legend? Ranke's attempted reconstruction of an independent Celtic lay of Tristan must remain hypothetical. Golther's assumption that the original story fell into three parts, may, however, be safely accepted. The three parts are: the Môrolt story, the saga of the princess with the golden hair, and Îsolt of the White Hands.

I. *The Môrolt story* is clearly of Celtic origin. It tells of the victory of a young Cornish hero over the giant Môrolt, who

[1] *Cligés* I.ff.

exacts human tribute. The David-Goliath parallel is obvious. After the young hero has been wounded, he is laid in a rudderless boat and pushed out to sea. The voyage in a rudderless boat to fairyland in search of healing reminds one of the favourite Irish tales of *imrama*,[1] although 'we have no reason to believe that the idea of such an adventurous voyage was confined to the Irish'. The popularity of this journey to fairyland is shown also by the legend of Arthur, and the story of *Guigemar* by Marie de France. The Môrolt story also provides us with the historical foundation of the saga. Mark, in some versions, is the sixth-century contemporary of Arthur; it has not, however, been possible to determine whether Arthur was originally connected with Tristan or not. The relationship—Arthur—Guinevere—Modred—might well have served as a model for the poet of Tristan. The date of that story must, however, in all probability fall after Geoffrey's *Historia* or after the popular tales about Arthur possibly prior to Geoffrey.

In Thomas and Gottfried, Mark and Arthur are not contemporaries. Mark himself was first mentioned historically in 884 in the *Vita Sancti Pauli Aureliani* by an Armorican monk. We can, with a certain reserve, arrive at important conclusions as to the home and subsequent travels of the saga from the etymology of the names of the various heroes. The name Mark (in old Celtic tales Eochaid) seems to signify an animal, i.e. 'equus' (Irish 'ech'). It is said that Mark had horse's ears, as Midas had ass's; cf. Béroul: *Marc a orelles de cheval*. The name Mariadoc is of Breton origin. Riwalîn, Tristan's father (in Eilhart called Rivalîn, in Thomas Rivalen, but in the French Romance Meliadus) appears in the Armorican saga as the ancestor of Breton princes. In a Welsh triad he is called Tallwch: 'Tristan, son of Tallwch, disguised as a swineherd, tended the swine of Mark, son of Meirchyon, while the swineherd went with a message to Îsolt.' Riwalîn's second name is Kanêlengres which, according to R. S. Loomis, suggests a corruption of Rivalon-Reis.[2]

The name Îsolt presents great difficulty: (Béroul) Iseut or

---

[1] Cf. Gertrude Schoepperle, *Tristan and Îsolt*.

[2] *The Romance of Tristram and Ysolt*; cf. also Golther *Tristan und Isolde*, p. 144 (*Kanoel + Langres*). *Parmenîe* = Ermenia (saga) = Armorica.

Yseut; (Thomas) Îsold, Ysolt, etc.; (Norwegian saga) Isond, (Sir Tristrem) Ysonde; (Eilhart) Ŷsalde, Îsalde; (Welsh) Esyllt. Probably the name Îsolt is of Franconian (Îswalda, Îshilt), not Cymric, origin. But we must not lay too much stress on 'the complete conformity to phonetic laws' as foreign names are often distorted. The name *Tristan* is most important, since it is at least Common Celtic if not definitely Pictish; cf. the Pictish saga of *Drust* in the Irish *Wooing of Emer*.

II. *The Quest of the Princess with the Golden Hair* goes back to a fairy-tale motif. Two other motifs are connected with it: (1) The dangerous journey to win a bride (gefährliche Brautwerbung, e.g. König Rother, Siegfried, Gudrun, etc.) which often brings in its train the fulfilment of a difficult task (the fight with a dragon). In this there are traces of primitive folklore, as for instance when it is said that Tristan cuts out the monster's tongue as evidence of his deed. (2) The motif of the nephew's love for the bride of his uncle and liege lord. The fact that Tristan goes to Ireland twice points to a certain vagueness in the tradition of the now composite saga. He undertakes the first journey for healing, the second to win the bride. We have already referred to the Celtic *imrama*. In the Irish elopement stories (*aitheda*) of *Diarmaid and Grainne*, and *Naisi and Deirdre* we find the second foundation of the Tristan romance, if the Arthurian material was introduced later. Whether Arthur's knights were originally mystic images of storm and sun, whether his Queen's abduction was an analogy to the rape of the flower maiden, whether his son Modred was a kind of Irish Midir, and finally whether Arthur himself was the personification of the enfeebled forces of Nature awaiting the new spring, are problems which we cannot enter into in detail here. The period at which Arthur came into the saga remains a matter of conjecture. The great Arthurian scholar R. S. Loomis says that Arthur was already connected with the Tristan story in a Welsh triad, but we may well ask, how then is it to be explained that Thomas and Gottfried omitted the popular Arthurian material?

III. *Îsolt of the White Hands* is of Breton provenance. The Classical parallels to this motif are the story of Paris and Oenone and the black sails of Theseus. Important romances in which the girl has the name of the hero's lost love are mentioned in G. Schoepperle's book; in *Horn* the names are Rimenhild and Reynild, in *Eliduc* Guildeluec and Guilliadun, in *Ille* Galeron and Ganor, etc. Above all, Arabian influence is shown in the seventh-century tale of Kais ibn Doreig, who in his grief at separation from his first love (*Lobna*) goes out to seek death. Here, as in *Tristan und Îsolt*, the name of his first love brings about his marriage to his second love, who bears the same name. Further Arabian influence appears in the legend of the two branches, which intertwine over the grave of the lovers.

The Popularity of the Tristan Story in Literature and Art

The popularity of the Tristan story soon led to amplification and to the interpolation of new or similar episodes, apart from the so-called *Tristan-Novellen* (e.g. *Chèvrefeuille*) which presuppose an acquaintance with the legend itself. The latter continues themes from general folk-lore: birth-stories, stories of human tribute to dragons and other monsters, single combat [see the list of island combats most carefully examined by G. Schoepperle: the duel between Henry and Robert (*Jocelin*), Arthur and Flollo (Geoffrey's *Historia* and Wace's *Brut*), Roland and Olivier (*Girard*), Ogier and Charlot (*Ogier*), Aeneas and Turnus (*Eneas*), Otuel and Roland (*Otuel*), etc.], the story of Philoctetes, the stench of whose wound is so unbearable that the Greeks expose him on an island, the healing at the hands of the enemy (cf. Telephus and Achilles, the *Sickbed of Cuchulainn*, etc.) love charms and the Irish *geis* which Deirdre puts upon Naisi, or Grainne on Diarmaid, the incident of the harp and the rote, and the legends of abduction (cf. *Etain, Guinevere, Sir Orfeo*). All these are either parallel stories or have sometimes directly, sometimes indirectly, enriched the material of *Tristan und Îsolt*.

Important for our knowledge of the Tristan romance are, moreover, the stories of the lovers' tryst beneath the tree (cf. *Pañcatantra*, and *Cukasaptati*), of the flour-strewn floor, over which Tristan leaps from his own bed to that of Îsolt, thus causing his wound to break open; the incident which only

Eilhart (not Thomas-Gottfried) relates of the wounding of Tristan on 'blades at bed' is old in its crudeness; it is, however, only a repetition of the flour-strewing motif (cf. the spreading of the flour on the floor in the *Master Thief*). The motif of the 'whittlings in the stream', which flows through Îsolt's chamber is also apparently very old.[1] The lovers' life in the forest, which Eilhart depicts as a rough, hard life and Thomas-Gottfried as a *wunschleben*, seems to go back to an old French poem: *Girart de Roussillon*. Thus not everything in the saga is originally Celtic, although, of course, this motif could have been Celtic. The influence of popular motifs is also to be found in the story of Brangaene ('the substituted bride'), of the pillow as a sleeping-charm (cf. Odin's sleep-thorn), of the faithful dog and especially in the incidents of Tristan's disguises as a fool, leper, minstrel, beggar, pilgrim, and monk; his disguise as a monk clearly points to the influence of the gleemen. The episode of the nightingale in *Domnei des Amanz* also points to the popularity of the *Tristan* romance.

Beyond the numerous motifs derived from literature, a glance at decorative art and book illustration bears witness to the immense popularity of the Tristan legend. We can only indicate some of the most remarkable works: first and foremost the Wienhausen embroidery—a masterpiece and unique of its kind, in Wienhausen near Celle. Its illustrations are based largely on Eilhart's *Tristrant und Îsalde*, although some are drawn from another source: this is true of the picture which shows Tantris being healed by the women, for in Eilhart's version Tristrant (here called Prô) did not see Îsolt during his first journey to Ireland, but was given the healing salve by a messenger: *die vil schône Îsalde/sante im dô balde/ein plaster daz gût was*. Other noteworthy tapestries are at Lüneburg and in the South Kensington Museum. Murals, too, depict scenes from Tristan (at Runkelstein near Bozen, St. Floret in the Auvergne, Palermo); ivory caskets (at Leningrad in the Hermitage; Forrer Collection, etc.), bed-quilts (South Kensington, Bargello, Florence), and tablecloths also bear witness to a widespread interest in our story. The motif of the 'tryst beneath the

---

[1] Cf. also Helaine Newstead, 'The Tryst beneath the Tree', *Romance Phil.*, 1956, p. 273.

tree' was often illustrated both on secular and religious objects: on misericords (Chester and Lincoln), corbels (Bruges and Bourges), combs (Bamberg), embroidery (Ratisbon), wooden caskets (South Kensington), and ivories (Paris). The famous Chertsey Tiles have been the subject of a special study by R. S. Loomis.[1] These tiles, which follow Thomas's version, are an important aid to the disentanglement of the Tristan legend. Also book-illustrations from the French School, German and Italian MSS., and woodcuts are an inexhaustible source dealing with our subject. The sculptures of the medieval German classical period at Naumberg and Bamberg must also be mentioned in this connection, although they have no direct bearing on the Tristan saga. As symbols of *hôher muot*, *zuht*, and *mâze* they represent the spirit of Gottfried's epic.[2]

URTRISTAN. ESTOIRE. BÉROUL-EILHART, THOMAS-GOTTFRIED. GOTTFRIED'S CONTINUATORS

The question of the original source, the *Urtristan*, has not yet been solved. The date of its composition has given rise to much controversy. Golther fixes it about 1150, but Bédier places it earlier and Schoepperle later. The number of lines in my abridged edition of *Tristan und Îsolt*, which was the first to appear in England, probably corresponds roughly to the number of lines in the *Urtristan*: 6-7000 lines. The *Urtristan* (*poème primitif*, *archétype*) probably did not contain the story of Tristan's childhood, nor the love story of Riwalîn and Blanscheflûr, and perhaps not the love-potion, if the *Urtristan* was initially modelled on the pattern of the Irish elopement stories. It probably ended with the life of the lovers in the forest.

Was the *Urtristan*, as Bédier, Golther, Vinaver and others assume, a work of high artistic value? Gertrude Schoepperle traces all the extant versions of the Tristan legend back to a single stage, the so-called *Estoire*, which already shows courtly tendencies and must therefore be considerably later than the *Urtristan*. The term *Estoire* is, however, rather vague, since it means something different to nearly every critic. Gertrude

[1] *Illustrations of Medieval Romances on Tiles from Chertsey Abbey*, Illinois Studies, II, 2.
[2] See *Art and Life*, by Hannah Closs, Shakespeare Head Press, Oxford, 1936.

Schoepperle holds the convincing view that the Tristan legend was 'conceived' on Celtic soil. At the same time, with her customary caution and modesty, she avoids an arbitrary construction of an 'independent' hypothetical Celtic epic, which to our knowledge does not exist. We can see how many Celtic motifs go to form the Tristan epic: the *imrama* (tales of voyages), the *aitheda* (defiant tales of elopement), the dog, the whittlings and the 'audacious water', etc.; the 'separating sword' is especially important as a symbol of Tristan's loyalty to his liege lord: In Gottfried's work Tristan, fearing Mark's arrival in the forest, places his sword between himself and Îsolt; Eilhart however 'explains' the separating sword as a mere 'habit'. The motif has evidently been inspired by Celtic tradition—Diarmaid puts a cold stone between Grainne and himself as a token of loyalty to his chieftain. The hypothetical Celtic *Tristan* which Ranke reconstructed is composed mainly of the above elements and contains no reference to the love-potion or the journey to woo Îsolt. According to that reconstruction the outstanding events of the *Ursage* would be: (*a*) Tristan fights with Môrolt; he then undertakes a hazardous voyage (*imram*) and is healed by a fairy versed in magic. He returns to Cornwall. (*b*) Îsolt is Mark's wife and falls in love with Tristan whom she forces to elope (*aithed*) with her. They flee to the forest accompanied by the faithful dog. Tristan remains loyal to his liege lord and lays a sword between himself and Îsolt. Thus Mark discovers them. (*c*) One day, as Tristan and Îsolt wade across a river, the water splashes up high against Îsolt's thighs. She taunts Tristan, and then only is Tristan disloyal to Mark. (*d*) Tristan throws whittlings into the water, and by means of these Mark discovers their hiding-place. Mark wounds Tristan, who, as he lies in the throes of death, embraces Îsolt and strangles her on his breast. The French Prose Romance has the same ending, but the motivation is different.

The *Urtristan* or *Le Poème primitif* was probably developed from a Celtic nucleus, but we may imagine that it was a self-contained poem of a somewhat later date and already to some extent French in spirit. Golther considers that the *Estoire* was the common source for Eilhart and Béroul, a source from which

Thomas derived nothing, but Schoepperle thinks that the *Estoire* is the very earliest common source accessible to us. Bédier fixes the date of the *Estoire* as 1154 (the year of Eleanor's departure from Normandy), but Schoepperle rejects Bédier's argument as lacking in evidence. The *Estoire* (about 1170?) was composed by a certain *Robert of Reims*, called *Li Kièvres*, and Béroul refers to it in the passage:

> Ne, si conme l'estorie dit,
> L(a) ou Berox le vit escrit.

This *Estoire* was the source of Eilhart's and Béroul's epics. We can reconstruct it more easily than the *Urtristan*, since we can deduce its contents by comparing the six extant versions of Tristan: Eilhart, Béroul, Thomas and Gottfried, the French Prose Romance, the *Folie*: the Berne MS., related to Béroul, and the Oxford Douce MS., probably a little earlier (dependent on Thomas).

With Eilhart von Oberge's *Tristan und Îsalde* (about 1180-1190) we tread for the first time on firm ground. Eilhart introduced the story of Tristan to the German public. Of the above six versions the German poem of Eilhart is perhaps 'the best representative' of the *estoire*. We know scarcely anything about his life. Like Heinrich von Veldeke, he was a Low German, but he wrote in the dialect of the West Rhineland, which was an important literary centre at that time. Oberge lies two and a half miles to the west of Braunschweig and three and a half miles north-east of Hildesheim. Eilhart's father was a *ministerialis* in the service of Henry the Lion. How did Eilhart von Oberge become acquainted with the story of Tristan? Possibly he had no German source and no direct continuators, and received the inspiration for his work at Mathilda's court. After her death (+1189), the literary zenith was quickly passed and a stern, religious spirit invaded the Saxon court.

Eilhart still follows the old technique and uses uncourtly expressions and rhymes; at the same time his tone is clear, popular and even blunt without being coarse. He does not worry about exact motivation, he does not explain how Tristan received the wound which breaks open as he leaps over to Îsolt's bed, but in Thomas and Gottfried we hear that Mark,

Îsolt and Tristan had been bled: *In einem tage er z'âder liez/als in sîn valscher rât gehiez/und mit im Îsot und Tristan.* On the other hand there is a convincing unity in the character of Mark; here Eilhart surpasses Thomas and Gottfried. Eilhart's uncourtly treatment of his courtly theme emerges clearly in the expression: *der vil unsêlige trang.* In his poem the love-potion retains its efficacy only for four years.

Gottfried probably knew Eilhart's *Tristan und Îsalde.* This would be borne out by his hidden diatribe against Eilhart. Gottfried's continuators, Ulrich von Türheim and Heinrich von Freiberg, drew from Eilhart and not from Thomas who was Gottfried's own source. From the time of Lichtenstein's edition of Eilhart no one seriously questioned Eilhart's influence on Gottfried until Gombert apparently destroyed some preconceived ideas by showing that Gottfried influenced Eilhart: 'Der Exkurs zur Minnetrankszene . . . hat dies ganz ausser Zweifel gestellt.'

The great popularity of Eilhart's epic is proved by the fact, mentioned above, that Gottfried's successors based their continuation of *Tristan und Îsolt* on Eilhart's version and not on Gottfried's and that the German Prose Romance also goes back in the main to Eilhart. Hans Sachs knew the Worms edition (1549-50) and composed five master-songs and a tragedy from its material: *Tragedia mit 23 personen, von der strengen lieb Herr Tristrant mit der schönen Königin Isalden.* The Czech Tristan, which consists of four parts, is also derived mainly from Eilhart.

Béroul's *Tristran* (after 1191), like that of Eilhart, is fragmentary. Both poets have certain motifs in common in their interpretation of Tristan. Béroul's world, like that of Eilhart, is clearly not the world of courtly love. It is in Thomas that *Frau Minne* first becomes the ruler of society.

The Anglo-Norman poet Thomas is Gottfried's source. As to the date of Thomas's epic, cf. Bédier, II, 55: 'la composition du *Tristan* de Thomas se place entre ces deux dates extrêmes: 1155-70'; Golther also suggests: 'nach Wace (1155) und vor dem Cligés (1170)'; according to R. S. Loomis, the heraldic evidence points to a later date (about 1185) than 1170. In Thomas we, for the first time, find the name *Îsolt,* instead of *Îsalde.* As compared with the *Estoire* and the series dependent on it, Thomas's depiction of courtly culture in England is new. Other characteristic modifications are to be noticed: the river now flows through the orchard, not through Îsolt's chamber; the life of the lovers in the forest becomes a dream-life in the grotto; the upbringing of the boy Tristan, and later the description of how Tantris educates Îsolt which reminds us of Abélard and Héloise; the hunting scene; Tristan's hall of images in Brittany—*La Salle aux Images*—all these reflect the spirit of courtly society. Thomas intensifies, simplifies and tones down his material; he makes modifications to suit courtly taste and extends the saga by depicting the minds of his characters, by interpolating soliloquies, reflections and conventional repetitions. The gallery of statues is an innovation on the part of Thomas, which changes the wild passion of the old saga into delicate emotion. At the same time he has a gift for lyrical narration, which is unique in the epic of the period; this is revealed in the wistful story of Riwalîn and Blanscheflûr, and in his enchanting description of the May-time festival at Mark's court.

There can be no doubt that the story of *Tristan* is in many ways the opposite of courtly: Îsolt suffers with Tristan; she dies of compassion. But Thomas has given it a courtly tone:

> He treats the characters impersonally. He is interested in them not only, perhaps not even mainly, for themselves, but as exemplifying a certain situation, which he expounds with a care for symmetry. Beginning with Mark, and his more or less negative type of suffering, he sets Îsolt and Tristan in the middle, not only as being the central characters of the poem, but also as undergoing 'duble turment' . . . while Îsolt aux Blanches Mains . . . forms a kind of pendant to Mark.
>
> The tone of this methodical exposition followed by an appeal to his readers is not unlike that of the so-called judgement of love recorded by André le Chapelain. . . . In some respects, therefore, Thomas's poem . . . may be taken as an illustration of the principles of courtly love. But the spirit of *courtoisie* and the spirit of the Tristan story are incompatible.[1]

Thomas has a talent for the psychological depiction of awakening emotion. A superb example of this may be found in the love-potion scene. He omits all that is unreal and incredible,

[1] C. B. West, *Courtoisie in Anglo-Norman Literature.*

as for example the tale of the golden hair brought by a swallow. (This story presupposes that the princess was unknown to Tristan. She is unknown to him in Eilhart's version, for the latter says that she sent a messenger to heal Tristan.) Yet Thomas's Tristan contains some inconsistencies; why should Mark fetch witnesses and why should Tristan flee and leave Îsolt behind? In the main, however, Thomas removes inconsistencies from the old saga and motivates everything: he refers to the political relations between England and Ireland in order to make Môrolt's demand for tribute justifiable; he gives a better reason for Tristan's second voyage to Ireland by telling of the Barons' hatred of Tristan. Especially important is his motivation of the love-potion episode: Mark too (in contrast to Gottfried later) drinks of it on his marriage night, while Îsolt spills her share of the potion. Hence Mark remains bound to her for all time, and for this reason, Mark's varying behaviour towards Îsolt after he had discovered her infidelity is apparently well motivated, but Eilhart's Mark shows more unity of character in his brutality. Although the setting of Thomas's Tristan is courtly, a certain lack of taste is sometimes to be found. Thomas is learned and rational. His learning breaks out triumphantly in the description of the Minnegrotte, which Gottfried later turns into a fairy palace. Thomas's hall of images is a counterpart to the love-grotto.

The contents of Thomas's *Tristan* (one-sixth of Gottfried's epic in size) can be supplemented. The main part of his fragment deals with the end of the Tristan legend, which is missing in Gottfried, so that each complements the other. The two versions have unfortunately only a few lines in common. The Norwegian Prose Tristan is a valuable source for the reconstruction of Thomas's version, as shown in R. S. Loomis' *Romance of Tristram and Ysolt*. But the complete specimen of this Old Norse *Tristrams Saga ok Isondar* of 1226, composed by the Norwegian Brother Robert, has come down to us in an Icelandic seventeenth-century paper manuscript. The Icelandic dancing-song, *Tristrams Kvaeði*, which has great poetic power, is based on the Norwegian version. The English *Sir Tristrem* (fourteenth century) was first published by W. Scott in 1804, who, however, wrongly supposed it to be the work of Thomas of

Erceldoun. Here, too, the lyrical passages have been omitted as in the Norwegian *Tristram* and only the bare story remains, yet this version is not lacking in dramatic vigour.

Before we turn to Gottfried, it would be well to refer again to Gottfried's continuators: Ulrich von Türheim from Thurgau (about 1240), who omitted the Minnegrotte altogether, and Heinrich von Freiberg (about 1290), who is also crude in comparison with Gottfried and Thomas. It is very significant that after Gottfried's courtly masterpiece, the realistic and archaic tone of Eilhart was again preferred to the polished art of Gottfried.

The relationship of the authors of the above versions of *Tristan* can now be indicated in the following table:

I	II
THOMAS (before 1170) group.	EILHART (1180-90) BÉROUL (after 1191) group.
La Folie Tristan (Oxford MS.).	*La Folie Tristan* (Berne MS.).
Gottfried von Strassburg (about 1210).	The French Prose Romance (between 1225-30).
The Norwegian Prose (1226). The Icelandic *Tristrams Kvaeði*. A Low Franconian fragment (thirteenth century).	Gottfried's continuators: Ulrich von Türheim (about 1240) and Heinrich von Freiberg (about 1290).
Some chapters of the Italian Prose Romance *La Tavola Ritonda* (about 1300).	The Czech Tristan (fourteenth century).
Sir Tristrem (fourteenth century).	The German Prose Romance (fifteenth century).

GOTTFRIED VON STRASSBURG: HIS LIFE AND HIS HOME

> ... der wîse Gotfrit
> von Strâzburc, der nie valschen trit
> mit valsche in sîner rede getrat.[1]

Among the medieval Tristan romances Gottfried's poem stands out as the unrivalled masterpiece. He is no mere translator who refashions his material with supreme skill. In contrast to his source, Thomas, he modifies the form rather than the motifs. Gottfried's originality lies in his artistic style, his interpretation of emotions, in the grace and musical beauty of his work.

[1] Rudolf von Ems, *Alexander*.

Strassburg, Gottfried's home, was rising in importance in the thirteenth century. The old *Argentoratus* had been destroyed during the troubled period of the Great Migration. Soon a new town sprang up, and the municipal by-laws show that in the twelfth century Strassburg was a busy market town and international trade was developing swiftly. Strassburg's commerce and population increased. From the exchange of commodities developed exchange by means of money and credit. According to a Dominican Chronicle at Colmar, Strassburg had only a few merchants in 1200, but in 1266 there were already eighty money-changers. According to Schmoller, the population of Strassburg was at least 10,000 in 1200. It had increased by 1228 and in the fourteenth century Strassburg was one of the largest German towns with about 50,000 inhabitants.

Gottfried himself was most likely a burgher. He is called *meister* in the Heidelberg Manesse Codex and by Ulrich von Türheim, Heinrich von Freiberg, Rudolf von Ems and K. von Würzburg; Füetrer (fifteenth century) calls him *her*. The author of *Tristan und Îsolt* must have enjoyed an excellent theological and religious education; he understood French with ease, and was obviously interested in education. All this we learn from his *Tristan und Îsolt*. He was probably *not* a cleric:

> dâ wart wol goffenbaeret
> und al der werlt bewaeret,
> daz der vil tugenthafte Krist
> wintschaffen alse ein ermel ist.

> *And so it was made manifest*
> *and proved to all the world by test,*
> *that Christ's law can be made to strain*
> *like any windswept weathervane.*[1]

In this ambiguous statement delivered at the ordeal Gottfried attacks superstition. He most likely attended a monastic school and found much inspiration in religious literature, as for example for his allegory of the *Minnegrotte*. No satisfactory solution to the problems of Gottfried's profession has yet been found. His remarkable description of the hunt might almost suggest that he had been in the service of the bishop in connexion with the hunt, though his marked aestheticism would

---

[1] Translated by E. H. Zeydel.

73

point rather to a career as amanuensis. Again, he may have been a master at the cathedral school in his home town, for he shows a special interest in education. A rather mediocre play about Gottfried's life, written by Fritz Lienhard, *Gottfried von Strassburg* (1902), leads us no further. Gottfried must have been an official of some kind, possibly at the bishop's court, and must have had plenty of opportunity to see and study courtly or knightly life as well as ethics—but one always has the feeling that he is an onlooker and not, like Wolfram von Eschenbach, an actor in the court or knightly life. Gottfried himself is the best source for our knowledge of his activities and desires. We hear that he experienced the joy and pain of love since he was a young boy. In contrast to Gottfried, Thomas avoids any such direct confession.

Gottfried must have been extremely cultured and have had refined, aristocratic tastes, for he knows the works of Ovid and Vergil. He is also well acquainted with the Bible and ecclesiastical authors. He must have composed *Tristan und Îsolt* somewhere around the year 1210, because, in his criticism of contemporary literature, he speaks against Wolfram and the latter answers. Besides *Tristan und Îsolt*, two songs have been attributed to Gottfried: a *Minnelied* and a *Loblied auf Maria und Christus*, both represented in the Heidelberg Manesse Codex. The *Loblied* is, on account of its impure rhymes, most probably not Gottfried's work; the authenticity of the *Minnelied* is also doubtful.

GOTTFRIED'S ORIGINALITY

The main problem which concerns us is the question of Gottfried's poetic originality. We have already given some indication of this: his style, his moral standpoint, his interpretation of the Tristan legend. Instead of describing directly, he often suggests the spiritual meaning of his poem to us through the form, as for instance in his introductory lines in which Gottfried from an almost scholastic tone works up to the pregnant expression:

> ein senedœre, ein senedœrîn
> ein man, ein wîp; ein wîp, ein man,
> Tristan, Îsot; Îsot, Tristan.

All external things have fallen away, the reader stands ready to be initiated into the whole mystery of *Minne*, which is in fact to Gottfried almost a substitute for religion. With Gottfried the *love-potion* is no longer reason and excuse, it is a poetic symbol and he perhaps kept the love-drink because it made an excellent climax. Love-potion or not—the climax in his *Tristan und Îsolt* was bound to come. A careful study of the text will confirm this. Îsolt's interest in his *lîp alsô gebaere* and her curiosity about Tristan's weapons are surely far more than objective inquisitiveness as to his birth and station in life; or does it smack of modern psychology to interpret her prolonged fury against him as something more than loyalty to Môrolt, anger at the deceit, and wounded pride? Then in the love-potion scene the manner in which she pushes him away:

> . . . habet iuch hin,
> tuot iuwer arme hin dan!
> ir sît ein harte müelîch man. . . .
>
> *Keep thy distance,*
> *I loathe thy arm embracing me,*
> *a bore thou art. . . .*[1]

when he tries to comfort and embrace her,—all this combines to create a crescendo that we feel the outbreak of their passion inevitable. This does not mean that Wolfram in contrast to Gottfried lacks all form. If the Classical serenity of Gottfried, who lived in the borderland between France and Germany, has much in common with Thomas in his poetic art and seems remote from Wolfram's expressive, rugged style which is so often claimed as characteristically German, we must not forget that Mozart, who too in some ways recalls Gottfried perhaps more poignantly than any other artist, also represents *one* side of the German's dual nature.

Thomas and Gottfried enhance the psychological content of the saga, but Gottfried is more steeped in its spiritual aspect than Thomas. We may claim that the Prelude was contributed by Gottfried, although the nucleus of many passages is to be found in Thomas. The acrostic which acts as a sort of captatio benevolentiae, reminds one of similar passages in the works of medieval poets. Gottfried speaks from his own experience while

[1] Translator, loc. cit.

Thomas denies any personal experience. The Prelude is significant, for here, as we have noticed, he reveals the moral and literary interpretation of his life and work. Gottfried's mood is one of mingled joy and sorrow:

> swem nie von liebe leit geschach,
> dem geschach ouch liep von liebe nie.

> *The man whom love could never bow,*
> *he's lived love's raptures nevermore.*[1]

Thus the mood of the lovers, too, alternates between joy and sorrow. Death alone can bring them relief: *ein líp, ein leben daz sîn wir*. In this way Gottfried reveals the profound tragedy of his Tristan; it is the alliance of life and death. But our poet lifts the tragedy from the aesthetic to an almost religious plane by allowing the lovers to yearn for the consummation of their love in death: *dirre tôt der tuot mir wol,/solte diu wunneclîche Îsot/iemer alsus sîn mîn tôt,/sô wolte ich gerne werben/umb' ein êweclîchez sterben*—an unmistakable anticipation of Richard Wagner's *Liebestod*, although Gottfried's lighter, even slightly frivolous tone is peculiarly his own, with its haunting Mozartian quality—hovering between joy and anguish, frivolity and the profound.

Richard Wagner's opera *Tristan und Isolde* (1857) is the most powerful of the modern Tristan dramas. To do it full justice one cannot separate the tragedy from its haunting music whose dramatic force Nietzsche even in the days when he had turned against Wagner, calling it a subtle poison, still found irresistible. Wagner borrowed the theme from Gottfried's poem which he read in H. Kurz's masterly translation (1844, 1877[3]), and was also acquainted with Simrock's (1855) rather prosaic rendering. He was, moreover, influenced by Schopenhauer, and probably by Novalis (see here p. 139), whilst his poetic emotion became intensified by his love for Mathilde Wesendonk. Wagner reduced the Tristan legend to three poignant scenes: (*a*) the apparent death-potion; (*b*) the lovers' tryst and the wounding of the hero; (*c*) Tristan's death-agony and final consummation, reunion of the lovers in death.

We now return to the Prelude, where Gottfried speaks of his

---

[1] Translator, loc. cit.

problems to the *edeliu herzen* as contrasted with the uncourtly world. One may be reminded here of the difference between *hohe* and *niedere Minne*, of Andreas Capellanus's *nobilitas cordis* and of Thomasin's *Wälscher Gast*. Gottfried in his interpretation of *Tristan und Îsolt* as a hymn of love for the '*edeliu herzen*' is unique. Even upon the basis of what has already been said, it is difficult to understand how Kelemina can deny Gottfried any measure of poetic originality. Here we may let a renowned French scholar, F. Piquet, bear witness to Gottfried's individual contribution in contrast to his source, Thomas:

> Nous croyons, après la minutieuse comparaison des textes que nous avons entreprise, avoir démontré que l'auteur du *Tristan* allemand ne mérite pas le nom de traducteur. Les nombreuses preuves d'originalité qu'il a fournies dans son ouvrage exigent qu'on l'apelle un imitateur, ou un adapteur, ou—plus simplement et plus exactement—un poète.[1]

A detailed comparison of Thomas and Gottfried shows that the latter was also an outstanding and careful psychologist. Gottfried's conception of love is not merely sensual, but love has for him a profoundly spiritual quality, which can be intensified until it becomes mystic. The clear motivation of Gottfried's poem has long been recognized. He depicts most charmingly the gradual awakening to love, Îsolt's maidenly shyness when she tries to approach her lover as if by chance. Gottfried endeavours to motivate events more skilfully than his source, as, for example, the scene with the cowardly steward, after Tristan has slain the dragon. Here Gottfried introduces the Cornish knights, whom Môrolt had taken captive at the Irish court, and describes their reunion with their relatives: *die von Kurnwâle ze Îrlant/ze zinse wâren gesant*. Gottfried also gives a more satisfactory explanation as to why there is a sword between Tristan and Îsolt: both fear that Mark will discover them: *wan sî des angest hæten*. Again Gottfried deepens the tone of Thomas's work in some places: King Mark and Brangæne, who is here not merely Îsolt's maid but her companion, are depicted with extraordinary sympathy. Mark is filled with *disem blinden leide*. He exiles the lovers, but for the time being conquers his jealousy and misery. The nobility of his character is revealed

[1] F. Piquet, *L'originalité de G. de Strasbourg*, p. 375.

in the farewell scene. He can force physical separation upon the lovers, but he can never separate their hearts: *und enkan doch an iu beiden/die liebe niht gescheiden.* He knows that it is no longer possible for the three of them to live together. Therefore he decides to stand back: *disiu gemeinde ist bœse.*

On the other hand, Gottfried condenses: e.g. the lament at the death of Blanscheflûr, and the medical details of Tristan's healing. Gottfried's tone is even more courtly than that of Thomas: e.g. Tristan does not drink of the love-potion first but courteously hands it to Îsolt. Gottfried carefully avoids un-courtly phrases (*rede, diu niht des hoves sî*). We must, however, not forget that it is far easier to improve upon a good source (like Thomas) than to create a work of great artistic value from an uncouth tale.

MORALITAS. THE ALLEGORY OF LOVE AND THE MAGIC POTION

Gottfried's originality is shown most of all in his moral philosophy, the courtly *morâliteit*, by which the courtly *moralitas* is meant, not the New High German word *Moral*. His ideal is the Classical Kalokagathia which can only be attained in the most sacred moments in the life of men or nations. Riwalîn is ruined through his want of *mâze : ûf gêndiu jugent und vollez guot,/diu zwei diu füerent übermuot.* The girl Îsolt is instructed in that *morâliteit* which ennobles her: *wol gesite,/schôn' und reine gemuot,/ir gebœrde süeze unde guot.* Music and poetry form part of her courtly instruction. Without *morâliteit* no one can have honour or possession. It teaches mankind to serve and win the favour of God and the World: *got unde der werlde gevallen,* but Gottfried lays more stress on the second—world; we must, however, not forget that this very world has a double nature, an inner and outer aspect, and it is the inner world which Gottfried exalts; cf. his Prelude.

He acknowledges that *Minne* is the force which dominates man's life. *Minne* is the source of *hovesite,* indeed of all virtues:

> lieb' ist ein alsô sælic dinc,
> ein alsô sæleclîch gerinc,
> daz nieman âne ir lêre
> noch tugende hât noch êre.

Love is so blissful in its thriving,
so blissful, too, in all its striving,
that no one man who lacks its teaching
virtue and honour can be reaching.[1]

Without *Minne* there is no honour. She is an enchantress who ensnares her victims. She is mistress of the world. She not only increases the torment of love, but also intensifies pleasure and alleviates pain. *Minne* is *virtus et passio*. In love's grief he finds bliss. A little anger, *zornelin*, is also necessary: cf. Publilius Syrus: *Amantium irae amoris integratio est*. Finally *huote* (surveillance) is lamentable: a chaste lady needs no watcher, while others are only incited by prohibition. Gottfried expresses his doctrine of love at least three times. We hear how *Minne* is kindled, how she acts and what she does in the hearts of those who can love truly.

Gottfried was indeed bold to adopt symbols from religious allegory for his own love-allegory of the Minnegrotte. Although he sees in God the sum of all virtues, his ideal is fundamentally aesthetic. His God is a 'courtly' God Who, even at the time of the ambiguous oath, sides with Îsolt.

The Minnegrotte of Thomas, as we have already mentioned, becomes in Gottfried's poem a wonderful palace. Gottfried's continuator, Ulrich, discarded it again. We cannot say that Gottfried's descriptions in this part of the epic are realistic: Tristan and Îsolt have no need of food; the bliss of love fills their lives. (How difficult it is to justify the fact that Îsolt later returns to her husband!) Gottfried drew this allegory of *la fossiur' a la gent amant* from the symbolism of the church: the rounded vault of the grotto represents the single-heartedness of love, the breadth love's boundless power, the height noble-mindedness, the white wall purity, the floor constancy; through the three windows (kindness, humility, good breeding), the light of honour shines into the house of love. Entrance is granted only to *edeliu herzen*, who possess delicacy of feeling. No medieval German poet has ever gone further than Gottfried in making a religion of love. In this lofty conception the difference between Gottfried and Eilhart and Béroul and the Celtic legends emerges most clearly. In the stories of Deirdre-Naisi or

---

[1] Translator, loc. cit.

Grainne-Diarmaid woman is nothing but a destructive force which against his will brings man to his ruin. In Eilhart and Béroul the love-potion is the excuse for the lovers' sin—which is therefore a sort of accident. G. Schoepperle rightly maintains: 'It is no doubt due to the fact that Lancelot did not blindly drink the poison of love, but sought the cup of his own will, that he superseded Tristan in the favour of many twelfth-century readers.' But in Gottfried's *Tristan und Îsolt* Tristan takes the burden of responsibility and their doom on his own shoulders: *sô wolte ich gerne werben/umb ein êweclîchez sterben*, though there is still a slight trace of the conventional conception of the love-potion, but we must remember that symbol and reality cover each other very closely in the medieval mind. Gottfried's conception of fatality lingers on to modern times: cf. Swinburne: *Tristram of Lyonesse, the Sailing of the Swallow*:

> Their Galahault was the cup, and she that mixed:
> Nor other hand there needed, nor sweet speech
> To lure their lips together; each on each
> Hung with strange eyes and hovered as a bird
> Wounded, and each mouth trembled for a word;
> Their heads neared, and their hands were drawn in one,
> And they saw dark, though still the unsunken sun
> Far through fine rain shot fire into the south.
> And their four lips became one burning mouth.

The love-potion is, as already mentioned, a symbol in Gottfried's poem and in the Norwegian version. Gottfried's love-potion does not cause love, but symbolizes it. The cause of love is thus no longer external, but lies in the souls of the characters themselves who are bound to each other by a love which, though unlawful in the eyes of the world, is in reality decreed by fate and enriches them with the perfect harmony of their hearts. Mark lacks this harmony; therefore his union with Îsolt is in the deepest sense immoral; according to the laws of the *edeliu herzen* Mark bears more guilt than Tristan. The pathos of the old spirit of revenge in the old Irish stories is almost lost in Gottfried. Mark realizes that honour and loyalty are powerless under the spell of love. Therefore he allows them to go to the forest, and God Himself sides with the lovers and gives His consent to their doctrine of love.

FORMAL PROBLEMS. GOTTFRIED'S CLASSIC SENSE

The literary *excursus* which Gottfried introduces in place of the knighting ceremony appears at an important point in *Tristan und Îsolt*. The *excursus* which Rudolf von Ems later imitates in *Alexander* could then be explained as showing the modesty of the poet, who does not feel that he is capable of describing the great knightly ceremony.

Many Classical references are to be found in Gottfried. How much he was attracted by Classical ideas is seen in his predilection for proverbs drawn from Latin sources. Also the love-potion was not unknown to Classical literature, cf. Ovid's *Ars Amatoria*, II, 106-7:

> Non data profuerint pallentia philtra puellis,
> Philtra nocent animis vimque furoris habent.

The invocation to Apollo and the Muses in Gottfried's time was a bold stroke. Gottfried calls on *Apolle und die Camênen,/der ôren niun Sirênen* to inspire him so that his song shall rise to the highest summit: *hin widere z' Êlikône/ze dem niunvalten trône*, and thus heaven almost appears a paradise for aesthetes. Nevertheless the Church was awake to the spirit of Antiquity, in so far as it could be of service to religion. Latin was the language of the Church. The seven arts formed the basis of education in the monastic schools where Classical authors were read: Cicero, Ovid, Horace, Vergil, Seneca; further, the stories of Alexander and Troy, also Publilius Syrus and Apollonius of Tyre. Besides this, Middle High German literature was enriched by a stream of important influences coming from the East through the crusaders, and from Arabian culture in Spain and indirectly through the South of France. The author of *Tristan und Îsolt* was more deeply steeped in the spirit of antiquity than any other medieval German poet. His perfect clarity of form sometimes caused him to fall into virtuosity. He also does not lack proverbial phraseology. But it is in the construction of his lines and the choice of words that he proved his greatness as an artist.

In his word-artistry Gottfried von Strassburg was a spirit kindred to Thomas. For Gottfried the play on words, antithesis and dialectic arguments appear a direct expression of the tragic tension between death and life, grief and joy, love and honour. Parallels, too, are favoured. Anaphora maintains the symmetry. Alliteration increases the musical effect. Nor does Gottfried's work lack humour, which is especially effective since it is embedded in his glittering virtuosity.

His style is a direct development of that of Hartmann von Aue, whose crystal-clear presentation of the *sin* (material) he praises. The content of a work must, Gottfried says, have internal and external beauty: in the moulding of the material and the words. In this exquisite harmony of form and content Gottfried has attained the supreme degree of perfection in Middle High German lyric poetry. The plasticity of his characters, events and nature is unique: Tristan on horseback; Îsolt's appearance at the Irish court; further single plastic features, as for instance when the boy Tristan sweeps back his hair and is too weak to move the deer (*sîn schoene hâr daz streich er nider . . .*), and the fascinating picture of the Rhine which becomes a small stream when divided into five arms (*sus wirt der michele Rîn/vil kûme ein kleinez rinnelîn*). Gottfried's love-epic is composed for the *edeliu herzen*, as he himself emphasizes. But his aesthetic world does not exclude heroic knighthood. We can see this for instance in the combat with Môrolt. Tristan is a warrior and a minstrel. In the modern version of the tale, *Tristan*, by Hannah Closs[1]— a work highly praised by the late poet Laurence Binyon—this undeniable quality in the hero's nature is emphasized and developed into a psychological problem.

Delight in beauty and grace, in exquisite form, subtle mannerism and polished speech provide a balance for the virile ascetic defiance of the fighter. Thus Gottfried von Strassburg seeks to maintain harmony on the brink of the abyss. For this reason his *Tristan und Îsolt* with its exquisite sublimation of passion remains for us today, even after Richard Wagner's *Liebestod*, an inexhaustible source of inspiration.

[1] Cf. also Estelle Morgan: *Some Modern English Versions of the Legend of Tristan and Isolde*, Die Neueren Sprachen, p. 420ff., 1952.

IV

Austria's Place in German Literature

Und was euch so entzückt mit seinen Strahlen,
Es ward erzeugt in Todesnot und Qualen.
                                    GRILLPARZER

WHEN GERMAN LITERATURE is spoken of, few are aware of the prominent part played by Austria in its formation, not only in modern times but more especially during the Middle Ages. The traditional picture of the 'gemütlich'—happy-go-lucky—Austrian has given rise to the proverb: 'In South Germany beats the German heart, in Berlin the German brain.' But Austrian history and literature tell another story. They were not created by dreams and tender melancholy alone, but also by noble deeds. Placed between East and West, Austria and especially Vienna has been the stage of many a mighty conflict.

Two thousand years ago, Vienna (Vindobona) was a Roman fortress. It was here that the royal philosopher Marcus Aurelius wrote his essay *Ad se ipsum*. Following the disintegration of the Roman Empire, the ravaging tide of the fierce Huns swept over the land, and after the death of their leader, Attila, the Ostrogoths, Langobardic tribes and later the Avars settled temporarily on the fertile soil of the Danubian valley.

It was, however, Charlemagne, who in his struggles with the Hungarians, first founded the so-called Ostmark (Eastern Marches) which constituted the germ of the later Austrian Empire, and from the end of the tenth century onwards the famous dynasty of the Babenberger, under whom the Austrian Minnesang lyric flourished, made Austria the protective gateway to the East. In 1273 the Hapsburgs came into power and held it for nearly seven hundred years until 1918 and the breakdown of Austria after the first Great War.

Vienna was destined to become a world-centre of culture.

Here as early as the fourteenth century the second German university was opened and soon afterwards it became the residence of the German emperors. With the Great War the political power of Austria was shattered, only the core of a vast country remains, but music, poetry and art yet retain their magic power. Here the South German genius wherein the religious but 'uncouth' Bavarian, the 'sensuous' Franconian, and specific Austrian characteristics are blended, has found its most perfect expression in the so-called Austrian Baroque. Illusion and reality are interwoven in poetry, and the Austrian theatre of the last centuries revels in 'Baroque' splendour and 'panache'.

Of the early struggle between Christianity and Paganism we know through two great poems of the ninth century, written in Bavaria: the *Wessobrunn Prayer* and *Muspilli*. Austrian literature is as yet silent whilst this Bavarian *Wessobrunn Prayer* tells us in alliterative verse of the creation of the world, when there was neither tree, nor mountain, nor sun nor moon nor the infinite sea, and whilst the second poem, *Muspilli*, describes the end of our world, in word and image reminiscent of the *Apocalypse*.

Only from the tenth century onward under the patronage of the Babenbergers in Vienna is it possible to speak of a specifically Austrian literature. After a long silence German literature awoke to a new spell of life. But we should know practically nothing of the early religious poetry of the eleventh and twelfth centuries if the invaluable Vorau MS. (in Styria) had not come down to us. Here alone we find mentioned the name of Ava (d. 1127), the first known German poetess, who probably was a recluse at the nunnery of Melk. The Vorau MS. also contains the oldest German version of the life of Alexander. Monasteries, such as those at Gurk, Millstatt, St. Paul, Ossiach in Carinthia, Vorau and Lambrecht in Styria, Melk on the Danube, harboured many a cleric poet and translator. I would make special mention of the Viennese *Genesis*. In the monastery of Melk which is now a magnificent Baroque building on the Danube near Vienna lived in the twelfth century Heinrich von Melk, who on account of his satires is termed the Juvenal of the Middle Ages. In his work, *Erinnerung an den Tod*, he paints the horrors of death and reminds us how transitory is man's existence.

A father rises from the tomb and tells his son of the agonies of hell-fire, and a wife stands at the bier of her husband. The poet reminds her of the 'truetlied' (lovesong) which he sang in honour of women. That leads us to the German Minnesang, which first burst into blossom, very largely independently of Provence, in Austria.

During the bitter struggles between Pope and Emperor a great revolution of monastic life and society came about. Literature, which had until then a mainly religious character, underwent a gradual secularization. Even in earlier times the 'Spielleute' (Vagantes) maintained the life of the old heroic stories, and in Germany knighthood under the influence of France created the 'court epic' with its immortal romances, *Tristan* and *Parzival.* The crusades opened up a new world. The social relation of man to woman underwent a change. The 'Frauendienst' (service of the knight to his lady), subject of so many poems, mirrors a sentiment that had become the ideal of chivalry.

Two great literary streams, then, flow parallel to each other, the Romance and the Epic. The latter found its noblest expression in the Austrian *Nibelungen.*

Like the rolling tide of the Danube, the epic of Siegfried's wooing and death, and the fall of the Nibelungs flows past the modern reader. The anonymous author whom we definitely know to be an Austrian betrays an exact knowledge of locality. As a comparison of this Middle High German *Nibelungen* with the Northern legend of the *Edda* shows, the Middle High German epic is imbued with the spirit of chivalry.

Usually the Middle Ages during their literary prime are looked upon as a period of asceticism. The theologian Harnack still spoke of its dualistic outlook, but we now rightly see, in the medieval conception of life, a unity through reconciliation of heaven and earth.

Beside the *Nibelungen,* Austrian literature of the thirteenth century gave birth to another epic—that of *Gudrun,* a paean of faithfulness in woman.

We have perhaps the most perfect expression of the Austrian genius in the Middle High German Minnesang, the lyric art of the twelfth and thirteenth centuries. The songs of one hundred

and forty-four minnesingers (troubadours) of Germany and
Austria are collected in the famous illuminated *Große Ma-
nessische Heidelberger Liederhandschrift*, compiled by the Manesse
family of Zürich.

Knightly love-songs immediately suggest the names of
Kürenberger and Dietmar von Eist, whose home was upper
Austria. These poems form one of the most precious legacies of
the Middle Ages. The lone woman on the heath, the falcon
soaring high in the air, the farewell of lovers at dawn of day,
the trysting of lovers under the lime tree, the lament for the
passing of the year, complaint against the spies or 'merkaere',
who prevent lovers from meeting, and the reckless mirth felt
at the coming of the spring—such is the burden of these songs.
Already in Kürenberger's poems the falcon symbolizes the
lady's lover. There he sings *Wîp unde vederspil die werdent lîhte
zam*: for, according to him, women and falcons are easily tamed.

The best beloved of all these Middle High German minnesingers is Walther von der Vogelweide from Austria, probably
from Bozen. He is the typical Austrian of tradition: tender,
courteous, at the same time almost relentlessly frank, ultra-
sensitive, and tinged with a melancholy which even revels in its
own pain. Walther von der Vogelweide passed most of his life
in Vienna. We must imagine him at the court of the Babenbergers singing in the presence of knight and lady this praise of
his country:

> He who would know virtue and love,
> Let him come to our land.

This poem has often been called the medieval *Deutschland,
Deutschland über alles*.

In his political verses he champions the cause of the German
imperium Romanum of the Hohenstaufen against the Pope.
Walther von der Vogelweide gave new life to the conventional
courtly Minnesang by transfusing it with the folksong. He sings
of the simple maiden, whom the cult of chivalry had for the
most part thrust into the background, in the unforgettable song:

> Under der linden,
> an der heide . . .

one of the most exquisite of German poems. Or again in his

poem *I sat cross-legged on a rock* (*Ich saz ûf eime steine und dahte bein mit beine*) he ponders on a possible reconciliation of the dualism between God and the World, between God's grace and honour and worldly wealth. One may well repeat the words of Hugo von Trimberg: 'Hêr Walter von der Vogelweide, swer des vergaez der taet mir leide' (He who could forget Walther von der Vogelweide is to be pitied).

Among the other Austrian minnesingers is Ulrich von Lichtenstein who, clad as Frau Venus, rode jousting from Northern Italy towards Vienna. Neidhart von Reuenthal, who lived in Melk and became a legendary figure, created the so-called village poetry of the German minnesang. Then there is the minnesinger Tannhäuser, symbol in medieval legend of a man whom a consuming passion drives to eternal doom; a tragic conception which Richard Wagner tried to improve on by the ultimate salvation of the hero.

The waning of the chivalric epoch is reflected in the verse tale *Meier Helmbrecht* by Wernher von Gartenaere, an Austrian poet, which gives a vivid description of predatory knights and burghers in the first half of the thirteenth century. So early did the decay of knighthood set in. The hero, Meier Helmbrecht, a peasant's son, returns home from his adventures as a robber-knight and shows off his knowledge of the various languages he has picked up by greeting his sister in Latin, his mother in Slav and the servant in Netherlandish. He is acknowledged by his father only when he calls the four oxen in the shed by their proper German names. Setting forth once more on his exploits he suffers a sorry death at the hands of the peasants whom he has derided and ill-treated. The circumstances are obviously based on topical events and point to Upper Austria as locality. The use by the Czech philosopher, Stitny, of the fourteenth century, of the name 'Helmbrecht' to designate a wanton fellow, proves the popularity of *Meier Helmbrecht*.

The gradual dissolution of knighthood was accompanied by a decay in literature. Not until the Renaissance did German literature revive, and once more Austria, especially Vienna, became the centre of culture. In the meantime in 1365 a university, which still enjoys fame throughout the world, had been established in Vienna by Rudolph IV.

Amongst the poets of the fourteenth century was Johann von Saaz, author of the *Ackermann aus Böhmen* (*The Ploughman of Bohemia*)—a masterly dialogue between author and death, who has robbed the former of his wife. A dialogue by Petrarch, *De rebus utriusque fortunae*, treats a like subject. Johann von Saaz foreshadows the art of polemical dialogue which the Humanistic age developed to perfection. It is also the first work in which an attempt is made to introduce the standard German used by high officials at the imperial Bohemian court. Here at Prague the Emperor Charles IV, who knew and corresponded with Petrarch, was the foremost patron of German Humanism.

The Renaissance brought with it a new attitude towards life. In Germany it took shape in the Reformation, but in Prague and Vienna sprang up a great circle of Humanists, the so-called 'poetae', notably the Viennese scholars Heinrich von Langenstein (member of the Universities of Paris and Vienna); Georg Peuerbach (interpreter of Vergil) and Aenea Sylvio de' Piccolomini, an impressive poet and orator, who later became pope Pius II, and was the author of the Renaissance story *Euryalus and Lucretia*, in theme very like Goethe's *Werther*. There was also Konrad Celtis, who wandered lecturing from university to university and finally settled in Vienna where he died in 1508. The age of Humanism opened full of promise, but later 'eloquentia' took the place of 'humanitas'.

On the threshold of the German Renaissance stands Kaiser Maximilian I ($+$1519), called the last of the knights, who held his court at Innsbruck and founded in Vienna (1502) the 'Collegium Poetarum et Mathematicorum'. Not only a patron of the Humanistic movement or Renaissance of the scholarly world, he was himself a poet. His epic, *Teuerdank*, describes the chivalrous adventures of his life; it is of distinctly allegorical character and the last product of the courtly epic. His prose work *Weisskunig* is a chronicle of battles and personal experiences.

The marriage of his grandson, Ferdinand von Österreich, into the house of Ladislaus secured the inheritances of Bohemia and Hungary for Austria. Austria, 'happy by marriage', was well on the way to the consummation of its power.

During the following years, however, Vienna had to stand its trial in the wars against the Turks. But even beneath the travail of the Thirty Years' War Austria's power remained unshaken, nor did the ravaging plague of 1679 and the second siege of Vienna by the Turks in 1683 blight its poetic vitality. During these dark years that rough diamond of an Augustinian monk from Swabia, Abraham a Santa Clara, held both citizens and court enthralled by his sermons, which later won the praise of Goethe, and were in part used by Schiller in his *Wallenstein's Lager*. Abraham a Santa Clara is one of the greatest German representatives of the literary movement called 'Baroque' which flourished especially during the reign of the Emperor Leopold I (+1705) in Austria.

In contrast to the art of the Renaissance, Baroque art has the reputation of being formless and overloaded. Its effect is often that of unrestrained magnificence. This style must ever seem incomprehensible to Classicists. But Austrian Baroque is not mere bombast. Leibniz has given it philosophical justification: 'The subordination of the atom to the whole and the simultaneous recognition of the atom constitute the formative principle of Baroque.' We find in German and Austrian Baroque art often that same peculiar intermingling of intellectual and sensual elements as in the English poets Donne and Crashaw. And we may note that in Austria Baroque architecture in the hands of Fischer von Erlach, Lucas von Hildebrand and Prandauer has a lightness, a musical flow, that removes it far from the overloaded Italian manner. Indeed it takes on a Romantic allure which enables it to blend with nature, as in the monastery of Melk, and in the little church of Dürnstein on the Danube, where its exquisite flowing curves echo the rhythm of the river.

As the genius of Goethe and Schiller rose Austrian Baroque fell into decay. After the golden age of Maria Theresa, Joseph II, her successor, set about to realize the great reforms dreamed of by his mother. Education was furthered, and State and Church revised on a wide basis. Mozart's dream of an enlightened mankind, as expressed in the *Magic Flute*, may indeed have been inspired by the spirit of Joseph II who opened the Austrian national theatre, to which every lover of drama wishes to make pilgrimage. The names of Schreyvogel, Laube,

Bauernfeld, Kainz, and Anton Wildgans have since added fame to the Burgtheater where frequent performances of Shakespeare provide a truly lasting bond between Austria and England. Stage art and music celebrated many a triumph here —but in the meantime Weimar had become the great cultural centre of literature and thought, and the spirit of Goethe, that universal genius of the modern age, shed its light on Austrian culture. At the same time Goethe himself gathered from the latter more than one inspiration, as, for instance, from the Orientalist Hammer-Purgstall and from the scholarly and literary circles in Bohemia, at Karlsbad, Teplitz, and Franzensbad. Moreover the theatre in Weimar, directed by Goethe, developed under the influence of Vienna.

The fall of Napoleon and the rise of Metternich brought about a reaction in Austria. We generally term this period the 'Biedermeierzeit'. Public opinion was suppressed and when at the Wartburg-Fest in 1817 rebellious young students made a bonfire of pigtails, corsets, and canes (the symbols of reaction) matters were only made worse. Two years later the student Sand murdered the diplomat-author Kotzebue, a deed which led to freedom being completely crushed.

Under this state of things the Austrian bourgeoisie sought refuge and sweet oblivion in the music and poetry of home and salon. The tumultuous wave of rebellion, echoing in Beethoven's daemonic symphonies, had ebbed. Schubert's gentler melodies soothed the troubled soul.

It would, however, be misconceiving the situation if this period, the 'Biedermeierzeit', was regarded as one of bourgeois spiritual tranquillity. We speak of it as the good old times— but in reality it was fermenting with revolutionary ideals. A new social class was fast rising, parliamentary reforms developing, and the press gaining universal power. Only in comparison with our own times does this period seem one of ease and security. The loyal Austrian loved his opera and sang his National Anthem to the melody of Haydn (1732-1809), inspired by *God Save the King*. And in the Schubert circle forgathered the so-called Schubertiaden—circles of leading poets, actors and musicians.

Here Grillparzer (1791-1872), Austria's first great poet since the Middle Ages, was a welcome guest. With him German literature experienced the Indian summer of its Classicism. In him were embodied many characteristic Austrian traits. He was, like Walther von der Vogelweide, of his age: solitary for all his sociability, dreamy, of a mind sensitive but slightly ironical, and with it all a conscientious official. Melancholy, disciplined subordination, frankness and irony—these specifically Austrian characteristics are expressed in his story of *Der arme Spielmann* (*The Poor Fiddler*), written in 1848. Whoever understands this poor fiddler will comprehend also the 'Austrian temperament', which falls precipitately from rapture into disillusionment, freezes in the sun and would fain flee far from the madding crowd.

In the Schubertiaden moved also the three sisters Fröhlich, one of whom was Grillparzer's life-long betrothed. 'Our hearts burnt but never melted', Grillparzer said of his love, and in his drama, *König Ottokars Glück und Ende*, which unmistakably alludes to the fall of Napoleon, the author commemorates his beloved Käthe Fröhlich.

It was long before his works were acknowledged by the public either in Austria or abroad. Bourgeois ideas and Schopenhauer's pessimism are voiced in his dramas. The freedom of one is the ruin of the other and man cannot strive against his predestined fate—this is what he says in his trilogy, *The Golden Fleece*. One might apply the words spoken by Grillparzer at the grave of Beethoven (+1827), to the work of the poet himself:

> Before us there have been poets and heroes, singers and visionaries, towards whom stricken mankind can turn to realize their origin and goal. . . .

As playwright Grillparzer stands head and shoulders above his contemporary, Raimund, the actor and author of fantastic burlesques, and above Nestroy, who from the stage flung many a home truth in the face of his public. Bitter contempt of state and society fell also from the lips of Karl Postl, generally known as Sealsfield when he became an American citizen. Second to Grillparzer in Austrian literature of the early nineteenth century we must place Adalbert Stifter from Bohemia. Artist, poet and novelist, he betrays a sensitive perception of light and colour in his description of landscape and not only seems to behold the magic power of God in great climaxes but also recognizes in the beauty of little things the wonders of nature.

This Wordsworthian attitude towards nature renders him especially dear to the English; and it is a curious fact that later on the philosopher Nietzsche, whose outlook on life was so far removed from Stifter's, should become one of his great admirers.

The year of revolution, 1848, saw the fall of Metternich but brought with it, none the less, disillusionment. This heralded a new era in Austrian literature. Ferdinand von Saar (from Vienna) was a forerunner in technical achievement long before the North German Arno Holz wrote *Buch der Zeit*. Saar also gives a moving picture of the Proletariat in his poems. Ludwig Anzengruber (from Vienna) provides a parallel to Ibsen in the character analysis of his dramas. Peter Rosegger (from Styria) seeks to lead overcivilized man back to nature. In his poetical stories of Alpine people the village-tale reaches its perfection. Karl Schönherr depicts the Austrian home in his dramas.

Much of this happened at a time when Naturalism was the triumphant fashion of the day in Berlin and Munich. Austria did not take the lead in this literary movement. Modern civilization appeared to the so-called Naturalistic authors as a product of man's milieu, of his surroundings, of inevitable historical development, influenced by man's striving for power, and the daemonic forces of hunger and sex.

In the movement that follows known as Symbolism Austria once more took a prominent part. About the year 1892, in which Gerhart Hauptmann's *Weber* was published, a reactionary tendency had become apparent, and in opposition arose a poetry of strongly individualistic character. Nietzsche is the poet-philosopher of this aesthetic and aristocratic literature. The ideal represented in his *Zarathustra*, uncertainly perceived by a spirit filled with ardent longing, inspired this school of decadent aestheticism, whose characteristic mood is morbid and suggestive of decay. In Austria, Bahr, Rilke, v. Hofmannsthal, and other participants in this movement, endeavour with subtle artistry and sensitiveness to atmosphere, to reveal the hidden regions of the subconscious and the irrational in human nature.

In the Viennese Hugo von Hofmannsthal, who died in 1929, the world has lost a great writer. All who have heard Richard Strauss's *Rosenkavalier* or *Electra* or *Salome*, the latter closely akin to Oscar Wilde's *Salome*, have been listening to von Hofmannsthal's libretto. And such as have enjoyed the yearly festival of music and drama at Salzburg will have heard his version of the medieval English morality play *Everyman*, in which the rich man forsaken by fortune has to account for his sins before God. In the drama *Das Salzburger große Welttheater* which is inspired by Calderon, von Hofmannsthal uses his favourite theme of the purification of mankind through death, and, as in Shakespeare's *As you like it* and in Goethe's *Faust*, the stage represents the world, where king, queen, beggar, peasant and workman play their transitory parts. This work is typical of literature in Austria on the eve of that country's doom. Melancholy and the unsatiated desire of life fill his poems. He throws a magic cloak around the world in order to quicken it.

Hugo von Hofmannsthal's early drama *Der Tor und der Tod*, 1893 (*Death and the Fool*), may be considered a characteristic example for the Romantic mood of this period. The hero Claudio is swayed between the world of deed and dream. Life and love are mere phantoms and only when death comes to him and plays a strain that calls up the shades of his mother, his beloved and his friend, does he recognize the worth of reality that he has let slip through his hands.

By the side of von Hofmannsthal and excelling him stands Rainer Maria Rilke (+1926). He was born in Prague, travelled to the South and to Russia, lived in Worpswede with a little community of artists whom he brought to public notice, and later enjoyed close intimacy with Rodin. His musical power over words, his rare subtlety of expression and his mysticism make it difficult for many to find access to his genius. In his verses echo the whispering of the trees, the raging of the storm, the awakening of spring and the murmuring of water. A certain mystic yearning is the key-note of Rilke's poetry:

> This is yearning: to be borne on the wave
> and to have no home in the flux of time....

In his description of man and beast (*Der Panther*) he endeavours to penetrate to the essence of all being; he himself says that his poems are experiences. He observes gestures, follows the flight of the birds and knows how the flowers grow. In the poem *Pietà* which forms a part of the cycle *The life of the Virgin Mary* the poet shows deepest insight into human feeling.

His *Stunden-Buch* (1906), a collection of poems, is for us a book of devotion. Amid the vast loneliness of the Russian steppes he meditates on human destiny. He loves not the harsh light of day, but the twilight of solitude and death. For him the modern city breeds falsehood, its children are but shadows, and the multitude becomes a herd, but the poet bursts these barriers in his striving towards God. In these and other poems Rilke has perhaps achieved the highest technical perfection in German poetry since Goethe. His translations of André Gide, Paul Valéry, Maurice de Guérin, Elizabeth Barrett Browning (*Sonnets from the Portuguese*), etc., display his sensitiveness to foreign poetry.

In his *Briefe an einen jungen Dichter* he expresses his inmost thoughts. Conceited criticism and irony, he says, are strangers to the true poet. Slowly, the poet must mature, like a tree, and stand against the storms of spring without fear that the summer may not follow.

Shortly before the First World War began a movement called Expressionism. Its aim, as the word implies, is to give not the outer but the inner impression of a phenomenon. Expressionistic feeling is illustrated by the paintings of Van Gogh, who reveals the internal processes of Nature with the sun as a symbol of life-giving force and the earth in a state of universal chaos. In literature a new sense of form is requisite for this, and a new language. Its language tends to renounce logic and to express the secret anguish and exultation of the spirit in a new ecstatic idiom, of a decidedly Nietzschean character. Bound up with this expressionism is the revolutionary tone which particularly during the First World War became a clamorous indictment of the past.

The designation 'the new man', 'brother of mankind', appears again and again in modern Austrian and German literature of that time. Weary of the sceptical outlook of the generation which looked to the past in order to escape the present, man is filled with a new desire to master his fate. The ultimate aim of life as conceived for instance by Franz Werfel (1890-1945), the Austrian, may be described as the realization of the human being in service to the community; he passionately desires to feel 'akin' to mankind: 'Dir, O Mensch verwandt zu sein'.[1]

In this brief survey a thousand years of German literature in Austria have passed before our sight. It has twice reached a summit in its development, in the Middle Ages, the time of Walther von der Vogelweide and the Nibelungen, and once again in recent years in Grillparzer and then followed by Rilke and Hugo von Hofmannsthal.

In 1935 appeared J. Weinheber's volume of poems entitled *Wien wörtlich* in which the poet of the odes and hymns falls into the broadest dialect. We hear the voice of the Viennese in all their suffering and their love for his native home, Vienna, whose decay he was doomed to witness, and whose great tragedy was that she was not spared the last ordeal—Vienna from which life had fled, where but the beauty of stone, and the Belvedere and Schönbrunn, stand as silent witnesses of a past glory.

[1] *Der Weltfreund*, 1911.

V

Goethe and Kierkegaard

GOETHE BICENTENARY, 1949

KIERKEGAARD CENTENARY, 1955

> There is a level of civilization on which the fate of the
> other nation is felt as if it were our own.
>
> GOETHE (motto of the re-established
> German Centre of the P.E.N. Club)

> Let the sons of Montaigne and Pascal, of Michelangelo
> and Dante, of El Greco and Cervantes, of Beethoven and
> Goethe, of Rubens and Rembrandt, become conscious
> of their fraternity with the country of Shakespeare—
> decimated as they are by a mad fury for which there is
> no strait-jacket and which is ready to burst loose at any
> moment.
>
> MAURIAC in *Le Figaro*, September 1945, see
> STUART ATKINS, *German Quarterly*, 1947, pp. 166ff.

WHEN GOETHE DIED in 1832, many Europeans felt that
they had reached a turning-point, the end of our
Western heritage. Since then many a warning voice
about the 'decline of the West' has been heard. The present
catastrophe was already prophetically foreseen by Nietzsche,
Oswald Spengler, and his contemporaries. Aldous Huxley's
Ends and Means (1937) stresses the need for reform and for
detachment. Others seek to solve the problems by planning,
others by dictatorship or the creation of new myths for the
masses, others by a sentimentality which is often nothing but a
masked 'cruelty which tries to drive mercy out of the world
by calling it names such as Humanitarianism'.[1] Our Western
civilization has been shaken to its foundations, the feeling of
security is gone, our belief in progress and in numbers has been
shattered, our democratic red tape can be almost as bad as
totalitarianism. There is more than ever a need for us to look

---

[1] C. S. Lewis, *The Problem of Pain* (1940).

96

backward as well as forward, to be conscious of our Western resources and to formulate our attitude to Goethe, who is a good tonic against our sordid pessimism and belief in man's total depravity. Although Goethe was born two hundred years ago, he is very near us. He is not only the greatest cosmopolitan of our age, but also Germany's most spontaneous and original poet and an eminent scientist. The fact that such a man could exist is in itself a miracle.

Goethe, as a poet and as a scientist, has a message to us, though, alas, the latter has often been misinterpreted or distorted. In the nineteenth century he was primarily looked upon as the creator of modern personality whilst we of the twentieth century see in him a unique challenge to our present standardization and over-specialization, and a central force reconciling 'the individual to his place in society as a whole'. In Goethe all activities (poetry, philosophy, scientific research) revolve round an organic centre. He is the last master of the balanced mean, perhaps the last and only European genius who can be called the equal of Homer, Dante and Shakespeare. If, according to Edison, a genius is 98% perspiration and 2% inspiration, there is certainly much more gold than dross in Goethe!

Goethe is truly a miracle of natural growth. In him poetry and philosophy and the problem of existence are inseparable. It is quite impossible here to re-assess the value of every volume of the Weimar Ausgabe which comprises one hundred and thirty-three volumes. And no single, normal human being can wade through the unfathomable ocean of modern research on Goethe: Goethe the Classic, the Romantic, the genius, the cosmopolitan, the statesman, the liberal conservative, the moralist, the scientist, the egoist, the Olympian, the Faustian, the German, the European, not to mention the enormous output of books and essays on him during the Bicentenary year. Judging by such works Goethe appears to have no character at all and yet we shall see that this is but a superficial view, because to the author of *Faust* the whole is more than its parts. This is his inner law, his central impulse, the key to the understanding of all his creative expression in life, science and poetry. He once (15 March 1799) remarked significantly to Knebel: 'I can only think in as far as I produce.'

He never regarded himself as isolated; he lived his poetic vision in a world of men, not in an ivory tower. He knew that life manifests itself in terms of opposites—but there was a unity behind the apparently bewildering variety.

He creatively experienced the unifying principle of science and poetry, he prophetically foresaw the scientific development of our own generation, i.e. the establishment of a 'single unified science' in which the process of the whole overrides that of the parts: 'In many situations the larger system must be considered before predictions can be made about the parts.'[1] Thus also the duality between the individual and society is reconciled by a unifying principle of all human efforts.

Especially now that our civilization is in mortal peril of becoming disrupted by the unbearable split between theoretical research and reality, science and society, mind and body, Goethe's profound conviction of the continuity of life and the oneness of centre and circumference is of vital importance to us all. The centre is to him more than periphery, but both, centre and circumference are one—a belief which, as we saw, became the basic principle of the approaching age of a new science in which the inorganic and the organic worlds are essentially united. There is indeed an urgent need for us to understand Goethe. We need not defend him. His reputation has long been established, though the full scope of his genius was not immediately recognized.

Before the year 1813 Goethe was mainly known in Great Britain and other countries as the author of *Werther* and *Götz*, who inspired Walter Scott in his translation (1799) and also in the composition of the *Waverley* novels. Byron's enthusiastic outburst about *Faust* is well known: 'I would give the world to read *Faust* in the original.' Shelley translated the majestic hymns of the three Archangels (in the *Prologue*). But the true apostles of the Goethe-cult in England first appeared in Carlyle and G. Henry Lewes. Whilst Carlyle as a Calvinist had weighed upon the educationist and the moralist in Goethe, the author of the 'pedagogic province' Henry Lewes emphasized the universal scientific breadth of the sage of Weimar, whose research had resulted in sensational discoveries in anatomy,

---

[1] *Scientific thought in the coming decades*, L. L. Whyte, *Horizon*, July 1948.

botany, optics and in theories of mineralogy and meteorology.

T. S. Eliot in *Selected Essays* says: 'Goethe is a man with the "sense of the age" . . . but by Baudelaire's time it was no longer necessary for a man to embrace such varied interests in order to have the sense of the age.'

Goethe no doubt had a sense of the age. His life covers a vast span of time: the Seven Years' War, the American War of Independence, the French Revolution, the rise and fall of Napoleon, the Viennese Congress, and the 1830 Revolution in France. His influence on his contemporaries must have been extraordinarily vivid. Wieland says of his first meeting with Goethe, that the latter made him feel like a dew-drop in the rising sun. . . . The later Goethe, however, appears to some observer as a God who rules through 'his serene remoteness'.

The centenary year of Goethe's death, 1932, witnessed many fervent expressions of homage from all parts of the world. In France, where especially Goethe's matchless poetry, his *Werther, Faust, Iphigenie auf Tauris, Tasso*, the *Wahlverwandt-schaften, Dichtung und Wahrheit*, and above all *Eckermanns Gespräche* have become popular, A. Gide paid Goethe an important tribute in the *Nouvelle Revue Française* (1932, III). Henry Lewes's *Life of Goethe* played no little part in making the poet better known in France. Even in recent French evaluations of German literature during the War of 1939-45, Goethe is not altogether discarded as the serene Olympian. Apart from François Mauriac's remark in *Figaro*, George Duhamel admits that 'the greatest achievement of Europe is the achievement of a few people, among whom must be counted the Germans'.[1]

In England, too, recognition is not grudged to Goethe. With an almost prophetic insight into 'the philosophy of the Wolf State', Dean Inge, in *The End of an Age*, explains how a combination of circumstances, each intelligible in itself, has driven Germany into the present apocalyptic catastrophe, also adding: 'The time may come when we shall be glad to see a strong Germany, the Germany that produced Kant, Goethe and Schiller, Ranke and Mommsen, the great musicians and the great scientists.' Against this stands T. S. Eliot's remark in *The Use of Poetry and the Use of Criticism*, lectures delivered at

[1] *Figaro*, January 1945 (cf. Stuart Atkins, G.Q., 1947).

Harvard University: 'Of Goethe perhaps it is truer to say that
he dabbled in both philosophy and poetry and made no great
success of either; his true role was that of a man of the world
and sage—a La Rochefoucauld, a La Bruyère, a Vauvern-
argues.' T. S. Eliot here re-echoes, possibly quite unconsciously,
Kierkegaard's provocative attack on Goethe's 'characterless-
ness'[1] or perhaps he still repeats Thomas de Quincey's pre-
judiced arguments as to Goethe's alleged lack of genuine
feeling, and hostility to religion. In his speech about Goethe the
sage, on the occasion of the award of the Hansische Goethe-
Preis in the Town Hall of Hamburg in May 1954, T. S. Eliot
frankly corrects his misjudgement of Goethe as a lyrical genius,
but there is no doubt that it is the *old* and *wise* Goethe who
receives that belated homage.

Nietzsche, who admired the *Conversations with Eckermann* as the
best of all German books, also did not take to the Faustian
Goethe. K. Jaspers, in *Die Wandlung* (1947), finds the sage of
Weimar 'out of touch with time', and tilts against windmills
when he tries to formulate his attitude to Goethe. F. Gundolf
justly praised him as the last universal visionary in our age.
Thomas Mann, however, rather narrowly saw in Goethe the
representative of the bourgeois period. If, in 1932, Goethe's
harmonious view of life was stressed by many admirers,
Nietzsche's warning against becoming a philistine must not be
neglected, for Goethe's serenity was paid for by heavy sacrifice,
the readiness for re-birth, the ever-recurring cycle of 'Stirb und
werde'.

Two hundred years have now passed away since Goethe's
birth. Can his books still speak to us? His life and work have
become for us a reality to which not only the individual may
turn but the whole world. *Faust*, apart from being a great confession, is doubtless the most gigantic achievement towards harmo-
nizing the intellectual and sensual chaos in our modern world.

We may find profound solace in his conviction that evil is the
servant of the good—this is the keynote and message of his
Faust—and solace in his passionate belief in the ultimate
salvation of human endeavours through God's loving kindness,
without which our efforts remain futile; in his call for selfless

[1] Cf. *Journals.*

activity for the good of the community and for self-recognition, e.g. in the *Zueignung: Know Thyself*, in *Urworte. Orphisch*: 'Du kannst dir nicht entfliehen'; cf. Hölderlin's *Rhein*: 'Wie du anfingst, wirst du bleiben'. Our mission, according to him, lies *within* us. This is not a fatalistic view, because we must *become* that which we really are.

In spite of the earthquake at Lisbon and the atrocities of the French Revolution and the social-political upheaval caused by the Napoleonic wars, Goethe, who certainly was no rebel, martyr, or adventurer, preserved his heart pure and always felt a sincere reverence, as he says in *Wilhelm Meisters Wanderjahre*, towards that which is in us, above us, and beneath us. In politics he stood for freedom, but not at the cost of order, in science for intuition, but not at the price of clarity—obscurity was to him no proof of profundity—in society and education he stood for a wide cultural background, though not to the detriment of a thorough training in a special profession, in religious matters for tolerance. Life, not death, was his deep concern, but by life he did not mean a vegetative existence, but creative activity.

Life is his deep concern. Yet death is worshipped as the immitigable deity all over Europe. There is the eternal conflict in us all—the conflict of Prometheus (symbol of the self-assertive will to live) and of Tristan (the self-effacing will to die). Both instincts have profoundly shaped the features of our civilization. They are enshrined in poetic images: Faust—Tristan, etc. To many observers, Wagner's *Tristan und Isolde* is characteristic of the German death-yearning, drowned in the music of the 'Liebestod'. There is a wild beauty in it, a beauty as fascinating as the rainbow over the storm-tossed abyss. But in the 'German expression' there is also subtlety and exquisite grace, in the smile on the lips of Eve at Bamberg, or in Gottfrid's epic.

Clemenceau, however, spoke of the German of death: 'These people love death. The divinity which they contemplate with fear, but with a fear mixed with ecstasy and intoxication, is death. . . . War is a pact with death. There the Boche encounters his best friend.'[1] Though the yearning for death does

[1] Tardieu, *The Truth about the Treaty*.

exist in many German authors, does it not also exist in other nations? That death-instinct is certainly not characteristic of Goethe. In him there is a balance between self-extinction and self-regard, the self-sacrificing anima and self-satisfied animus. Life is for Goethe a gift which we must not throw away. But this is no contradiction to the mystic view which is also Goethe's conviction: i.e. 'He who will find life must lose it'—Man must give himself to a cause greater than his own personal existence.

Now this view seems to be overshadowed by the modern outlook which is distinctly sombre. According to the philosopher Martin Heidegger, 'the dulling influence of everyday life and our herd instincts prevent us from realizing true human existence'. Life to us is 'Sorge' and 'Angst', not only because of the slums and poor hygiene but 'by reasons of the very constitution of the human self' (D'Arcy) 'life is a cancerous growth or at best a long sitting in a dentist chair'—frustration and despair—only 'betweenness having birth and death as its limits'.

Goethe, too, experiences the curse of petty cares which corrode our happiness and energy: 'Care at the bottom of the heart is lurking',[1] but in him there is care and detachment. Goethe did believe in the ultimate goodness of the Universe, in God and immortality. Now, according to Nietzsche God is dead or He is in the opinion of many contemporary nihilists the Lord 'of nothingness'.

The death of God 'contributes indeed the greatest event in Western thought since the end of the nineteenth century'.[2] To such a view life is accidental and full of paradoxes; there is (in sharp contrast to Goethe's view) no inner continuity— only a continual dying and a continual daily boredom, the rule of the herd, a vulgar mass-slavery: 'They say, they believe, they do, they think. . . .' But Goethe gives us a vision and an example of personality which is *not* swept along by the wheel of time and which does not float in a spiritual void. The law of day and night, give and take, of 'Diastole' and 'Systole' is the principle in Goethe's philosophy of life.

His favourite metaphor of 'weaving', cf. the Erdgeist:

[1] *Faust*, I.   [2] Introduction to G. de Ruggiero by R. Heppenstall.

> a fluctuant wave
> a shuttle free,
> birth and grave,
> an eternal sea,
> a weaving, flowing,
> life all glowing . . .

reflects that ceaseless activity and continuity, whilst those of 'leap' and 'repetition' show a lack of any continuity 'in the web of becoming'.

Boredom has become our modern curse. 'How terrible tedium is—terribly tedious . . . the only thing I see is emptiness, the only thing I move about in is emptiness. I do not even suffer pain. The vulture constantly devoured Prometheus' liver; the poison constantly dripped down on Loki; that was at least an interruption, even though a monotonous one. . . . My soul is like the Dead Sea, over which no bird can fly; when it has flown mid-way, then it sinks down to death and destruction.'[1]

However, Kierkegaard vanquished this despair through the confession that suffering is the meaning of life, and that man represents the bridge between time and the eternal. The 'moment' through which Goethe's Faust seeks to clasp eternity remains according to Kierkegaard ambiguous:

> Nature's security is due to the fact that time has no significance for it. Only in the instant does history begin. Man's sensuousness is by sin posited as sinfulness and therefore is lower than that of the beast, and yet this is because here the higher life begins, for now begins the spirit.[2]

According to such a view of life, 'the error of humanism' and of Goethe does not lie in this emphasis on the dignity of man, but in their failure to affirm man's ultimate independence of the world as personality. Personality does not and cannot fully exist within society. As a person man cannot be completely a citizen of the world.

It is on this point that Goethe is attacked most violently by those who are haunted by fear and despair and who see in the author of *Werther* and *Faust* a seductive deceiver who transforms our world of horror into a mirage of loveliness.

Compared with Goethe's time, the whole present age seems to be a period of despair, in fact, as Kierkegaard says, 'the age

---

[1] Kierkegaard in *Diapsalmata* in *Either-Or*.   [2] *The Concept of Death.*

of the Wandering Jew' . . . an age which tries to substitute for
life a blind passion for history and science. In the stories of
Job and Abraham who were doubly rewarded for what they
sacrificed, Kierkegaard found a simile for the spiritual values of
suffering. In this connection the religious category 'Repetition',
which expresses that restitution of one's sacrifice through a
manifold reward, attains a special significance in his philosophy.

The concept of 'Repetition' is brilliantly illumined. Life is
seen as a repetition without which the world would cease to
exist, and without which there would be no life, no beauty.
Such an affirmation needs courage, the courage of Goethe's
Die and be re-born, Stirb und Werde, and Schiller's soldiers in
Wallensteins Lager:

> Und setzet ihr nicht das Leben ein,
> nie wird euch das Leben gewonnen sein. . . .

Kierkegaard also stakes everything on his idea. He was
ready to lose everything, but in the end, like Job, he was doubly
rewarded. He knew that to live only on hopes would be coward-
ice, and only on recollections would be a sensuous illusion. As a
true Christian he seeks the 'imitatio Christi' and renounces the
poet's dream.

Kierkegaard was convinced that only through fear and
despair can we find our salvation, as they compel us to the
decision of our inmost freedom, a freedom which we thus owe
to ourselves. In this struggle to decide our own fate we stand
alone, but God's eye watches over us. It is that loneliness to
which we are condemned, deprived of every earthly help and
human community, which in a different way is also the theme
of Kafka's terrifying trilogy of utter human melancholy:
Der Proßess, Das Schloß, America.

Kierkegaard, however, shows man the way out of this hope-
less despair, in that he thrusts the mystery of our religious
awakening into the very misery of our forsakenness. The
decision and the courage to accept one's fate is the first act of
our inner freedom and of the way towards true self-knowledge.

Did Goethe, as Kierkegaard and J. Jaspers maintain, really
not experience the magnitude of suffering? Although it can be
truly said that despair constitutes Kierkegaard's moral message,

Goethe too, both as man and as poet, profoundly experienced the mystery of suffering. Through Eckermann's mouth (I, 106) he gives the lie to the shallow legend of his serene happiness:

> . . . Im Grunde ist es nichts als Mühe und Arbeit gewesen, und ich kann wohl sagen, daß ich in meinen fünfundsiebzig Jahren keine vier Wochen eigentlich Behagen gehabt. . . .

Moreover, it need hardly be testified that he was not impervious to the suffering of his fellow men. He who had once shrunk with horror from the revolutionary aftermath of the storm of the Bastille, in his *Wanderjahre* (1829) at the age of eighty still betrayed quick sympathy with the bold reform plans of the Count of Sismondi, with Jeremy Bentham's desire to provide the greatest possible happiness for the greatest possible mass of people, and with the philanthropist Robert Owen. His *Märchen* is doubtless a conscious, artistic manifestation of the rising social unrest and the new order of his own age.

But Goethe, as a philosopher as well as a poet, believed in organic evolution, not revolution. He opposed any attempt to totalitarianism and standardization: 'Alles Große geschieht in der Minorität.[1] The social and political unity of a people must grow from within, and not be superimposed from above.[2] Narrow party politics was loathsome to him: cf. the *Xenie*:

> Wo das Gelehrte beginnt,
> hört das Politische auf. . . .

We must realize the political and social conditions in the Germany of Goethe's time if we are to do him justice. The German word *human* expressed her deepest thoughts, but the word *national* was really meaningless then. Germany had no metropolis yet, the German authors lived in a spiritual isolation—unthinkable in France and England at the same period—with Weimar as Germany's soul, and also there was no public to support it.

In order to stem the tide of suffering he visualizes in his *Wanderjahre*, the new state on the basis of real Christianity, a state of democratic citizens, without the absorbing domination of a metropolis, without the levelling aspect of uniformity, but with a strong authority and a human, penal law. Schiller's

[1] *Eckermann*, II, 65.   [2] Ibid., 271.

arresting vision of the ideal equilibrium in man's conflict between the purely sensuous and purely formative urges in modern culture, as depicted in his thirteenth letter, *Über die ästhetische Erziehung*, may well be applied to Goethe himself:

> . . . Sobald der Mensch nur Inhalt der Zeit ist, so ist er nicht. . . .
> Sobald der Mensch nur Form ist, so hat er keine Form . . .

Goethe found a balance between the two opposing principles. He came to see human existence in symbols. 'Alles Vergängliche ist nur ein Gleichnis'—the fleeting appearance of things attuned to a deeper significance; the individual was raised to the universal. This is, I think, also the meaning of the words of renunciation in the *Wanderjahre*:

> . . . Und dein Streben sei's in Liebe,
> Und dein Leben sei die Tat. . . .

Such an attitude to life was liable to be misinterpreted as cold indifference and selfish detachment. Goethe, certainly, did not allow his creative genius to become a fanfare of humanitarian pathos. On 20 October 1830 he said to Eckermann: 'Wenn Jeder nur als Einzelner seine Pflicht tut. . . . Ich habe es in meinem Beruf als Schriftsteller nie gefragt: was will die große Masse und wie nütze ich dem Ganzen? . . .' Only that which concerned or touched him directly, became productive in him.

To Schiller, the world's history was the world's judgement. To Goethe it was the symbol of an ordered cosmos. He who had developed into a full personality in the conflict between self-surrender and the Promethean longing for self-realization sought a meaning in the demonic and apparently illogical in history. Such a conception of our existence differs fundamentally from that of Kierkegaard and Arthur Schopenhauer, who could find no sense in the chaotic appearance of events. Kierkegaard experienced how fear and adversity drew people together and produced 'beauty and harmony in life's relationship, just as the cold of winter produces ice-flowers on the window-panes', but without that compulsion of fear its beauty vanished. It seemed to him no mere coincidence that his initials were S. A. and thus stood in mysterious inverse relationship to those of Arthur Schopenhauer's A. S. In contrast to both stands the hymn of Lynkeus with its affirmation of human existence, cf. *Faust* II:

> Es sei, wie es wolle,
> es war doch so schön.

So much concerning Goethe's alleged indifference to human suffering. Anything that was a paradox or violent in its development was distasteful to Goethe as it was later to Stifter, the author of *Nachsommer*; cf. also *Eckermann*, 17 April 1825. As to that demonic element in life, Kierkegaard in his attack on science in the *Journals* stresses the *miracle* which can be exhibited as a miracle but never be understood. Also Goethe saw and experienced the magnitude of the demonic in life: 'Alles Große bildet, so bald wir es gewahr werden';[1] or cf. the moving chapter *Antikes* in his appreciation of Winckelmann, where Goethe admires the demonic totality of our human existence reincarnated in Winckelmann. He loved the Greeks; they lived, created and shaped life on a grandiose scale, in art they taught him serene repose, they showed him how to exist under the violent onslaught of our stark reality and his Faustian vision.

Even in *Werther*, though darkened by Ossianic Weltschmerz, the strife of the individual is presented to us like a demonic spectacle. In his *West-Östlicher Divan* it becomes a simile of typical universal experiences, cf. *Hegire*, written in 1814:

> Nord und West und Süd zersplittern,
> Throne bersten, Reiche zittern.

Also in his *Campagne in Frankreich* in the face of conflicting party interests he stands aloof: 'Der Dichter aber, der seiner Natur nach unparteiisch sein und bleiben muß, sucht sich von den Zuständen beider kämpfenden Teile zu durchdringen'; but this detachment is not a cowardly escape and must end tragically if reconciliation is impossible. In encountering the masses he seeks to protect the rights of the individual from political coercion.[2] As an artist and a thinker he perceives all that happens in an ever-changing and ever-recurring cycle of existence. He affirms life and death and immortality, for he believes in lastingness and change: *Dauer im Wechsel* and *Eins und Alles*.

[1] *Eckermann*, 16th December 1828.   [2] *Eckermann*, III, 316.

In these two poems lies the keystone of his entire outlook on the world. Existence is an enigmatic metamorphosis and a levelling-out of all forces.

To Eckermann on 11 March 1828 Goethe said: 'Der Mensch muß wieder ruiniert werden!—Jeder ausserordentliche Mensch hat eine gewisse Sendung, die er zu vollführen berufen ist. Hat er sie vollbracht, so ist er auf Erden in dieser Gestalt nicht weiter vonnöten. . . .' In *Urworte. Orphisch* he called this mystery of our fate the 'daemon' in us who compels us to action, and who destroys us after the completion of our task. Thus the necessary becomes transitory, the essential accidental again. Only for a moment destiny is suspended. It elevates us when it destroys.

It is a favourite thought of Goethe that we are saved from the fear of annihilation and from annihilation itself by memory. In his *Euphrosyne* he sings the praise of the poet who enshrines man's deed in his immortal song and thus in the friend's memory ('Erinnerung'):

> Wen der Dichter aber gerühmt, der wandelt, gestaltet,
> Einzeln, gesellet dem Chor aller Heroen sich zu. . . .

Goethe's conception of death is differentiated from that of Kierkegaard (and also that of Rilke) by his decisive, vital power. This overcoming of death is often accounted to him as ruthless or egotistic indifference. But to Goethe life is immortal. This is so above all in the creative personality who signifies for him the highest stage in the completion of our existence. Thus Goethe could say: 'Höchstes Glück der Erdenkinder ist die Persönlichkeit.' There is something irrational in this cult of personality. The final unity of the ever-changing absolute in us and around us is God Himself:

> Und alles Drängen, alles Ringen
> Ist ewige Ruh in Gott dem Herrn.

Such a concept of life, however, does not exclude the inward strength which ignores personal security and which, as in the case of Socrates or any heroic mind, stakes the individual life, and is a healing well in moral conflicts.

Aldous Huxley, at the end of his *Time Must Have A Stop* arrives at a similar recognition of the secret of inwardness when through Bruno Rontini's mouth he demands: 'Find out how to become your inner not-self in God while remaining your outer self in the world . . .' and when he offers the following interpretation of Hotspur's motto: 'It is only by taking the fact of eternity into account that we can deliver thought from its slavery to life. And it is only by deliberately paying our attention and our primary allegiance to eternity that we can prevent time from turning our lives into a pointless or a diabolic foolery. The divine Ground is a timeless reality.'

This urge toward inwardness and towards a new order of values in our life bears different names in different modern philosophical systems. They all reflect the vast cleft between our materialistic standardization or over-specialization and the freedom of our conscience. Goethe, whose capital sin, according to Kierkegaard, was egoism, did not yet suffer from the torturing awareness of this modern dualism.

The repeated charge of egoism leads Kierkegaard to a sharp criticism of Goethe's women characters, e.g. Clärchen and Margarete. Already in a short attack on *Poetry and Truth* he accuses the author of taking 'himself out of everything'. Similarly, Clärchen is cast into insignificance by Egmont's overwhelming personality and Margarete by that of Faust. As to women in his private life, Goethe does tell us through Eckermann that man admires in her the youthful beauty and not so much the intellect. But such a remark must not be generalized and is quickly counteracted by his *Wahlverwandtschaften* or by his admiration for Frau von Stein and sympathetic words about the character and intelligence of the Großherzogin Amalie, whom he calls one of the best and most important women of his age and one who would always be it even if she were no princess: 'Sie ist eine der besten und bedeutendsten Frauen unserer Zeit, und würde es sein, wenn sie auch keine Fürstin wäre. . . .'

In his *Wahlverwandtschaften* (1807) Goethe quite unromantically praises married life as the pivot and summit of all culture, whilst Kierkegaard saw in woman the seductive tempter of his genius, and suddenly and consistently broke his betrothal with Regina Olsen. In his decision he was faced only by an Either-Or. Goethe was at heart conciliatory. In his ballad *Paria* (1823) he re-created poetically the experience of man's higher

and lower instincts. He significantly makes God create woman
out of good and evil. Her head is divine, earth-bound her body:

> So hat Brahma dies gewollt . . .
> . . . Und so soll' ich, die Brahmane,
> Mit dem Haupt im Himmel weilend,
> Fühlen, Paria, dieser Erde
> Niederziehende Gewalt. . . .

As we can see in Goethe's life, Kierkegaard's hostility to
marriage is by no means characteristic of the attitude of the
creative genius. Wolfram von Eschenbach, though the poet of
most passionate dawn-songs, sings the praise of married love:
'. . . ein offen süeze wirtes wîp kan solhe minne geben . . .'
('an openly known sweet wedded wife can give such love').
John Sebastian Bach—one of the greatest musical geniuses in
Europe—was married twice and the happy father of twenty
sons and daughters. Goethe's own union with Christiane can
serve as proof to us that married life need not check or frustrate
one's creative activity through biological relaxation or satiation
of the sexual unrest, nor did it induce him to abrogate his own
authority.

There is, no doubt, a long road from Goethe to the 'hard-
boiled nineteen-thirties'. Intellectualism and mere reflection
are, according to him, the misfortune of our civilization, as are
heartlessness, mockery, and wit. In order to defend marriage
nowadays one must be able to 'enchant its licentious inclination' with *The Seducer's Diary* (Kierkegaard).

About a hundred years after Goethe's death during those
same 'thirties, we were faced with blasé indifference and
intellectual conceit which sneered at the very mention of Goethe's
cult of personality or at anything 'Romantic' and which finds
its echo in the acrid *Bagpipe Music* by Louis MacNiece:

> . . . It's no go the Yogi-Man, it's no go Blavatsky,
> All we want is a bank balance and a bit of skirt in a taxi. . . .

But now, if I see the European development aright, feeling
veers in the direction of a revival or a revaluation of Goethe.

A return to 'pathos'—by this I do not mean 'false pathos', also
not the grand heroic style, but the outspoken need of a new
idealistic faith—seems the only way out of that spiritual

stagnation and out of doubt, sensuality, and despair. Faust was
to Kierkegaard personified doubt, Don Juan personified sensuality and Ahasver personified despair. These three demonic
elements—doubt, sensuality, despair—represented to him life.
Doubt, like the other two, must go under, and it therefore would
have pleased Kierkegaard if Goethe had not saved his Faust;
'His conversion merely reduces him to a more everyday level'.
According to Kierkegaard, Faust is the apostate of the spirit
and goes the way of all flesh. He is the arch-doubter who must
silently offer himself as a sacrifice to mankind. Kierkegaard
thus gives a sharp but one-sided criticism of Goethe's Faust,
whom he considers too wordy a seducer:

> Faust is a demoniac figure like a Don Juan, but higher. . . .
> His countenance is not wreathed in smiles, his brow is not un-
> clouded and happiness is not his playfellow; the young women do
> not dance into his embrace, but he frightens them to him. What
> he seeks is not merely the pleasure of the sensuous, but what he
> desires is the immediacy of the spirit. . . .[1]
> Nothing less erotic can be imagined than this talk about the
> future, which is usually the result of one's having nothing with
> which to fill the present. If only I am present, then I have no
> such fear, for I can make her forget both time and eternity. If
> a man does not understand how to put himself in rapport with a
> a girl, he should never attempt to deceive, for then it will be
> impossible to escape the two rocks: questions about the future,
> and a catechization about fidelity. Hence it is quite proper that
> Gretchen should conduct such an examination of Faust, since he
> has been imprudent enough to display his chivalry, and against
> an attack from this source, a girl is always armed.[2]

For Kierkegaard, the aesthetic hero has an easy conquest,
the religious hero, however, is the sufferer. He thus rejects
Faust's salvation. But Faust did not fall into the paradise of
wisdom as Kierkegaard wishes us to believe. He passionately
abandons himself to the tortures of sin, so that thereby he might
in suffering learn the power of evil. His ultimate salvation is
based on a purely Christian spirit:

> Und hat an ihm die Liebe gar
> Von oben teilgenommen,
> Begegnet ihm die selige Schar
> Mit herzlichem Willkommen.

[1] Kierkegaard, *Either-Or.* [2] *Diary of the Seducer,* in *Either-Or.*

The counterpart to Faust is the story of the Venus in the *Hörselberg*, the symbolic meaning of which Kierkegaard profoundly admired. It is the motif of the man under a spell, 'who has to play the same piece backwards, and every time he makes the slightest mistake has to begin again from the end. . . .'

In *Eckermanns Gespräche* we are expressly warned against considering Goethe's *Faust* within the narrower limits of a single idea continuing throughout the drama. But Kierkegaard judges it pitilessly from the moralist's aspect.

No less bitter is his attack on Goethe as a scientist which, at the same time, is an attack on science itself. 'Almost everything that flourishes nowadays under the name of science (particularly natural science) is not science at all but curiosity. In the end all corruption will come from the natural sciences. We have lost our reverence towards God in whom alone is certainty.' Goethe who was not religious seemed, according to Kierkegaard, to have put science above the existential and when 'science' is undoubtedly supreme, religion has as good as completely disappeared. Those are the two poles which Kierkegaard uses for casting the horoscope of his generation. He summarizes the situation by the remark: 'A Professor of Theology is greater than Christ.' Kierkegaard here speaks more to us than to Goethe or Goethe's contemporaries, as, to Goethe, centre and circumference are inseparable, i.e. a true scientist must also be a good citizen.

We certainly are intoxicated with science, especially in these days of unparalleled triumphs in atomic research, but if we desired to follow Kierkegaard 'it would require a world revolution to drag a man out of this drunkenness'.

In Goethe's universality life, science, and poetry are united. He does not put science above existence. He is the last European master of the balanced mean, the spiritual ruler, full of Christian inwardness and an antique faith in living—a miracle of natural growth towering high into the approaching struggle between rootless, mechanized forces and civilized humanity.

He is a message to us all—a touchstone of quality. He is not only the greatest German poet but the voice of Europe.

VI

Friedrich Hölderlin

(1770–1843)

An das Göttliche glauben
Die allein, die es selber sind.

*Things divine are believed in
But by those who themselves are so.*
Trans. J. B. Leishman

CENTENARY

A HUNDRED YEARS AGO, Friedrich Hölderlin, one of the greatest lyric poets of the world, died at Tübingen. Of the seventy-three years of his life only about seven were poetically creative. They belong to the rich harvest of German Classicism, when Schiller and Goethe were drawn to one another in a close literary friendship and the Jena Romantics were united in a common effort—their journal, the *Athenäum*. In the year 1800 which saw the publication of Novalis's *Hymns to the Night*, Schleiermacher's *Monologues* and Schiller's *Mary Stuart*, the author of *Hyperion* experienced a period of intense creative activity. But almost immediately afterwards 'Apollo', as he put it himself, 'vanquished' him. The long night of madness descended on his genius to obscure it for forty years.

Only recently, despite some vague memory of his tragic doom, his odes and his elegies and hymns which move us to awe, he was for most of us really little more than a name. Yet his words, fearless, strong, and richly sonorous, might well prove an important spiritual force and a message of hope in our troubled times. And the work of scholars and writers such as R. Peacock and J. B. Leishman, E. M. Butler, F. Prokosch, M. Hamburger, M. Montgomery, etc., has by now made Hölderlin familiar to a wider circle in England.

Even as a student at Tübingen Seminary, Hölderlin betrayed rare spiritual qualities. He loved the piano and the flute, and as Schwab tells us, he moved through the room like Apollo. No wonder that Hölderlin felt an affinity to Schiller even if he was naturally repelled by the cynicism of the former medical student. Indeed, Schiller remained the only contemporary poet for whom Hölderlin retained a life-long respect and awe. Schiller recognized in Hölderlin his own violent subjectivity and advised him to attempt more concrete description. Nevertheless, to the author of *Hyperion,* reality remained but the shadow cast by the light of his abounding fantasy: 'Ich glaube, daß die Scheue vor dem Stoffe . . . auf eine Zeit so zuträglich ist, . . . weil sie die Kraft in sich zurückhält, weil sie das verschwenderische jugendliche Leben sparsam macht.'[1]

Hölderlin was born under an evil star. On the occasion of his very first visit to Schiller's house in 1794, he felt that he had forfeited Goethe's sympathy for ever since, not recognizing the famous stranger, he had treated the latter with clipped, highhanded reserve, whilst Schiller's refusal in 1799 to co-operate in a previously planned periodical, the *Iduna,* which was to aim at a reconciliation of science and life, threw Hölderlin into literary isolation. A further letter to Schiller, in which Hölderlin begged the latter's assistance, remained unanswered.

Of these biographical incidents the general reader may perhaps be aware, though he knows little of Hölderlin's mission as a poet and his problem:

How can I suffer the tribulations of this life and yet keep my soul unsullied?

How can I interest myself in politics and yet retain spiritual poetic integrity?

How can I, seeing my life's ideal crumbling to dust, still affirm life and build it anew?

What is the meaning of death? . . .

Such were the problems that beset the poet's mind.

In *Hyperion* he sought to bridge the gulf between spirit and matter through the idea of sacrifice; he struggled to discover unity in life, to discover it only in rare moments of grace. His most fervent desire was to fathom the deepest problems and to

---

[1] Letter to Schiller, 1797.

love the very essence of life: 'Wer das Tiefste gedacht, liebt das Lebendigste.'[1]

Nature and his love for Diotima revealed to him a unity of simple loveliness and highest culture. His love for Diotima— his pseudonym for Susette Gontard, wife of a Frankfurt banker —became indeed the mainspring of his imagination. All that the intellect of mankind had thought and produced throughout the centuries seemed to him nothing in comparison with one moment of love, a love that was for him the truest affirmation of life: 'Everything is within us.' To live and love, Hölderlin's Hyperion drinks from the fountain of youth. For freedom is only in the child ('im Kind ist Freiheit allein') who is not 'contaminated' by social rules, and who is immortal because it knows nothing of death: 'es weiß vom Tode nichts'.

In *Hyperion*, the first of the spiritual landscapes which are so characteristically Hölderlin's own, the idea of man's power of renewal after the complete annihilation of his ideals is resolved in elegiac chords. Hyperion, after being wounded in body and soul, struggles to create life anew, but Diotima passes into the realm of death. Her letter of farewell is preceded immediately by the renowned *Schiksaalslied*, which recalls so vividly Pindar's eighth ode and Goethe's *Parzenlied*. The ruthless antithesis of our human lot and the gods' beatitude is echoed in the rhythm itself:

Ihr wandelt droben im Licht
Auf weichem Boden, selige Genien. . . .
. . . . . .

Doch uns ist gegeben,
Auf keiner Stätte zu ruhn,
Es schwinden, es fallen
Die leidenden Menschen
Blindlings. . . .

You roam above in the light,
On yielding meadows, fortunate Genii! . . .
. . . . . .

To us though is given
To find no place for repose.
We fall and we vanish,

1 *Socrates und Alkibiades.*

115

We suffering mortals,
Blindly from one hour
On to another,
As waters are hurtled
From boulder to boulder
Down through the years to we know not where.[1]

The idea of sacrifice is accentuated far more strongly in his tragedy *Empedokles* than in *Hyperion*. Empedokles is guilty of flaunting his pride before the gods. His suicide becomes a festival of nature, for through it the broken harmony between heaven and earth is restored. Through his self-sacrifice which reminds one of the death of Christ, life is renewed:

Am Tode entzündet mir das Leben sich zuletzt.

Hölderlin was far more definitely than any before him a poet of prophecy. The magnificent formal patterns into which he ultimately cast his ideas were achieved only shortly before his spiritual eclipse, as though his prophetic lips had been closed before his lyric tongue outstripped the limit of human utterance.

In the belief that he stood in the midst of life, but actually only shortly before his ruin, he wrote one of the most lovely of short lyrics, *Hälfte des Leben*, in which personal emotion is transfused with a mystic attitude towards nature, raised to the power of myth, for the realm of the gods ever remains superior to that of nature. The aether, the heavenly element, is the home of the eagle and of Zeus. Similar concepts may be found in Hölderlin's interpretation of the rhythm of day and night, his mythical rendering of the Alps in *Heimkunft*, of the oceanic god in the great elegy *Archipelagus*, or in his hymn on the *Rhein*. The impassioned apotheosis of perfected life finally seems to disrupt every limit of form. And yet his hymns in 'free rhythm' bear witness to a sense of harmony. In the latest hymns this becomes particularly apparent through their tripartite construction.

The latter is a necessary result of Hölderlin's attitude towards life, his belief in the Eros myth with its three elements—Aether, Earth, Light—and his concept of our threefold cultural

[1] Translated by J. B. Leishman. (In the German text I have corrected H.'s spelling generously.)

development which, rooted in the 'classical antique', struggles from the 'Christianity' of man's childhood towards ultimate consummation, in 'Universal Love'. Hymns such as *Der Rhein, Der Einzige, Die Wanderung, Patmos* and also the elegies *Brod und Wein, Der Wanderer,* etc., clearly demonstrate this type of structure which recalls Herder's ideas of human development and Schiller's dream of Greece. According to Herder we step from the naïve state of the antique world into the period of conflict typified by Christianity, and thus gradually attain to regeneration and a nobler state of religious society, namely to the union of Classic paganism and Christianity.

Seen from this angle Hölderlin's mysterious utterance, 'He who thought deepest loves life most', becomes apprehensible. This central idea of his poetry found expression in his late hymn *Patmos*, in which St. John's Revelation takes place on the Greek island. Here Christendom and Greece are reconciled.

Only a poet who believes in the nobility of life and nature can create images of such power. His favourite symbols of the union of god and men are lightning and tempest. Euripides must have suggested the image of Bacchus begotten by the lightning stroke; Bacchus-Dionysos, the creator of the vine that sprouts from the fecund earth, remains Hölderlin's favourite god under whose protection he stands as visionary and as poet.

As we have seen, Hölderlin was from the start aware of his sacred mission. In the poem *Buonaparte* he calls the poets the sacred vessels in which the spirit of the heroes and the wine of life is preserved. To Hölderlin, man is divine when he dreams and a beggar when he thinks: 'O ein Gott ist der Mensch, wenn er träumt, ein Bettler, wenn er nachdenkt' (*Hyperion oder der Eremit in Griechenland*). He celebrates the great heart, not the limit of rational thought. Thus he bears us away on the flight of his song which is often lightly dismissed as all too ethereal. Hölderlin gave to poetry and to life both dignity and power. Life, ever spending never spent, meant everything to him: 'Einiges, ewiges, glühendes Leben ist Alles.'

As poet he triumphs over matter. His words hold the ocean in a tea-cup, and to him a single moment of divine inspiration compensates lifelong suffering and striving. Hence Hölderlin can speak more poignantly of Fate, having suffered more

deeply at her hands. As poet he is doomed to stand bare-
headed beneath the onslaught of the tempest that, grasping the
divine lightning with his own hand, he may bestow the heavenly
gift 'enveloped in song' on his people, cf. *Wie wenn am Feiertage*:

> Doch uns gebührt es, unter Gottes Gewittern,
> Ihr Dichter! mit entblößtem Haupte zu stehen. . . .

The wide rhythmic span of his periods is here matched to the
tempestuous breath of poetic inspiration. Characteristic
features of his verse are the parallel constructions which give
a sort of rhythm to the apparently unbounded tide of his verse,
and through which Hölderlin, moreover, gives the subject-
matter a fitting form: 'Hölderlin has here made us share,
physically, the terrible agitation of which he speaks.'[1] Unlike
the modern expressionist poets, he is not obsessed by single
words or sounds, but allows his periods and phrases liberal
expansions, a quality to which may be ascribed that sense of
fluctuating verbal rhythm apprehended already in his earliest
poems. It may be noted that the noun usually appears at the
end of the sentence, whilst cleft participles are welded to a
forceful unity in a tumultuous tide.

In the above poem, *Wie wenn am Feiertage*, the spiritual landscape is introduced by a natural phenomenon—just as the
Archipelagus opens with a picture of the sea. Also in *Brod und
Wein*, landscape and soul are played off in fateful interrelation
against one another. Both are rooted in a divine origin, and
Hölderlin's invincible faith in that concept is his greatest
message to us, whilst it is not so much suffering or experience
that reveal to him man's fate as above all this significance of
man's birth. A similar thought is expressed in Goethe's *Urworte.
Orphisch*.

Ideas of this kind are continually cropping up in Hölderlin's
work. Examples of the divine origin of blind Fate are for him
Rousseau and *Der Rhein*, the symbols of the free man. Characteristically this hymn which terminates in a paean of Universal
Love is of symmetrical and harmonious construction.

Most recently it seemed to have been the fashion (resulting
from an all-too-strict imitation of Norbert von Hellingrath's

---

[1] S. S. Prawer, *German Lyric Poetry*, p. 108.

great Propyläen-edition) to divide Hölderlin's work and concept of life into a system of beliefs, e.g. nature, heroism, Greece, love, etc. But we must not lose sight of the direct and tragic line of development that leads from the first shattering of his youth's dreams to new faith through Diotima—the embodiment of the divine on earth:

> ... Und ins volle Götterleben
> tritt die sterbliche Natur. ...

and thence to renewed despair and once more to the triumph of Universal Love. Indeed we may say that Hölderlin's later hymns were only possible when shortly before his spiritual eclipse he gave himself completely to the mythical interpretation of our entire existence and dedicated all poetic utterance to the praise, the celebration and adoration and the invocation of the divine. Thus the personal element gradually faded ever more from his word which became the voice of his religious and poetic vision.

To Hölderlin poetry appeared to spring from cosmic forces. Therefore the question of his political convictions can only be regarded in the broadest sense. Buonaparte was for him the symbol of an elemental outburst of the creative spirit, while at that time Goethe regarded Napoleon as the welder of chaos. Hölderlin sought political freedom, not order by force. The less he knew of the State, the happier he felt, he writes in the spring of 1801.

His dream fantasy was nurtured by the Greek ideal and the dream of Germany's regeneration. Love of Greece and of his home meant to him but love of a new noble order of life in the cosmic process, and faith in the return of the divine essence and its absorption in nature—elements being seen in relationship to his fatherland.

In his invocation of Greece in *Archipelagus* he had sung the praise of Attic culture and the creative power of the Classic age which he says still retain their influence on us today and awaken yearning for a new hope. In *Brod und Wein* the rhythm of day and night suggests the coming and fading of godlike powers, but not as the apotheosis of Greek beauty alone but of the divine in general: the pagan-Christian unity, Dionysos-Christ.

Hölderlin had now reached a maturity that enabled him to give poetic interpretation to the problems of his own country and to comradeship with his fellow men. His vision was no longer directed to the Greek past, but to the future of his own land.

After the World War of 1914-18 the growing generation found a source of inspiration in Hölderlin. Under the stress of party politics, his spirit was, alas, soon obscured. Nevertheless, though often ignored or forgotten, he remains the immortal exponent of a happy balance between a proud sense of personal responsibility and humble surrender to life, between self-affirmation and sacrifice. Over his emotions joy and sorrow held ever-changing sway—a ceaseless shift of balance recognizable in his style in which we so often find long sustained sentences matched by the most succinct phrases. Interpolations accentuate the tension of his later hymns. Like nature, words themselves are often not only intellectual metaphors, but a revelation of sacred powers.

To us, who once more ponder on the secret of human origins or our fate beneath the dance of death, Hölderlin brings the message of divine life, triumphant still—around and within us.

HELLAS—CHRISTIANITY—GERMANY[1]

With Hölderlin, rhapsodic verse may be said to reach its zenith, not only in Germany, but in modern literature as a whole. He might well be called the German Pindar, the true bard of 'sacred enthusiasm'. Hölderlin's poetry is more than an outpouring of personal emotion and experience. It has nothing in common with Anacreontic frivolity or the embroidered perfection of the mere virtuoso, nothing with the decadent atmosphere of *Fleurs du Mal* or the priestlike ritualism of the George school. His poetry combines rapture and clarity— in Stefan George's words: 'Sparta's steel-bound prowess wedded to Ionia's grace' ('Spartas gebändigten mut/Ioniens süsse vermählt').

With Hölderlin, Klopstock's dream of a truly German poetic

[1] The two chapters inevitably overlap, though in the second part here the analysis is more detailed.

form found its fulfilment. And yet Hölderlin's vision of the unity of Hellas, Christendom, and fatherland remained a closed book until Nietzsche's time. Dilthey was the first to pave the way for a real understanding of Hölderlin, yet it was the profound veneration felt by the Stefan George circle for the author of *Hyperion* which finally brought about his resurrection from semi-oblivion. This was in part due to George's so-called 'Third Hellenism' with its yearning for intoxication and illumination—Rausch und Helle—and a deep-rooted affinity between the two poets, although George's approach to Hellas differs essentially from that of Hölderlin. Both worship the divine in the earthly as in their conception of Diotima and Maximin, both decry a vague romanticism and the overvaluation of the intellect. Both know the Northerner's yearning for the South, both are seers demanding sacrifice of their fellow human beings, and, lastly, both invoke the three primal forces of life—'Kairos, Eros, and the holiness of the moment.'

Yet each speaks a different tongue. Hölderlin draws a long breath sustained from sentence to sentence and even from verse to verse, whilst George's language is often angular, not to say harsh. In this respect Hölderlin's rhythm might rather be compared with the luminous breadth of Turner's landscapes than with the poetic or visual designs of William Blake, who is sometimes said to bear affinity to the German poet.

Further, Hölderlin and George approached the Greek ideal by different paths. Hölderlin's mighty rhythm was inspired by Pindar, whilst it was Classic sculpture that directed George to his goal. The latter, moreover, surrounded himself with a circle of poets and intellectuals amongst whom was Norbert von Hellingrath, the editor of Hölderlin's works, whilst the former was destined to tragic solitude.

On the second of December 1802, Hölderlin writes that Apollo has vanquished him:

Und wie man Helden nachspricht, kann ich wohl sagen, daß mich Apollo geschlagen.

After a brief Icarian flight to the heights of Olympus he was hurled headlong to the lowest depths of a forty years' span of spiritual darkness, so that the author of *Hyperion* becomes for us, as it were, a figure of myth himself, the tragic bringer of light. To him Hellas was a religion. He spoke with the tongue of the spirit rather than with words. Even in the night of madness, especially in the first bitter years, he still lets us dream of the eagle's soaring flight. His tragedy was unique. Heinrich von Kleist put an end to his own life, Shelley was torn from this earth all too soon, Novalis found the consummation of his yearning in death, but Hölderlin was doomed to the protracted silence of years. Of the seventy-three he spent in this world, only seven were given to creation. He who had communed with gods, became a stranger even to himself, sometimes seeking a sorry identity with the puppet of his benighted fancy, Scaliger Rose or S(c)ardanelli.

His poetry reveals the presence of the Divine Nature in and around us:

> Denn es waltet ein Gott in uns.

Hölderlin is concerned always with the wholeness, the physical and metaphysical unity of life. Art is for him the flower of nature, i.e. of perfected nature. Thus, too, he regards society as a whole:

> Es ist nur ein Streit in der Welt, was nämlich mehr sei, das Ganze oder das Einzelne? . . .

Characteristic of his utterances in this respect is a passage from one of his letters:

> Ich scheue das Gemeine und Gewöhnliche im wirklichen Leben zusehr. . . . Das Reine kann sich nur darstellen im Unreinen. . . .

Such an attitude towards life was bound to throw the poet into profound solitude. In spite of the terrible anguish he felt at his own and his people's destiny, his vision remains full of hope and directed towards a happier future. Hölderlin cannot, therefore, be called at bottom the poet of Weltschmerz or of suffering, but rather the prophet of sacrifice. Even amidst his own desolation and ruin he felt the hand of God: 'Apollo hat mich geschlagen'. In his above-mentioned poem, *Wie wenn am Feiertage*, he speaks of the vessel of the God; he faces the lightning flashes of the tempest that he may grasp the divine fire for mankind through his verse.

His faith in the unity of man and divine nature gives him
strength. Like Kant and Schiller, Hölderlin also stood above
the limitations of Enlightenment. Both writers and the Greeks
were the heroes of his youth:

> Schlag vier bin ich Morgens auf, und koche meinen Kaffee
> selbst und dann an die Arbeit. Und so bleib ich meist in meiner
> Klause bis Abends; oft in der Gesellschaft der heiligen Muse,
> oft bei meinen Griechen; jetzt gerade wieder in Hrn. Kants
> Schule. . . .
> . . . Kant und die Griechen sind beinahe meine einzige Lektüre.

But a certain alienation from Kant in favour of the theories
of Leibniz may be noted quite early in his career. Hölderlin's
vision is not abstract. He desired at all costs to preserve the
totality of life which Kant's dualistic concept with its division
into subject and object threatened to sever. Here Hölderlin's
and Schiller's paths may be said to cross each other: cp.
Schiller's *Künstler* with Hölderlin's *Hymne an die Göttin der
Harmonie, Das Schiksaal,* and especially *Natur und Kunst oder
Saturn und Jupiter.* Hölderlin also invokes Urania, but not the
goddess of truth. It is harmony he worships. For Hölderlin, as
for Goethe, moral freedom is not essentially antithetical to
nature's laws, whilst for Kant and to a great extent for Schiller
it appears as irreconcilable with nature. The debt that he owed
to Schiller both as man and poet, was frequently and grate-
fully acknowledged by Hölderlin himself:

> Ich wußte wohl, daß ich mich nicht, ohne meinem Innern
> merklichen Abbruch zu thun, aus Ihrer Nähe würde entfernen
> können . . . weil ich Ihnen so viel seyn wollte, mußt' ich mir
> sagen, daß ich Ihnen nichts wäre. . . .

Hölderlin's poetic vision revolves round the trio *Diotima,
Hellas, Nature.* His hero-worship and faith in the community
were rooted in that trinity. It is impossible to conceive of one
without invoking the other two. The poet's development,
however, from the hymns of his youth to a first despair and
thence to the story of his spirit's healing through Diotima and
the rebirth and sublimation of his ideal to a dream of universal
love, must not be obscured by formal categories.

It is hardly possible to analyse the philosophical and religious elements of Hölderlin's work without violating the lyric mood of his poetry, which is marked by its extraordinary simplicity and profound culture. His words in *Hyperion*; 'Man is a god as soon as he is man. And if he is a god, he is beautiful', recall Herder's 'humanus', Goethe's concept of humanity and the ideal of the 'kalokagathos' expounded in Schiller's *Ästhetische Briefe*.

Again Hölderlin writes of art that it is the 'first-born child of human, divine beauty . . . beauty's second daughter is religion—religion is love of beauty'. In such a divine concept of life, man is at the centre of nature. Love alone is able to find that unity which Herakleitos called the One embracing all aspects of the same thing (ἕν διάφερον ἑαυτῷ). Unity of the sensual and intellectual marks the zenith of existence, but can only be obtained through sacrifice and by a noble nature. It is through this idea of sacrifice that Hellas, Christianity and fatherland are reconciled in Hölderlin's later work.

Everything is subordinated to Nature, the divine creative power:

> Fühlt neu die Begeisterung sich,
> Die Allerschaffende wieder.

In Nature abide the sources of rapture. Nature brings the spring, the fullness of summer, the maturity of autumn. She presents us at the same time with a symbol of a heroic life. So palpably do the forces of Nature rise before Hölderlin that they transform themselves to myths before his very eyes. In Nature we find intensity and ecstasy as well as clarity. It is this unity of the elements that Hölderlin seeks in poetry:

> Und was Du thust, thue es nie in der Hitze. Überdenke kalt! und führe mit Feuer aus! . . .

We must here take heed not to fall into the all too ready cliché: Dionysos *versus* Apollo. As in nature we find in Hölderlin's verse an interweaving of rapture and stillness, of conflict and reconciliation. Herein lies perhaps the very secret of his peculiar rhythm. His poetic vision embraces the totality of life. His path leads from Greece through Christianity to the realm of universal love. Perfect love of nature, love of all things, is also the foundation of an ideal which precludes one-sidedness, an ideal which Hölderlin longed to see realized in his own country. In such poetry a superficially impressionist technique can find no place. Hölderlin's aim is to paint with wide, generalized brush-strokes; take for example the etherealized landscape in *Mein Eigentum*: Herbsttag, Traube, Hain, Obst, Blüthen, etc., or his letter to Neuffer:

> Ich kann Dich nicht mit Reisebeobachtungen plagen . . . ich bin meist mit dem Totaleindruck zufrieden.

Whereas Schiller in his *Ideal und Leben* complains of the unbridgeable gulf between the joys of the flesh and the soul's beatitude, Hölderlin does not separate spirit and flesh. Rather he venerates in Nature what he considers to be her three great principles—the Earth, the Aether, and the Light—the trinity with which man has been acquainted since the Eros-myth of Plato's *Symposium*. The conception of Aether was probably also inspired by Pindar, Goethe's *Ganymed* and Heinse's *Ardinghello*. Schelling's *Weltseele* is also usually regarded as an influence, but here Hölderlin was giver rather than receiver, as Schelling introduced the aether concept into his philosophy at a later date. The above trinity of forces is expressed in Hölderlin's poetry by his beloved tripartite structure: cf. *Germanien*, *Wanderung*, *Mutter Erde*, *Patmos*, etc.

It is evident that this threefold construction has here a metaphysical significance. (1) Childhood: Hellas; (2) period of combat: Christianity; (3) perfection: universal love (All-Liebe) and reconciliation of Hellas and Christianity. Yet a real synthesis of those three forces was achieved by Hölderlin but seldom, for his passion belonged primarily to Hellas. Stefan George's caustic criticism of Enlightenment and Romanticism in his own poem *Hyperion* is born of the spirit of Hölderlin:

> Klagend an ach welchen wassern
> Weinend an ach welchen weiden
> Nach—welchem glücke.

> *Wailing, alas! by what waters,*
> *Weeping, alas! by what willows,*
> *And for what pleasures.*[1]

---

[1] Translated by O. Marx and E. Morwitz, *The Works of Stefan George.*

We have seen how Hölderlin everywhere seeks manifestations of the divine essence. Philosophy, art and religion are for him priestesses of nature:

> Philosophie und schöne Kunst und Religion, diese Priesterinnen der Natur.

Unlike Schiller and Goethe, he discovered the divine ideal in life itself, in the image of Diotima. Goethe could only satisfy his being by dividing himself between earth and heaven—Christiane Vulpius and Frau von Stein. Schiller, for his part, laments the loss of harmony (*Das Ideal und das Leben*).

In Greece, Hölderlin recognized an essential manifestation of the divine. The *Archipelagus* revealed to him the Greek ideal of a perfect age of harmony. At the same time Hölderlin's vision did not lose sight of the future of his own country. His very hatred of the present was born of a longing for a noble world in which the hero appears as the mediator between God and man. Herein Hölderlin betrays an affinity with Pindar whose influence is no less marked in his style. Yet a clear distinction must be drawn between the style of the two poets—namely, in regard to the dynamic use of the verb which appears in Goethe's poems of the Storm and Stress period and especially in Hölderlin's late poems in 'free' verse, whereas it is by no means characteristic of Pindar's.

For Hölderlin the hero, as for instance Napoleon, denoted the sublimation of *natural forces*. Hölderlin demanded political liberty, not order by force:

> Je weniger der Mensch vom Staat erfährt und weiß, die Form sei, wie sie will, um desto freier ist er.

He invokes in nature the elemental expression of free life. Lightning and tempest are for him an image, reflecting the mystery of the poet's creative power. They are the nuptials of God and man. Dionysos, generated from the lightning of Zeus, is Hölderlin's favourite amongst the gods. How overwhelming must have been for him an experience of nature's titanic conflict:

> Von den Alpen, die in der Entfernung von einigen Stunden hierherum sind, stehe ich immer noch betroffen, ich habe wirklich

einen solchen Eindruck nie erfahren, sie sind wie eine wunderbare
Sage aus der Heldenjugend unserer Mutter Erde und mahnen an
das alte bildende Chaos, indeß sie niedersehen in ihrer Ruhe. . . .
Ich fühle es endlich, nur in ganzer Kraft ist ganze Liebe.

Hölderlin stands in awe of nature, apprehending therein the
cosmic forces of life. In his faith in universal nature is rooted
also his concept of culture. With what anguish he realized how
often natural perfection is violated in the world of fact! In his
despair over the destiny of human kind he wrote that most
popular but moving poem *Hyperions Schiksaalslied*, which Brahms
set to music and Klinger welded to visible form. That fierce
indictment of his 'barbaric countrymen' at the end of *Hyperion*
('. . . Handwerker siehst du, aber keine Menschen, Denker,
aber keine Menschen, Priester, aber keine Menschen . . .') was
born of the same spirit. Hellas became for him more and more
a symbol of the true world—a world which his country had so
sore a need to inherit, a legacy to which through the nobility
of its poetry it possessed a right.

Unlike George, Hölderlin does not see in man the ruler of
nature. Again and again he maintains the necessity of a
religious reverence for nature. His vision is thereby directed
above all towards the future, not the past, and the above
indictment of his countrymen is balanced by his readiness to
make every sacrifice. The Rhine, striving towards the North
and the Danube making towards the South are to him symbols
of his country's destiny. He knew nothing of politics in the
narrower sense of the word. A comparison of the *Schlacht* with
its second version (*Der Tod fürs Vaterland*) is significant. In the
second version the revolutionary tendencies are diminished in
favour of more universally human traits:

First version: Knechte, Neulinge, Unterdrückern.
Second version: Würger, Jünglinge, Ehrelosen.
A further comparison with Klopstock's impassioned *Schlacht-
gesang* and Schiller's dramatic *Schlacht* is no less illuminating.

Love of the fatherland meant for Hölderlin a new path of life
in the cosmic order, faith in return to nature and a merging
with its divine powers. The gods of the Classic age are now
joined by Christ, but Hölderlin's passion for Greece burns
unquenchable right into the period of the elegies and 'free

rhythms'. These much-discussed hymns in 'free rhythm' are closely related to his growing love for songs of his fatherland. Nevertheless, we can find some earlier instances of this type of verse: e.g. *Die Bücher der Zeiten* (1788), *An die Vollendung, An Luise Nast, Am Tage der Freundschaftsfeier, Hymne an den Genius Griechenlands, Da ich ein Knabe war, Hyperions Schiksaalslied, Buonaparte*, etc.

To look on these later poems as a product of his madness is hence just as much a mistake as to look on Hölderlin (as some do on Van Gogh) merely as a madman, for it is particularly in some of his last 'free rhythms' that Hölderlin attains an unmatched equilibrium of rhapsody and clarity, freedom and form. We may well, in spite of many a critic's assertion to the contrary, find in those hymns and in the elegies a supreme manifestation of his genius. It is true that he never wrote a lyric in the purest and narrowest sense of the word 'Lied'—a fact which, however, did not prevent him from writing one of the most exquisite and poignant short poems in the German language, namely *Hälfte des Lebens*:

> Mit gelben Birnen hänget
> Und voll mit wilden Rosen
> Das Land in den See,
> Ihr holden Schwäne,
> Und trunken von Küssen
> Tunkt ihr das Haupt
> Ins heilignüchterne Wasser.

> Weh mir, wo nehm' ich wenn
> Es Winter ist, die Blumen, und wo
> Den Sonnenschein,
> Und Schatten der Erde?
> Die Mauern stehn
> Sprachlos und kalt, im Winde
> Klirren die Fahnen.

> *Half of Life*
> *With yellow pears leans over,*
> *And full of run-wild roses,*
> *The land into the lake,*
> *You gracious swans,*
> *And, drunk with kisses,*
> *You dip your heads*
> *In the sacredly-sober water.*

FRIEDRICH HÖLDERLIN

Where shall I gather though,
When winter comes, the flowers, and where
The dappling shine
And shadow of earth?
The walls will stand
Speechless and cold, the wind-swung
Weather-vanes clatter.[1]

As for those hymns themselves they may be called unparalleled
in spiritual exaltation and control of form and theme, in depth
of thought and imaginative power, in 'sacred passion' and
audacity of formal structure.

Hölderlin bases his ideas on the supposition that the Germans
are in contrast to the Greeks 'nüchtern' and intellectual:

> Deswegen sind die Griechen des heiligen Pathos weniger
> Meister, weil es ihnen angeboren war, hingegen sind sie vor-
> züglich in Darstellungsgabe, von Homer an, weil dieser außer-
> ordentliche Mensch seelenvoll genug war, um die abendländ-
> ische Junonische Nüchternheit für sein Apollonsreich zu erbeuten,
> und so wahrhaft das Fremde sich anzueignen. Bei uns ists
> umgekehrt.

A consideration of Hölderlin's work as a whole may give us
the key to the understanding of the late elegies and hymns, the
germ of which seems already to be hidden in the *Ideale der
Menschheit* of the Tübingen period. After that world of ideas was
shattered:

> Todt ist nun, die mich erzog und stillte,
> Todt ist nun die jugendliche Welt. . . .

Hölderlin found a new and profounder affirmation of life
through Diotima who in his Hyperion period gave him a proof
of the divinity locked in the human form:

> Lieber Freund! Es gibt ein Wesen auf der Welt, woran mein
> Geist Jahrtausende verweilen kann und wird. . . . Es ist auch
> wirklich oft unmöglich, vor ihr an etwas Sterbliches zu denken
> und eben deswegen läßt so wenig sich von ihr sagen.
> Mein Schönheitsinn ist nun vor Störung sicher. Er orientiert
> sich ewig an diesem Madonnenkopfe. Mein Verstand geht in die
> Schule bei ihr, und mein uneinig Gemüth besänftiget, erheitert
> sich täglich in ihrem genügsamen Frieden.

In this Frankfurt period his poetic genius freed itself

[1] Translated by J. B. Leishman.

completely, to which purely external facts bear witness; for the youthful hymns of humanity in rhymed verse now give way to the ode. With the coming of Diotima, he abandons rhymed verse altogether.

But his bitter realization of the duality of existence remained. Hyperion was broken on the wheel of life. Apart from lamentation, nothing remained to him but a yearning for annihilation and death. He knew that the ideal is that which nature once *was*, and that the future will strive towards such a state again. The present seemed to him lost. Yet in the Homburg period Hölderlin once more acquired a faith in life through a self-dedication to Nature that thought no sacrifice too hard. And now his poetic genius glowed more resplendent than ever. He prophesied Empedokles's heritage to his people. In death, life was rekindled anew.

Hölderlin's last great poems are woven around his dream of Greece, Germany and Christianity. His late poem on peace, *Friedensfeier*, the MS. of which turned up in London not until 1954, mentions the Prince of the Feast who is probably Christ or Hölderlin's conception of Napoleon or both in one person. The Peace of Luneville (1801) has certainly provided the background of this ode, but Hölderlin has, most characteristically, created his poetic vision of the end of revolutionary struggles and the return of the Golden Age.

How deeply he was still rooted in Hellas is proved by his translations from the Greek, the thunderous wave of Pindar's verse, the weight of the Sophoclean chorus, and lastly his own 'free rhythms'. For all their 'sacred passion', they are controlled by a Classic sense of form. The external signs are manifest. The essential germ of thought is often enclosed in the poem's centre: *Wanderung, Germanien, Der Rhein, Der Einzige, Patmos.* In spite of an apparent freedom of form, the sequence of the verses is frequently as in *Der Rhein* or *Patmos*, etc., symmetrical: 5+5+5. The widely spanned rhythms in *Am Quell der Donau*, etc., are based on a system of parallelisms, and the position of the words betrays a distinct formal sense: e.g. *Wie wenn am Feiertage.*

The three-tiered internal and external architecture of some of the poems is particularly striking. The images taken from

nature are of tremendous symbolic force: e.g., Regen =
Begeisterung; Strom = junger Held; Adler = Mittler zwischen
Erde und Himmel; Quell = Ursprung; or Gewitter, Weinlese,
etc.

The audacious rupture of the syntax is not cacophonous,
e.g.:

> Daß schnellbetroffen sie, (Unendlichem
> Bekannt seit langer Zeit,) von Erinnerung
> Erbebt, und ihr, (von heilgem Strahl entzündet,)
> (Die Frucht in Liebe geboren,) (der Götter und MenschenWerk)
> Der Gesang, (damit er von beiden zeuge,) glückt.

> *Which, stricken of a sudden, known so long*
> *To Infinitude, quivers with recollection,*
> *And from it, enkindled thus by the sacred bolt,*
> *That fruit in love begotten, that labour of gods and men,*
> *Song, to bear lasting witness of both, will leap.*[1]

Through similar rearrangement of words the rhythmic arch
is swelled to bold proportion. The most important noun is often
placed at the end of the sentence: e.g. *Wie wenn am Feiertage*:
'Natur', 'Begeisterung . . . die Allerschaffende', 'Die Alle-
bendigen, die Kräfte der Götter', 'Der Gesang'.

A true valuation of Hölderlin's poetry necessitates a study
of earlier versions of the same poem, and of his method of work.
He was in the habit, it seems, of jotting down his chief ideas and
emotions in a rudimentary fashion on a piece of paper. These
he would then develop and rearrange. We may also trace a
connection between various poems: e.g. *Da ich ein Knabe war,*
Hyperions Schiksaalslied, Hälfte des Lebens. One sequence grows
out of the other, e.g. the poem *Versöhnender, der du nimmerge-*
glaubt, which is the germ of the three poems: *Der Einzige,*
Brod und Wein, Patmos. In his elegy *Brod und Wein* and the hymn
Der Rhein, out of which the famous hymn *Patmos* was one day to
develop, we may recognize some of the essential features of his
ideas and his poetry.

In *Brod und Wein,* originally called *Der Weingott,* Hölderlin
predicts the birth of a new culture and a new religion. The
work consists of three principal parts subdivided into a further
three: I (*a*) The coming of the Night, (*b*) the influence of the

---

[1] *As when on a Holiday,* translated by J. B. Leishman. (The brackets are mine.)

Night, (c) the yearning for the ideal, for Greece; II (a) the evolution of ancient Greece, the 'house of the Gods', from out of the Greek landscape, (b) the development and ennoblement of the Greek gods, (c) the zenith of Greek culture and religion; III (a) the godless present and a new heroism, (b) a humble genius appears as comforter and hope, (c) promise of fulfilment:

> Aber indessen kommt als Fackelschwinger des Höchsten
> Sohn, der Syrier, unter die Schatten herab. . . .
>
> *Meanwhile, waving his wakening torch, the son of the Highest,*
> *He, the Syrian, comes down to these lingering shades.*[1]

Just as bread and wine are created out of the divine (the light) and the earthly (the earth) so the new perfection of mankind will be born of the union of God and nature.

The 'free' verse poem *Der Rhein* betrays a mysterious symmetry in subject and construction (3×5 verses). The great river is here the symbol of the free hero; cf. also Goethe's *Mahomets Gesang* and Hölderlin's *Der gefesselte Strom* and *Die Wanderung*. Whereas Goethe's poem expresses the rebellion and stress of youth, Hölderlin sings of the terrible, divine origin of blind Fate and the unbridled fury of the demi-god. Hölderlin's confession: 'as you began, you will remain': 'Wie du anfingst, wirst du bleiben', re-echoes Goethe's *Urworte. Orphisch* about the laws of destiny which govern us.

> Nach dem Gesetz, wonach du angetreten,
> So mußt du sein, dir kannst du nicht entfliehen.

Even in those humble later years, the memory remains. But poet and hero are singed by the holy fire. Rousseau is Hölderlin's model. The author of *Der Rhein* admits himself a disciple of the religion of Universal Love. Nature is good, to her the sons of earth must return. But only for a moment in this marriage of God and man does existence seem for Hölderlin to attain the perfected harmony. In memory alone the dream lives on. His friend Sinclair, he says, was also blessed with divine vision, in the prison of daily life as well as in the 'chaos of night'.

This hymn is in thought closely related to *Hyperion* whilst

---

[1] Translated by J. B. Leishman.

formally it rather recalls the *Andenken*. In the middle of the poem we once more find the central idea, and the tumultuous episodes of our human drama merge in the credo of Universal Love. In that same concept of love the mighty chords of the hymn of *Patmos* ultimately resolve themselves whilst the trinity—Mother Earth, Father Aether, and Light as mediator between them—rises triumphant before the poet. All three, says Hölderlin, not only the spiritual idea of Christianity, must receive our worship —a reconciliation which to him appears already to have been foreshadowed symbolically by the Revelation of St. John which took place on the Greek island.

VII

Novalis

HYMNS TO THE NIGHT

Where Love awakens,
The dark despot Ego dies.
JALÂL-UDDÎN-RÛMÎ

WHAT IS MORE sudden than lightning?—Vengeance.
What vanishes most swiftly from sight?—Unlawful
possession. Who knows the world?—He who knows
himself. What remains an eternal mystery?—Love.

Such are the riddles of the Sphinx as they appear in the fable
at the end of the first part of the fragmentary novel, *Heinrich
von Ofterdingen*, by Novalis. They are the ore of his own
Weltanschauung, washed ashore by the limpid ripple of his
rhythmic prose.

Novalis's writing possesses neither Hölderlin's tragic tension
nor Schiller's divine 'Pathos'. None the less, it is unique in its
graceful, almost childlike fervour and sincerity. In his sombre
and magnificent *Hymns to the Night* (*Hymnen an die Nacht*) he can
indeed rank with either poet in power of imagery and creative
imagination.

The terms 'Classic' and 'Romantic' are often played against
each other in order to debunk Novalis's work. But no great art,
not even the 'Classic', lacks something of the 'Romantic' flux.
In her study, *Art and Life*, Hannah Closs puts this truth into the
memorable line: ' . . . a harmony of finite form in which yet
lingers other music of infinity'.

To Novalis as well as to Goethe and Schiller art is the
highest achievement of human existence and fundamentally an
expression of life, no Romantic escape from life. It is misleading to say that the German Romantic contributions of
significance are 'secondary or editorial ones, rather than

134

original literary productions.'[1] A. W. Schlegels' translations of Shakespeare, and the Arnim-Brentano anthology, *Des Knaben Wunderhorn*, and the brothers Grimm's *Kinder-und Hausmärchen* are of course not original works in the deepest sense of the word, yet those 'Hymns', written in rhythmic prose and free verse, represent not only the finest product of German Romanticism but belong with Hölderlin's and Goethe's works to the rarest treasures of European lyric poetry.

Immeasurably sad they may appear at first. Wilhelm Dilthey, in his book, *Das Erlebnis und die Dichtung*, called them an interminable lament drawn through the depths of night. Actually, however, they reveal themselves not only as the expression of Novalis's yearning for love and death but as the promise of a new and nobler world. Goethe rightly said that Novalis might have become the 'imperator' of German literature. But it was his fate to die before he had completed his twenty-ninth year. Novalis is the true poet of the German Romantics. Untrammelled imagination is for him the essence of all reality. Soaring above the material, his poetry is yet divorced from the earth. Only the world of the spirit is as true to him as that of the senses. Herein lies the key to an understanding of his poetic personality.

The ways of men are dark and enigmatical, those of genius unfathomable. Whom the gods love they often snatch away in the bloom of life, or as Plautus says: 'Quem di diligunt adolescens moritur.' Michelangelo, Titian, and Goethe seem to be exceptions. Giorgione was thirty-two when he died, Catullus about thirty-three, and Keats, Shelley, Schubert, Wackenroder, J. Chr. Günther, Hauff, Büchner, Graf von Strachwitz, Trakl, and Novalis never even reached the age of thirty-two. Hölderlin was about thirty-two when his spirit was enveloped in darkness, yet he had to live on with broken powers for four more decades.

While an iron necessity lies over Hölderlin's terrible fate, Novalis' life is illumined by a never-fading shimmer of grace. The poet of these *Hymns to the Night* was neither an unhinged Werther nor a rebellious Prometheus. He accepted the practical work of everyday life and led us through it to the 'blue flower'

[1] R. Tymms, *German Romantic Literature*.

of his desire. The suddenness of his poetic outbursts reminds one of the shocks and changes in the lives of the mystics.

Novalis (a pseudonym for Friedrich von Hardenberg) was born on 2 May 1772 in the county of Mansfeld on the estate of his Moravian relatives, which had once been a medieval nunnery. He was the second eldest of eleven children. His father, Herr von Hardenberg, was director of the salt-works of Saxony and later introduced his son Friedrich into the business of management. Ludwig Tieck, Novalis's friend, tells us how an attack of dysentery overtook the nine-year-old boy and, after recovering from it, his intellectual powers suddenly awoke. The quiet, dreamy boy with the brown eyes and the almost transparent, hectic complexion now changed to a youth of spirited gaiety.

Friendship became a necessity to him. In Jena he saw Schiller, and in a letter to the Kantian philosopher Reinhold in October 1791 he writes of the first momentous meeting with the 'dream-vision' of his boyhood: 'Schiller's look cast me into the dust and raised me up again. I placed the most complete, most unlimited confidence in him from the first minute. . . . I recognized in him the higher genius, which exerted its influence over centuries. . . .'

After the completion of his years spent as a student in Jena, the decisive hour of his life arrived. He met Sophie von Kühn for the first time, on the estate of Grüningen near Weissenfels. She had only reached her thirteenth year and was ten years younger than Novalis himself. Her memory is perpetuated in the figure of Mathilde in *Heinrich von Ofterdingen* and in the Klarisse of the *Verstreute Blätter*. He comments on Sophie's childlike, often capricious manner: 'She wishes to please everyone' . . . 'her coyness and yet innocent truthfulness . . . her tobacco-smoking, her affection for her mother when a child' ('Once she received a beating from "*ma chère*" '), 'her outspokenness towards her father . . . her confirmation . . . her face during obscene stories, her talent to imitate' . . . 'She wishes me always gay. I shall not see her wound. She does not allow herself to be addressed *du*. . . . She thinks more of others than herself. . . .'

Sophie was already ill in the autumn of 1795. In the following spring she was operated on for a tumour of the liver. In March 1797 she died. His day, Novalis says, had been turned into night as he looked into the red sunrise. Four years later, on 25 March 1801, he himself died of tuberculosis.

His experience of Sophie meant for him the unfolding of his poetic powers. Just as Dante was once changed by Beatrice, so was Novalis by his youthful bride. His life had become a blazing flame. In his darkest hours of despair he went to Sophie's grave to conjure up her picture; at home lay the clothes of his beloved, and through them he could feel her nearness. How was it then possible that he became engaged to Julia von Charpentier less than two years after Sophie's death? Nevertheless, it does not presuppose unfaithfulness towards Sophie who had become to him the image of all that was good and valuable in life. The ideal of true womanhood mingled with the realistic features of the original. We are here reminded of Marcel Proust's affection for Albertine in the eleventh volume of his *A la recherche du temps perdu*: 'Nowhere do there bud so many flowers, forget-me-not though they be styled, as in a cemetery.... And was it not natural that now the cooling star of my love in which they were condensed should explode afresh in this scattered dust of nebulae? They all of them seemed to me pleasures and sophisticated caresses, both of which are transient.' But whilst Proust could not detach from a desire for affection 'all that embroidery' of his memories of Albertine's body, the core of Novalis's love for Sophie lay in himself—Sophie drove him on to a passionate longing for death. This was the fundamental experience for Novalis and it reflected itself in his majestic hymns.

Novalis' *Hymns to the Night* indeed belong in the main, together with Hölderlin's odes and hymns, to the mightiest of European lyrics. They are inspired by a vision in which the finite is reflected in infinity and the accidental becomes a symbol. For him the world of poetry is the real one. Mathematics becomes religion, the individual the universe. His poetry is more than seeing, hearing or tasting—it is the language of his innermost self: he is no sickly pervert hankering after death. His poetry is just as far removed from Catullus's *Vivamus, mea Lesbia*. In the *Fragmente*, *Blütenstaub*, and *Aphorismen* he unfolds before us hitherto unknown treasures of deep worldly wisdom. They are rare seeds of poetic insight. He tries to give an 'encyclopaedia' of poetry and science which to him belong together. Like Herder and Hamann, he sees in both a redeeming and ever-developing unity. The way to true knowledge is for him self-examination and this inwardness is only one step from mysticism.

Novalis wrote his *Hymns to the Night* about 1798. They were published for the first time in 1800 (in the Romantic journal *Athenäum*) in rhythmic prose. The version in free verse was discovered in manuscript form in the Novalis archives only in 1901.

In the *first* Hymn the poet sings of light which lives in the stars, plants, and animals. Night is lonely—but she only appears to be so. Her eye is 'deep' and eternal. 'In sweet intoxication' she unfolds the soul's heavy wings.

In the *second* Hymn he praises sleep who slumbers in the golden sea of grapes, in the oil of the almond-tree and in the brown sap of the poppy. Sleep is the silent messenger of infinite secrets.

With the departure of light vanishes also sorrow (*third* Hymn). In the *fourth* Hymn the last morning is announced, and with a sensuous shudder the poet experiences the ecstasies of ravishing death. His hope lies in the freedom of heaven and the return to the wonderland of the night and to death's 'youth-giving wave'.

The *fifth* Hymn lets us glance back into the history of human culture, and refers to Christ's Resurrection. The *last* Hymn turns to Jesus, and the Sweet Bride and Beloved. To the unorthodox Novalis, Christ is also the God of Night who leads mankind back to its origin—a view very different from that of Stefan George or of Schiller, who in his *Götter Griechenlands* laments the fall of the Greek gods on the arrival of the Christian God. Novalis is doubtless a 'Romantic', but not an anti-Christian lover; cf. also M. C. D'Arcy's penetrating study on Eros and Agape, *The Mind and Heart of Love*.

The very experience behind these 'Hymns' is clearly revealed here. Pain at the loss of the beloved awakens the poet's enthusiasm for the night and his readiness for death. Yet the sorrow is softened by the sight of the heavens and of the landscape that rises steeply. The dream disappears, yet the reality remains—namely, the unshakable faith in the beloved. This dream-life is quite conscious. Sophie and Christ overcome death. They return to the light of day, to a new world.

We see that the poet's longing for death is not 'romantically' and morbidly confused, but full of delicacy of feeling and self-possessed. So also was his life. He always betrays a sensitive nature and also one that is gay and sociable and free from doubt. He chose the practical profession of a mining official—in contrast to Goethe's *Werther*. He, moreover, loved mathematics because they were to him absolutely free from everything unintellectual, and like a pure child of the mind, like Athene, who sprang from Jupiter's head. Thus pure mathematics became religion to him. Whilst Hölderlin in his *Hyperion* says: 'We are nothing, what we seek is everything', for Novalis everything, even the most insignificant object on earth, became a source of poetic inspiration. Although he is irresistibly drawn towards night he does not curse the 'desolate' day as the dying hero does in Wagner's *Tristan und Isolde*, the high-soaring song of a love finding its fulfilment in death.

The influence of Novalis on Wagner was penetrating. Moreover, one cannot fail to recognize Schopenhauer's creed of world renunciation as an influence on *Tristan und Isolde*. Wagner could find in the philosophy of *The World, considered as Will and Idea* the conception that man's greatest fault is to be born, and that Death is an atonement, for Death says to us: 'You are the product of an act which should never have taken place; therefore you must wash it away—die.' Death is no evil. Already Theognis declared: 'Optima sors homini natum non esse, nec unquam adspexisse diem.'

Richard Wagner, however, not only discovered in Novalis's *Hymns to the Night* poetic inspiration for his opera, but occasionally also borrowed passages from the 'Hymns' almost literally. The similarities are striking; cf. 'wenn der letzte Morgan sein wird—wenn das Licht nicht mehr die Nacht und die Liebe scheucht' (IV) with Wagner's 'Der öde Tag/Zum letzten Mal!' (Act II, Scene 3) or Novalis's reference (II) to 'Night's consecrated ones' in:

Heiliger Schlaf!
Beglücke zu selten nicht
Der Nacht Geweihte

with Tristan's words:

O nun waren wir
Nachtgeweihte!
Der tückische Tag. . . .
. . . Seine eitle Pracht,
seinen prahlenden Schein
verlacht, wem die Nacht
den Blick geweiht . . .
(II, 2),

and the passage in the hymn: 'The Mother despatched me to dwell in your world':

Schickte die Mutter mich
Zu bewohnen deine Welt (IV)

with Tristan's answer to King Mark:

Es ist das dunkel
nächt'ge Land,
daraus die Mutter
mich entsandt. . . .

When in his 'Hymns' Novalis asks the dark night: 'Have you, too, a heart as mortals have?' Eros, Death and Night merge into one great conception. Night transforms all things again into a new conscious existence. Night is here more than a Romantic transfiguration with winged spirit and 'infinite eye'. Night flows cool and refreshing, she grants us joy and holy sleep, she is eternal, dark and inexpressible—Night is the path to inner being, the way to poetry, to creation.

E. Young's *Night Thoughts* have a similar ring: Out of the depths of secret night flows all *Life* . . .; cf. also Akhnaton's grandiose hymn: 'Thy dawning is beautiful', and *Psalm* CIV.

Towards the end of the free-rhythmic 'Hymns' Novalis turns to depicting traditional Christian ethics, and the spirited word lapses into rhymed expressions of naïvely Christian fervour, as already in the fourth Hymn:

Hinüber wall ich,
Und jede Pein
Wird einst ein Stachel
Der Wollust sein. . . .

This sanctification of the night contrasts strongly with the ideas of Goethe, who is continually leading us back to humanity.

In his essay, *Die Christenheit oder Europa*, Novalis speaks with the deepest emotion of the Church.[1] He desires a religion of feeling and swears by the golden age when Europe was a Christian country and when a great common interest was a reality— a visible Church, ignoring all State boundaries. His idea for a unity of cultured peoples should find today an impassioned echo amongst the stricken nations in the heart of Europe. In his *Geistliche Lieder* (*Spiritual Songs*), in which he sings of Good Friday, Easter, Whitsun, and other holy feast-days, he speaks of a religious union of all people resulting from a similar fervent belief in the Heavenly Mediator Who, at Golgotha, gave His life for us as the supreme sacrifice.

In this connexion the attitude of Novalis's friend, Schelling, to Christianity is revealing. Both approached God by dreaming in a trance-like state. Both were engaged in this creation of a new modern mythology. The myths of Greece, however, remained for Schelling the highest example of the poetic world. Of the Christian angels, only the fallen Lucifer offered him mythological material; Christ Himself was for him the image of the voluntarily suffering God, and Mary, the Virgin Mother. Friedrich W. J. von Schelling, like Novalis, demanded that 'poetry must disclose its origin. It must stand as a symbol: it must show us the tears and laughter of God confronting His own being . . . creation as well as destruction. God must be depicted as nature, and the picture must be precise. It must be finite, while simultaneously describing the infinite: finite and infinite "falling together" (*symballein*).'[2]

In Novalis's *Heinrich von Ofterdingen*, an apotheosis of poetic art, we meet, in the fairy tale of Arktur and Sophie, a new Olympus. The work is clearly impregnated by Jacob Böhme's mystical philosophy of the fall and the redemption of nature and man's return to the eternal land of light.

Also the thirteenth Hymn of Novalis's *Geistliche Lieder* is significant:

---

[1] T. F. Hiebel *Novalis*, University of North Carolina Press, 1954.
[2] *Horizon*, Sept. 1945, K. T. Bluth.

Wenige wissen
Das Geheimnis der Liebe,
Fühlen Unersättlichkeit
Und ewigen Durst.

The theme—the Last Supper—is not orthodoxly formulated, but pantheistically coloured as a religious ecstasy and the longing to unite with the true breath of the world. Christian religion is to Novalis a religion of ecstasy. In his *Moralische Ansichten* he speaks of the sinful man as the more Christian man, as perfect union with the Godhead is the purpose of sin and of love (*der Zweck der Sünde und der Liebe*). Instead of a belief in the eternal recurrence of the identical (compare *die ewige Wiederkehr alles Gleichen*, an ancient belief reappearing later in Nietzsche's philosophy), the poet prophesies for us a new world. He feels nature not as an enemy, as Fichte did. She is blood of his own blood. He, like the Dutch philosopher, Hemsterhuis, demands the training of the senses, so that the abstract should be made visible, the mind be materialized and the senses spiritualized. According to Novalis and Hölderlin there rests within us a close relationship both with the powers of the spiritual world and with the earth. But whilst Hölderlin sang the praises of the ether, it is in the flower, in the water, in the animals, and in the moon that Novalis discovers the supernatural. And whilst Hölderlin's poetry vacillates in a fiery rhythm of rising and a tragic descent, we here look, as it were, into a crystalline clearness.

How little, Novalis laments at the end of *Lehrlinge zu Sais*, have we sunk into the secrets of the flux. His vision of life's eternal flow is given a unique poetic expression: the universal spirit manifests itself 'in thirst, this mighty longing for that which flows. The intoxicated feel only too well this celestial bliss of the flux, and ultimately all the pleasant sensations we have are manifold fluctuations and the stirring of those primeval waters (Urgewässer) in us. Even sleep is nothing but the flow of the invisible world-encompassing sea, and waking the beginning of the ebb. How many men stand near the intoxicating flood, and do not hear the lullaby of these mother-waters (mütterliche Gewässer), and do not enjoy the charming play of the eternal waves. In the golden age we lived like these waves. Among multi-coloured clouds, among these surging seas and springs of the living on the earth, the races of humanity were begotten and lived in never-ending play: visited by the children of heaven; and then in that great event which the holy legend calls the flood of sin, this golden world was annihilated; and the earth was laid low by some hostile being. . . . It is not merely as a reflection—the sky lying in the water—but a tender friendliness (Befreundung), a sign of neighbourliness, and when unfulfilled desire wants to rise to immeasurable heights, blessed love gladly sinks into the infinite depths.'

This attitude to nature is remote from the pernicious and 'blind sentimentalism that finds an enduring peace in "nature" and mistakes a presumed unself-consciousness in the plant and animal world for happiness and contentment'; cf. W. Bowyer Honey, *Science and the Creative Art*. It is also opposite to D. H. Lawrence's belief in the 'natural' forces of the primitive man. Novalis *did* know that life meant conflict, and he believed in Christian ethics, in beauty and compassion.

Novalis shows a genial capacity for friendship. This is shown in his attitude towards his literary contemporaries and especially to Friedrich Schlegel, Tieck, and Wackenroder. In Tieck's allegorical poem *Der Traum* we can clearly discern the prototype of Novalis's '*blaue Blume*' the symbol of Romantic poesy. The flower motif is, of course, ancient. It appears also in Dukas's musical composition *La Péri*, where, however, the lover who wanders through Iran has to choose between the flower and the fairy whose kiss brings him death.

Tieck was one year younger than Novalis. Wackenroder and Sophie had already died when they met in Jena in the summer of 1799. A. W. Schlegel introduced the two poets. Soon afterwards Tieck visited Novalis in his Herrnhuter home at Weissenfels. Köpke, Tieck's biographer, tells us, in an illuminating anecdote, how pious and austere the atmosphere was there. On one occasion Tieck heard Novalis's venerable father, Hardenberg, apparently giving vent to a violent outburst of rage in the next room. 'What is the matter?' he inquired anxiously of the butler who entered at that moment. 'Nothing,' replied the latter dryly. 'The master is merely holding his devotional hour!'

The legend of the 'etherial' and even that of the sexually

supersensitive poet Novalis is entirely misleading. In his
Fragmente he calls understanding the secondary order of things
only a weaker form of life or one which has died out. As a true
poet he grasped nature better than many a profound scholar.
He passionately believed in some mysterious connection between man and the universe. The awe he felt for mathematics
('pure mathematics equals religion') was symbolical of that
oneness of finite and infinite in the soul of the artist. Novalis
was also deeply interested in hypnosis, galvanism, animal
electricity, and in Brown's physiology, also in mineralogy and
geology, which he studied under the guidance of the eminent
professor and 'vulcanist' Werner in Freiberg.

In his *Lehrlinge zu Sais* Novalis hails nature as the source, the
comforter, the priestess, the worker of miracles. We have
already hinted at the affinity with Schelling's philosophy:
nature is visible spirit, whereas Schiller in his ballad *Das
verschleierte Bild zu Sais* speaks of the unveiling of truth as an act
of heavy guilt. For Novalis the surpassing of the earthly limit
was no crime. He finds nature again in the woman and the
mother of things, Rosenblüt. So he solves the riddles of nature,
in contrast to Schiller and also to Kant's great disciple, Fichte,
for whom everything leads back to oneself:

Einem gelang es—er hob den Schleier der Göttin von Sais—
Aber was sah er?—er sah—Wunder des Wunders, sich selbst.

Novalis's self-examination is closely related to F. Schleiermacher's demand in the *Monologe* to become that which one *is*.
Men must not be afraid to see what they have done, what they
have been and who they now are. Their inner freedom and
eternal youth lie in their strength of will and lively imagination.
And Schleiermacher's words, 'Be not modest in your actions',
must not be misunderstood. He also advocates striving after
order and moderation. Schleiermacher clearly states, 'Free is
the man who seeks and knows himself', and likewise for Novalis
the appearance of nature is not in itself autonomous, but a way
to inner understanding. The 'Non-Ego' is to him a symbol of
his own ego and serves as an understanding of his own experience and feeling. The world is, as he subtly says, 'an universal
trope', and an 'encyclopaedic index' of the mind.

Again and again he reveals his inner instinct for nature. This, indeed, is the poetical core of his whole work, especially in the *Lehrlinge zu Sais*. The germ of this fragmentary novel is the captivating fairy tale of *Hyazinth und Rosenblüt*, who are in love and whose lives are steeped in nature. But one day there comes a man with a book. From now on, Hyazinth without guidance has no peace, and wanders away. Turmoil has entered life because of this separation of man and woman. Desire makes them long for reunion. In his dream-world Hyazinth finds the mother of creation, the veiled maid of nature, and when he lifts the veil, Rosenblüt falls into his arms.

The fairy tale was for Novalis the basic form of poetical expression. Here all the natural orders of life are mingled haphazardly together in the anarchy of creation, and Chance is revered.

In *Heinrich von Ofterdingen* (begun in 1800), for example, every man assumes the mantle of poetry. The novel aims at dissolving the world into the realm of the spirit. The dream is overshadowed by the symbol of the 'blue flower' ('blaue Blume'), which was the favourite symbol of Romanticism. The supersensual is interwoven with the sensual. The story tells how Arktur, having been spirited away, lives with his daughter Freia in the North. Casting his weapon into space, he wakes Eros, the child of Heart and Sense, from sleep, and draws him to Freia. Meanwhile, however, the poet depicts the turmoil on earth. Heart and Sense are captured. After a period of trial Eros and Freia are finally united and set up to rule.

To the author of such a poetical spectacle, Goethe's novel, *Wilhelm Meister's Apprenticeship*, must indeed have appeared, in its basic concept at any rate, as too tangible and material, as a camouflaged 'dish of wood shavings' or as a pilgrimage to attain the 'diploma of nobility', although it is precisely Mignon, Harfner, Philine, and others who struck in the ears of the Romantics a new note of revelation. Did they not indeed call *Wilhelm Meister*, the French Revolution, and Fichte's *Wissenschaftlehre* the three most important 'tendencies' of their own Romantic age?

Novalis himself is the poet of Romantic yearning. His *Hymns to the Night* are, as we have said, without question the most powerful lyrical product of the Jena circle and German Romanticism in general. Hölderlin's unique and solitary genius stands outside the movement. Novalis is its exponent.

The path he trod leads, as we have noticed, ever more inward to a yet purer integration. Creative activity of the spirit, unalloyed and untrammelled by utilitarian purpose, is his goal. Everything he expresses must spring from the fountain of moral freedom. Everything aggressively loud or near offends him, till he has removed it to a rarefied plane. He sees only the symbol and desires a creative independence from material things, but, as said, not a complete divorce. The purpose, he feels, of all poetry is to raise man above himself to a vision of the universal. In a letter to August Wilhelm Schlegel his brother, Friedrich, says of his friend Novalis: 'Fate has laid into my hands a young man who may rise to anything. . . . I never saw such serenity in youth. His emotion has a certain chastity which is rooted in spiritual integrity, not in lack of experience.'

For us today, and above all for the Germans, Novalis should have a special significance. Unfortunately, we learn little from history, and facts are, as Novalis rightly said, certainly not the essential influences. Science and education, through political abuse and a barbaric lust for over-specialization, have often enough proved themselves equally bankrupt. The ultimate truths of existence cannot be solved through evolution, scientific analysis or the rivalries of intellectual ambition. The only hope of rebirth lies, according to Novalis, in a recognition of the spiritual realities of beauty and a reverence for the mystery of nature, creative activity, the totality of life, and last, not least, in a full understanding of the individual's right of freedom and responsibility towards mankind.

Herein lies the real significance of Novalis's work. His art touches the secret heart of our existence through the power of imagination and intuitive sensibility. We saw how he nevertheless always maintains the balance between nature and the ego, and between phantasy and reason.

Novalis's song is at once individual and universal, born both of a chastening and a mighty inebriation of the spirit.

VIII

Nihilism and Modern German Drama

GRABBE and BÜCHNER

Quid igitur timeam, si aut non miser post mortem, aut
beatus etiam futurus sum? Quamquam quis est tam
stultus, quamvis sit adulescens, cui sit exploratum se ad
vesperum esse victurum?

CICERO, *De Senectute*

*What, then, shall I fear, if after death I am destined to be either
not unhappy or happy? And yet is there anyone so foolish, even
though he is young, as to feel absolutely sure that he will be
alive when evening comes?*

Translation by W. A. FALCONER

IN HIS MEMOIRS, the Russian writer Ivan Turgenev (1818-83)
maintains that he coined the word 'Nihilism'. But this word
is actually much older. It was already used by Friedr.
Heinrich Jacobi in 1790 in a letter to Fichte, and by Jean Paul
in his *Aesthetics* (1804).

By the term 'Nihilism' we mean not only the philosophical
doctrines of extreme revolutionism which aim at overthrowing
the constituted order of society but in general also the rejection
of current religious and moral beliefs. Almost the whole history
of German literature of the nineteenth and twentieth centuries
casts a shattering reflexion on our present-day situation—one
could rightly say that it is a mirror of the modern crisis of belief.
So the study of the drama of a people has a profound meaning
which goes beyond the narrow analysis of style and text and
touches the core of our existence.

The German rebel and playwright, Georg Büchner, was
still an impressionable schoolboy at the time of the revolution
of July 1830. In many references to Brutus and Cato he glorifies
the liberties of 1789, and in his farewell to the Gymnasium at
Darmstadt he compares Cato to the standards of the age that
judges him:

A day of dwarfs can measure no man. Who shall point their way to eagles, their wings spread wide to bend a stormy course among the stars? Who cares to count crushed flowers, broken on a windswept earth, whose gathered fogs had thickened, brooding over life? What child dare set the measure of its own thoughts or motives, when monsters are abroad—to say which is most monstrous? Events and their conclusions should not be judged as they present themselves to our eyes—we should seek to pierce the deepest of their meanings.

I feel this must be said, and I may show in my handling of so difficult a theme the point from which all judgment of such a man—the judgment of a Roman—may be attempted.

His voice can find no echo in the opinions and principles of a later age. . . .[1]

In the French Revolution human greatness is revealed to Büchner in the fight for freedom, but, as we shall see later on, he by no means idealizes its leaders and their people. Yet his concept of the human scene is great as well as tragic. We ask ourselves: What is meant by 'great'? It is that which strives for a thing far superior to the satisfaction of one's own personal, egotistic aims, because that which achieves such greatness alone is true.

And what is meant by 'tragic'?[2] It is that which in such a conflict between ego and a greater course knows of no escape. Tragic may be applied to the insoluble conflict in activity (e.g. Caesar, Napoleon, Hannibal), or the very existence of man can be tragic (e.g. Hamlet, Socrates, Egmont).

In such tragic issues death is no essential condition; guilt, too, is not essential, for a criminal (such as Macbeth) can be as tragic as a man or woman of pure and inviolable heart (e.g. Desdemona, Ophelia, Luise). It is certainly tragic when in the moment of the greatest happiness there follows the sudden fall (e.g. in the story of Lohengrin and Elsa), or when the bonds of inner sympathy and human love are torn to pieces, as in the struggle between families (e.g. in *Romeo and Juliet*), or between two personalities (Wallenstein and Max Piccolomini, or Wotan and Brunhilde), or between two peoples (as during the suicidal World Wars of 1914 and 1939) and two religious creeds (cf.

[1] *The Plays of Georg Büchner*, translated by G. Dunlop, London, 1927.
[2] Cf. A. Pfeiffer, *Ursprung und Gestalt des Dramas* (1943); T. R. Henn, *The Harvest of Tragedy* (1956), etc.

Erasmus and Hutten). Last but not least, we also sense tragedy in the guiltless, and at the same time, guilty entanglement of mankind in the iron net of environment (as in Hebbel's *Maria Magdalena*), or in the curse of biological inheritance (Ibsen's *Ghosts*).

However, the great tragedy ultimately does not depend upon merely external things, which can oppress the human victims through hunger, social and pathological conditions, and financial worries. Every man in the last resort is responsible for his own lot. It is an inner fatality, from which there is no escape— the tragic element lies in ourselves.

Each one is answerable for his own self alone. In his boundless arrogance or passion or will, man sins against the will of the universe. Boundless are the actions of the relentless hero (in H. von Kleist's dramas), boundless too, the uncompromising beauty of Hebbel's Agnes Bernauer, boundless the superhuman purity of a Genoveva.

Moreover, the German tragedy of the nineteenth century is sharpened by philosophical deliberations. Schopenhauer, Schelling, and later, Nietzsche among others probe into the depths of the interminable and insoluble conflict between the individual and the world. According to Schopenhauer, man's worst guilt is to be born at all. The original sin—the primeval evil—is nothing more than the guilt of existing. A release is only to be found if the individual sacrifices himself voluntarily to the infinite.

It is a mystical conception that God divides Himself into two parts through His creation and seeks to reunite Himself by means of man gaining knowledge of his origin and striving to return to God once more. Hebbel turns this mystic idea into a heroic one when he states that every capable man must be resolved into a greater self if ever he attains to self-recognition and an assured use of his powers.

According to a conception such as this, *God* Himself is made to fall into sin through the creation of the world. The individual becomes therefore *no* longer the free originator of his deeds, but the fulfiller of a higher will. Even God Himself becomes questionable, for He is the root of all conflict. God and man need that conflict, for that very dualism is the great wound of the

world which alone can lead to salvation through man himself—
that is to say, man must die for God, he must be crucified. To
write poetry, according to Hebbel, means to kill one's own self.

The truly tragic being accepts with determination this world
of horror and despair despite its sombre promise of destruction.

There can be no question that since Büchner, Hebbel, and
Nietzsche our present conflict has been unparalleled in severity.
For many God is dead. The Christian martyr drama (e.g. the
Romantic *Genoveva* by Tieck or the consecration play, *The
Annunciation*, by Claudel) culminates in a heavenly triumph, in
an atmosphere of salvation whereby the real tragedy is raised
from guilt and sin. Yet for the godless Nihilist only senselessness
prevails, whereas Nietzsche was still seeking to overcome our
futile monotony and deadening sameness by means of the forceful personality.

But Goethe already knew of the primeval contradiction of all
existence when he says in his *Wilhelm Meister*:

> You lead us into life, you let the miserable creature
> be guilty and then you surrender him to torture, for
> all guilt is avenged on earth.

And Hölderlin's *Song of Fate* laments the hopelessness of mankind's urge. The Danish philosopher Kierkegaard has accepted
the terrible suffering of man as the basis of the whole ethics of
human existence in his work. His God is a God of terror.

In order to understand modern tragedy, the fundamental
difference between the ancient Greek and present European
concept of tragedy must not be overlooked. With Greek tragedy
our fate is god-willed (e.g. Oedipus), the individual stands
under the rule of the gods. The latter are all powerful; the
human creature is merely small and worthless; and he suffers
mystically (like Oedipus). In Shakespeare, however, the
individual is not pressed like this against the Fate of the Gods;
rather the responsibility or opposition lies in his own breast.
In this way the tragedy is planted in the character of the
individual. And yet another point: according to our Idealistic
or Marxian interpretation of history, the impact of tragedy is
either sharpened or softened or nullified: Mme. de Stael once
said, 'Tout comprendre c'est tout pardonner.' But the genuine

tragic figure requires an 'Either-Or'—a situation in which opinions relentlessly clash with opinions, free will stands against compulsion, personal sense of right against duty (e.g. in H. von Kleist's *Prinz von Homburg*), order against chaos (e.g. Schiller's *Räuber*), self-surrender against self-assertion (e.g. Goethe's *Faust*), or the victim struggles in vain against the cruel necessity of circumstances or against the curse of biological inheritance.

Every real tragedy will make us feel that, although we suffer, it is greater to be crushed than not to be touched at all by the events of life.

There is, no doubt, a fundamental difference in the interpretation of history by the Classic writers and the Marxists. In Schiller's view the history of the world is the world's own judgement. For Goethe it is the norm of all activity. It is, of course, quite wrong to deny all tragedy in Goethe's drama, but he conquered the tragedy of existence by his belief in 'change and permanence', in cosmos and order of life. In him we find no counterpart to the courage of despair of the Nihilists, who would rather be guilty than sink into bottomless nothingness once again. Against this gloomy outlook Goethe puts his belief in a higher order of the universe, e.g.:

in his *Seefahrt* ('er stehet männlich an dem Steuer');
in his *Proœmion* ('jeder Schritt ist Unermesslichkeit'); and
in his *Symbolum* ('Stille ruhen oben die Sterne und unten die Gräber').

Goethe does not struggle like Grabbe or Nietzsche to glorify the powerful personality in a cruel and purposeless world. Existence for Goethe is not the fall from God, or Satan's lot, but conflict and readiness to accept both the permanence and change (*Dauer im Wechsel*). After Goethe and Schiller and Hölderlin, however, the nineteenth century scene becomes darker and darker. The more 'godless' that Europe becomes, the more fearful is its despair.

Today the two philosophical trends often stand irreconcilably opposed to each other: (*a*) One group of thoughts attempts to relate all significant events or catastrophe only to individuals as if for example beside Hitler perhaps Bismarck, Friedrich II of Prussia, or even Luther might bear the whole blame for the present evil. (*b*) The others are disciples of Karl Marx and explain historical phenomena and personalities solely by temporal environment, social conditions, etc., as if the shoe made the cobbler! To Goethe, on the other hand, the fortunes of birth and the infallible daemonic quality of existence are presented as an undeniable fact.

These two opposite views are distinctly reflected in the German tragedies of the nineteenth and twentieth centuries. We can now see before our very eyes how everywhere the foundations are cracking, how moral values, which until now have remained unshaken, have become meaningless and empty. The way from Lessing, Goethe and Schiller to Büchner, Hebbel, and Grabbe is, as we shall see, the way of German tragedy. Society has changed. The conflict between the material and spiritual life is already clearly defined in Büchner's letter to Karl Gutzkow:

> You set out to reform society from above, by means of the educated classes. Impossible! Our time is strictly materialist. If you had gone more directly to work, you would soon have reached the point at which all reform would have stopped of itself automatically. You can never bridge the gulf between the educated and uneducated. I have convinced myself that any well-to-do minority, no matter what concession it may wring from the people in power, will never be willing to give up its privileged position to the great masses. And what of these masses themselves? For them there are only two levers—want and religious fanaticism. Any party which understands their use will succeed. Our time needs iron and bread—and then perhaps a cross or something like it. I believe that in social questions the only thing to do is to go from a fundamental principle—build up the people to a new spiritual life and let the worn-out society of today go its own way to the devil. Let it die. That's the only new thing it is capable of.[1]

Perhaps the following comparison of Goethe's and Heine's views on important events in 1830 will be sufficient proof of the above change of attitude:

Heine in Heligoland . . . was convinced of the essential futility of all human effort—knew that progress was nothing but the ebb and flow of the tides. 'The red-hot news arrived from the mainland

[1] Translator, Dunlop, loc. cit.

in a thick packet of newspapers. I felt I could set the North Sea—
the very Pole—on fire. I was a son of revolution.' . . . At about
the same time a visitor to the aged Geheimrath was puzzled and
a little scandalized at being greeted with enthusiastic exclamations
on the great event in Paris. Then it turned out that there had been
a slight mistake. The 'great event' was the settlement of a controversy in respect to 'The unity of composition in the animal
kingdom' between Cuvier and Geoffrey St. Hilaire, and St.
Hilaire had won. But Heine's boatman, who had rowed him out
to bathe every day, may be given the last word. He too was over-
joyed at the news. He turned it over in his mind, and came to a
conclusion. 'The poor people,' he said, 'have won a victory.'[1]

We shall now turn to concrete examples in the development of
the German tragedy since Lessing and Goethe and Schiller:
Faith in the heavenly order of things on earth still prevails in
Lessing's *Emilia Galotti*. Here there are no rebellious uprisings
or grumblings, no opposition to God, no acts of vengeance.
The tragedy offers three possibilities: (*a*) Emilia will be left to
the unscrupulous prince and evil will triumph; (*b*) Emilia's
father raises his sword against the villain and incites the
suppressed peoples to revolution; (*c*) self-sacrifice—and this the
father does in Lessing's drama when he destroys his daughter,
and so does not rebel. By this he remains true to the given order
of things, but with the knowledge that a Heavenly Father
passes judgement on us all.[2]

With Goethe and Schiller, too, belief in the given order
remains unbroken, although not unchallenged, because both
recognize in the greatness of remaining an individual at the
same time a curse—for here on this earth self-assertion stands
in direct opposition to self-denial. This is the theme in Goethe's
lyrical drama, *Faust*, which is profoundly tragic in its conflict of
self-will and self-surrender:

> Mark how beneath the evening sunlight's glow,
> The green-embosomed houses glitter. . . .
> . . . Ah that no wing can lift me from the soil
> Upon its track to follow, follow soaring. . . .
> . . . Yet in each soul is born the pleasure
> Of yearning onward, upward and away. . . .

[1] Ibid. (Professor Brandes's two records).
[2] Cf. Benno von Wiese, *Die deutsche Tragödie von Lessing bis Hebbel* (2 vols.),
Hamburg, 1948, a masterful study of the problems concerned.

A comparison of Goethe's *Tasso* (1790) with Grillparzer's
Sappho (1818) is particularly illuminating, because it brings out
clearly the difference between Goethe and the younger generation of his time. Both Tasso and Sappho are artists; the very
existence of both is precarious. But for Goethe's Tasso art
remains supreme while for Grillparzer's Sappho life means
more. She believes that she can renounce her art in order to
find freedom and happiness in her love for Phaon, but she
fails tragically. Her love is rejected by Phaon for the sake of the
young and charming Melitta, and now Sappho can no longer
find her way back to art, to her true self. Suicide is her only
way out; it is escape from the world, renunciation—not
liberation. For Goethe's Tasso, however, art is and remains
triumphant in spite of the fact that his passion and poetic
imagination play their part in his personal accursed fate. The
faith in his creative activity remains unbroken.

Schiller, like Goethe, recognized the essentially tragic
character of a great personality (e.g. Wallenstein, or Demetrius
the deceived deceiver). But Schiller, the champion of freedom,
does not shake the foundations of the traditional order: in his
Robbers the noble robber Karl Moor hands himself over to
justice. Here, as well as in other tragedies, Schiller places the
hero in the immediate environment of crime. He shows, as
Goethe does, that the active hero is in the end without conscience. The deed shapes the character and not the opposite.
This applies especially to his *Wallenstein*, where Schiller
shows that the desire for freedom can create both good and
evil.

Wallenstein is one of the very great German tragedies. Here
the idealist is in direct opposition to the modern Nihilists (e.g.
Büchner, Grabbe, Toller, Borchert). Wallenstein is a noble
character, but it is impossible for him to remain guiltless. He is
a man of action and as such he asserts himself, but not without
guilt. We still move here in a world of moral values. In his
famous monologue (I, 4, *Wallensteins Tod*) he says:

> And is it possible? Is there no more
> return, even though I would? Must I in truth
> fulfil the deed, because I ponder'd it,
> and cast not forth the tempter from my soul?

. . . wear the face of guilt. . . .
. . . Stern is the aspect of necessity;
nor without shuddering does the hand of man
dip into destiny's mysterious urn.
In mine own breast my deed was still mine own,
but, once, escaping from that dark concealment,
the heart's recess, its own maternal home,
let it but wander forth to light and day,
and it belongs to those capricious powers,
whom man still strives, but strives in vain, to soften. . . .

So far, no treachery as yet has crossed Wallenstein's threshold.
Now only a slender boundary divides the two paths in his life.
Wallenstein still hesitates. But he knows his fate—'When I have
ceased to act, I cease to be' (I, 7). He cannot sink into utter
nothingness. He does not believe in chance or blind accident.
'The world within, his microcosm' (II, 3) is his fate, the deep
perennial fountain from which all his deeds and thoughts
must flow. So we can foresee the current of his actions.

Thus, once Wallenstein has decided, he can say 'My breast
is free, my soul's clear again':

'Twas done with inward strife,
while yet the choice was mine;
but now 'tis past,
Necessity is come, doubt flies at last,
I battle for my head and for my life.[1]

The fifth act, in particular, is filled with an unbearable,
heavy tension. The tighter the net is drawn round Wallenstein,
the more contented he becomes. He now no longer believes in
the stars, but in himself. He is fearless, unrepentent, unlament-
ing even in the face of Max's voluntary death, with which the
flower in Wallenstein's existence has faded. He greets life for the
last time; he wishes to dismiss his servant, for the latter believes
that good fortune has deserted his master. Only a noble mind
can speak as Wallenstein does in this scene, but he remains the
man of action who can no longer go back without being
obliged to surrender.[2]

Wallenstein meets his death at the hands of treacherous,

[1] III, 10.
[2] Cf. K. May's excellent analysis in his *Friedrich Schiller. Idee und Wirklichkeit im
Drama*, Göttingen, 1948.

ambitious murderers who, because of a sudden false report that
the Swedish troops are advancing, prepare his end. The
deceitful cunning of intrigue in the ranks triumphs over the
great hero, who at the very last hour of loneliness in his fortress
at Eger, towers high above his petty opponents. The essence of
this tragedy is Schiller's recognition of the fact that all freedom
of action (even of noble action) only brings about its undoing.
The honourable man, through the guilt of his conscience, is
inexorably drawn into the net. Fate plays its treacherous game
with him. But with his death the belief in the divine order of
our universe remains undisturbed.

With Hebbel (1813-1863) the situation is distinctly sombre—
for instance, in *Maria Magdalena*. Force of circumstance works
like a blind fate on Klara and draws her without mercy to
suicide in order thereby to save her father, Meister Anton, at
least from shame. In contrast to Goethe and Schiller, the
individual—entangled in a petty bourgeois milieu—is here
already completely submerged in the process of tragic
fatality.

With C. D. Grabbe (1801-36) the late-born son of the warder
of a jail in Detmold, life becomes utterly futile and senseless.
According to his *Herzog Theodor von Gothland*, man reads goodness into history, since he is too cowardly to confess its horrible
truths to himself. This is a rejection of Hegel's philosophy. The
only way out of the senselessness of life would be to purify the
earth with fire and sword, war and plague, like Attila or
Caesar. The poet, according to Grabbe, is the surgeon or the
satyr who plays with chaos.

Instead of belief in the divine order of things, only sorrow
rules in a world in which the deeds of heroic virtue become
deeds of crime. Even death does not free—it is no illusion, no
triumph as with Goethe's Egmont. Death, like life, is a means
of torture and pain. This earth is hell—not guilt—but we must
take this hell upon ourselves, otherwise we are cowardly
philistines. We are humans (in Grabbe's sense), humans with
eagles' heads, but our feet are rooted in the mud.

In his tragedy *Hannibal* the noble hero goes under in a chaos
of commonness. Yet the one solace remains: 'We don't fall out
of this world.' Napoleon, too, is conscious of his historical

mission even at the hour of his defeat when he says: 'It is my fortune which falls, not I.'[1]

A short comparison of Goethe's *Faust* with Grabbe's *Don Juan und Faust* also clearly indicates how very much Grabbe's Nihilism differs from the Classic belief in the divine world order. Grabbe's Faust is a wretched person, self-destructive and grotesque. He is, as the devil mocks, much less than a devil— only a human being. But the imposing thing about this drama is that volcanic 'will to power' which, in spite of knowing suffering, is fulfilled in activity alone, even if nothingness waits furtively behind sorrow and desire. If he cannot create, he can still destroy.

Georg Büchner (1813-37), born near Darmstadt, the son of a district medical officer, is, next to Grabbe, perhaps the most uncompromising German Nihilist of the nineteenth century. I have already referred to his remarkable schoolboy essay about ancient virtues and our 'contemporary rotten civilization'. To Büchner, who died at the age of twenty-three, human freedom was a farce. This world is godless and guiltless, but a curse is on the world.

The stark tragedy, *The Death of Danton* (*Dantons Tod*, 1835), is no defence of the revolutionaries. The facts are treated too honestly for that, e.g. II, 14:

> PHILIPPEAU: Well, what do you want?
> DANTON: Rest.
> PHILIPPEAU: Rest is in God.
> DANTON: In nothing. Could I sink into anything more peaceful than that? If God is perfect rest, is not nothing God? But I'm an atheist. That damnable phrase, 'Nothing is made from nothing'— and here am I something. What a pity!
> Creation has spawned, and now there's no more emptiness. All swarming. Nothing has killed herself—creation is her death-wound and we are blood-drops from it. The world's a grave; we congeal in it. That sounds crazy. There's some truth in it. . . .
> ... We're all buried alive. Like kings, they nail us down in three or four coffins—under a sky, and in houses, then in shirts and coats. We scratch for fifty years on coffin lids.
> Yes, it would help a man to believe in annihilation. No hope in death; it's a stiller sloth. Life is more complex, better organized;

[1] Cf. B. v. Wiese's analysis of this 'Gebundenheit des Lebens in der Einseitigkeit', loc. cit.

that's all the difference. And yet! I'm used to one kind of stagnation, the devil knows if I shall get used to the other. Oh, Julie, if I could go alone, if she'd leave me alone! If I could fall to pieces and dissolve utterly! But when I crumble to atoms, I shall still be a heap of longing dust. Each grain could find rest only in her. I won't die—no, I won't die! They haven't cut us yet. We must roar at them—make them fight every blood drop from our limbs.[1]

As we see, there is no idealization of events and characters. In a letter to his family of 5 May 1835, he asserts that he had been true to history and that he portrayed the revolutionaries 'as they really were: bloody, debauched, energetic and cynical'— that is to say, without abstract ideology. The latter quality is, however, embodied in the inhuman Robespierre who sets himself up as the 'Messiah of Blood', and whose terrible fanaticism presents the strongest contrast to the epicurean Danton, for whom sensuous pleasure seems to be the only salvation from the miserable monotony of human existence. Robespierre is opposed to all compassion, to all mercy. He erects the despotism of freedom against tyranny: 'The weapon of the Republic is Terror, the strength of the Republic is Virtue.'

Thus the rule of the Revolution becomes a Saturn who devours his own children. Danton is for moderation because when the emergency ceases, murder begins. But Robespierre refutes him in a scene which is his comrade's undoing. Yet, Danton has no illusions any more, for freedom is to him a dream—and life a comedy—and dying means only 'coming from one dung-heap to another'. Here is Act I, Scene 6:

ROBESPIERRE: I tell you, who holds my arm when my sword's out, that man's my enemy. His intentions are nothing. Who hinders me for my good, kills me as surely as if he stabbed.

DANTON: Where defence ends, there starts murder. I see nothing that compels us to go on killing.

ROBESPIERRE: The social revolution is unfinished. Who makes revolutions by halves, digs his own grave. Aristocrats still live; the sap and power of the people must rise in place of these degenerates. Vice must be punished. Through terror purity shall triumph.

DANTON: Punish! Oh, that word! I don't understand it. You

[1] This and the following extracts from Büchner's plays are given in the translation by G. Dunlop.

and your purity. Robespierre! You've fingered no bribe, eh—and made no debts, and never slept with a woman? You've worn a decent coat and never been drunk? Robespierre, you're revoltingly righteous. I'd shame myself to go trotting thirty years between earth and heaven with the same moral face, and think men worse than I for taking their miserable pleasures. Man! Is there nothing in you, no little whisper, just a twinge now and then, that calls you liar—Liar?

ROBESPIERRE: My conscience is clear.

DANTON: Conscience is a mirror that monkeys shudder at. Each ape makes himself as smart as he can, and goes off into the world to take his pleasure. Why grumble at that? If a man spoils your game, defend yourself—that's natural. But what right have you to make the guillotine a wash tub for other men's foul clothes, or turn their heads to balls of soap to wash 'em with, simply because your own damned coat's so spotless? Protect yourself, yes, if any man spits on it or wants to tear holes. Why care, though, if they leave it alone? They're not ashamed to go ragged. Does that give you a warrant to lock them up in graves? Are you God's constable, eh? If you're too dainty to see what God Almighty does without blenching, hold up your handkerchief, man, and don't look!

ROBESPIERRE: You deny purity?

DANTON: Yes, and vice too. Men are Epicures—coarse or fine. Christ was the finest. And that's the only difference I can make between 'em. Each follows his bent. He does what does him good. Old Incorruptible! Am I cruel to tread the heels from your shoes, eh?

ROBESPIERRE: Danton, there are times when impurity is treason. . . .

Death is the only inexorable opponent in this cruel strife. In spite of Danton's mockery of the meaninglessness of human existence the feeling of comradeship in the common suffering of the prisoners and the self-sacrificing love of Julie, Danton's wife, and Lucile, Camille Desmoulin's wife, cast a transforming gleam on Danton's last hour in the prison and before the scaffold.

Danton recognizes that life itself is not worth living. What is there to fight for? Human beings are foolish ghosts, or caricatures, boring and sometimes amusing. Only when we reach death does the horrible worthlessness of all existence arise in awful and hateful proportions before us. Thus for Danton, life is a whore who plays tricks on her pitiful victims. His words before the last journey to the scaffold are without illusion: 'We are ragged pipers—our bodies are the instruments.' We are children who are roasted in the fiery Moloch arms of this world and who are tickled by rays of light so that the gods are delighted with their laughter. . . . The world is chaos. Nothingness is the God of the Universe. . . .

Danton is certainly no fanatical enthusiast for revolution. He does not believe in a utopia. He does not consider his corpse as 'a dung-heap of freedom' . . . The guillotine is the best doctor for his suffering in a godless world.

Who can speak of human guilt here? And the fellow-prisoner Thomas Payne declares: 'Remove our imperfections—then can you demonstrate your God. . . . God might satisfy your reason, but your feeling denies Him and rebels. We can deny evil, but never pain. . . . The smallest stab of pain, if it only stirs an atom, cracks your creation from top to bottom.'

Face to face with *Death*, existence seems to Danton to be a living grave, but he had loved life to desperation. Caught in the mechanism of a political trial, he views his fate in these terms:

> LACROIX: You shouted bravely, Danton. If you'd taken such care of your life a little sooner, it might have been another story. Death may be impertinent. She may breathe in man's face and be damnably familiar.
>
> CAMILLE: If she'd only fight you down—throw her arms round you—and tear you limb from limb. But with all these formalities it's like the wedding of an old virgin—with contracts to be signed, and witnesses called, and Amens to say; and then at last she raises the sheet very gingerly and crawls in on you with her cold feet.
>
> DANTON: Yes, better fight, fists and teeth. I feel I've fallen in a mill wheel, and my arms and legs are being torn off me slowly—with icy strength. God! to be killed so mechanically!
>
> CAMILLE: And then afterwards to lie by yourself—very cold—in a dank reek of sloth. Listen! Suppose death tortured the life out of you by inches—one fibre at a time—and you knew all the while you were rotting away.
>
> PHILIPPEAU: Quiet, my friend! We are meadow saffron in autumn. It bears seed when the winter's done. In this only do we differ from uprooted flowers. The experiment will stink a little. Is it so bad?
>
> DANTON: An uplifting prospect! From one dunghill to the

other! Your divine class-order, eh? From the first to the second,
then to the third and so on. I've had enough of school benches.
I have corns on my rump from sitting like an ape so long.

Danton knows that only those are the fortunate ones who can
still get drunk. Tomorrow he will be a broken fiddle, an empty
bottle.

Death apes birth, for when we are dying we are as helpless
and naked as new-born babies. Of course we get a shroud for a
napkin. What will it help? He wants to die effortlessly—like a
star falling—like a ray of light burying itself in clear waters.
But to be without pain is an illusion.

Büchner's Nihilism becomes still more pronounced in his
tragedy, *Woyzeck*, in which Woyzeck is driven to murder and
suicide. Here is a scene which is significant: Scene 5: the inside
of the booth:

> MARKET-CRIER (*produces the donkey*): Show yer talent—show yer
> brutish reason. Spread the 'ot flush of shame on the face of
> 'uman *Société*.
> Gentlemen, this is a moke—four hoofs, one tail and all the
> usual appendages. Was once professor at a university, where the
> students learnt ridin' and fightin' from 'im. His understand' is a
> simple one, but 'e 'as 'is compound reason. What do you do when
> you think with your compound reason? (*The donkey behaves
> indelicately.*) What—when you think with your compound reason?
> Tell me now, do you see one moke in all this cultured assembly?
> (*Donkey shakes his head.*) You see—that's reason. What difference is
> there between a man and a moke? Both dust, sand, and dung!
> Their expression, however, is various. A donkey speaks with 'is
> 'oof.
> Tell these gentlemen what time it is. Which of you gentlemen
> can pass me up a watch? A watch please.
> SERGEANT: A watch? (*Extracts a watch with slow majesty.*) There
> you are, sir.
> MARIE: Oh! Do let me 'ave a look. (*She clambers into the front
> seats.*)
> DRUM-MAJOR: You're a fine girl! (*He helps her.*)

The following fairy tale of a grandmother about a forsaken
child symbolizes the desperate loneliness of man in a world of
dissipation and cruel boredom:

> Once upon a time, there was a poor little child, and no father
> it had, and no mother it had—all dead. And no one any more in

161

all the world. All dead. So off it went to look for them all night long and all day long. And there was nobody any more in all the world, so it tried to fly up to heaven—and the moon blinked her eyes and looked so kind; but when it came to the moon, the moon was just an old bit of wood. So then it went to the sun; and when it came to the sun, the sun was no more than a dried-up sunflower —and when it came to the stars, the stars were just little golden flies stuck about like a shrike would stick 'em on a sloe—and when it wanted to go back to earth, the earth was just an overturned mug. And it was all alone, and so it sat itself down and cried. And there it sits now still—all alone.[1]

I end this grim conclusion with a brief reference to Wolfgang Borchert's recent radio play, *The Man Outside*, perhaps the most radical tragedy of Nihilism which appeared in Europe after the end of the last War. Borchert was born in Hamburg and died in 1947 at the age of twenty-six. *The Man Outside* is the drama of a German prisoner of war who returns from Siberia to shattered Germany. His parents are dead, his home is destroyed. His compatriots do not want him. There is no room for him any-where in a world of apocalyptic destruction. It is the old theme of the homecomer (cf. *Wunder um Verdun*, 1930, by Hans von Chlumberg), written in a revue-like sequence of scenes and in the style of expressionist drama. The figures in the play are nameless: *the* undertaker, *the* old-man, *a* girl, *her* husband, *a* colonel, *his* wife, *his* daughter, *his* son-in-law, *a* cabaret-pro-ducer, *a* roadsweeper; only Frau Kramer and the River Elbe are named.

Borchert herewith presents a world, morally lost, a state of hysterical mass-man, a Europe of unspeakable misery and cynicism, neither of which can give an answer to any of the burning problems which beset our mind. Büchner's *Danton's Death* is still a great drama, but with the above play by Borchert European Nihilism has reached its total negation of human existence, and at the same time, the end of true tragedy.

Since Darwin and now after 1914 and 1939 many writers do not believe in the ultimate goodness of nature any more, nor in a golden age, not in a 'hortus conclusus' which shelters us from the apocalyptic vision of destruction in an age of science and ideological wars—the 'forest fears' (cf. Kenneth Clark,

[1] *Woyzeck*, Scene 21.

Landscape into Art) are written in our faces—therefore now, more than ever, the artist needs faith in life, in the sanctity of our human existence, confidence in nature as a source of consolation, mystery and inspiration in spite of insoluble conflict and suffering which we must accept.

True tragedy can only breathe in a world of human values to which we must return if we do not wish to perish.

IX

Georg Trakl

AN AUSTRIAN POET (1887-1914)

In order really to be a great genius a man must be the
exception. But in order that his being exceptional should
be a serious matter he himself must be unfree, forced into
the position. There lies the importance of his dementia.
There is a definite point in which he suffers; it is impossible for him to run with the herd. That is his torture.

Translated by A. Dru, The
Journal of Søren Kierkegaard, 1850

GEORG TRAKL, THE passionate admirer of Dostoevsky, is a
true child of his tormented era. He was only twenty-
seven years old when in the beginning of the First World
War, sick in spirit as in body, he died in the military hospital
at Cracaw. One year before he had completed his first volume
of poems. Of his work, as of his life, nothing is left but fragments,
yet they testify to his genius.

A native of Salzburg in Austria, Georg Trakl was by profession a dispensing chemist. Quite early in his career he fell a
victim to alcohol and drugs. Since his death in 1914 the little
volume of verse in the Inselbücherei *Gesang des Abgeschiedenen*
had, for some time, become almost the only means of rescuing
his name from oblivion, for the public was practically un-
acquainted with the volume of Trakl's collected verse published
in 1919 (Gesamtausgabe). None the less, Georg Trakl, like
Georg Heym and Kurt Heynicke, is incontestibly one of the most
significant lyric poets figuring in the expressionist anthology,
MenschheitsDämmerung (1920).

He shares their macabre hankering for the morbid and
terrible, for death and decay. In Trakl, however, these are
mingled with tender melancholy which none the less cannot
be dismissed as mere traits of decadence and irresponsible

aestheticism, but should be considered far more as a prophetic warning on the eve of cataclysm, an admonition—media vita in morte sumus—in the midst of satiety and smugness. Under the light of the autumnal moon the rats emerge from the latrines and scurry through the rich granaries (cf. his poem, *Die Ratten*).

Georg Trakl's poetry is not so simply explained away, as some would have us believe, by references to the hallucination of alcoholic and narcotic addiction, or the general decadence of a fin-du-siècle period, even though his images often reveal an obsession with disintegration; cf. Charles Pierre Baudelaire's *Une Charogne*, Richard Dehmel's *Der tote Hund*, Franz Werfel's *Jesus und der Äserweg* (also here as in Dehmel we find the motif of all-embracing Christian love that does not shun even a decaying carcass); moreover, Gottfried Benn's *Mann und Frau gehn durch die Krebsbaracke* and Georg Heym's morbid description of Ophelia's corpse, her hair floating in a nest of young water-rats in *Ophelia*, or Heym's poem, *Die Morgue*.

Likewise, Trakl betrays that hatred of the metropolis so typical of his age, e.g. in *Abendland* ('You mighty cities, built of stone . . .'), a poem that in the rich suggestiveness of its metaphors reminds one of Hölderlin's rhythm, and which may perhaps rank as Trakl's most poignant vision of the Götterdämmerung threatening our civilization: 'You dying peoples! Pallid wave breaking on the shore of night, falling stars.'

Whilst the German naturalists, e.g. Julius Hart, and some impressionists, e.g. Johannes Schlaf, author of the novel, *Das dritte Reich*, greeted the city Berlin with jubilation, Rilke and Hugo von Hofmannsthal fled from it with horror. Thus Rilke in his poem, *Denn Herr, die großen Städte sind/Verlorene und Aufgelöste* . . . speaks of townspeople who live anxiously and evilly. Hugo von Hofmannsthal is moved to his poignant lamentation in the *Ballade des äußeren Lebens*, whilst the apocalyptic ecstasy of expressionism breaks out in curses on the 'daemon' of the metropolis, e.g. the distorted imagery of Ernst Stadler in *Judenviertel in London*; Johannes R. Becher in his poem *Berlin* invokes the monster spider (Spinnenungeheuer) Berlin; Georg Heym in *Der Gott der Stadt* describes the furious god Baal sitting astride a block of houses, the big towns kneeling round him:

'Er streckt ins Dunkel seine Fleischerfaust. Er schüttelt sie. Ein
Meer von Feuer jagt durch eine Straße. . . .'

Just as the metropolis with its desert of houses (Riesenstädte,
Häusermeer, Steinwüste) sapped his spirit, war drained the
life-blood from Trakl's heart:

> . . . umfängt die Nacht
> sterbende Krieger, die wilde Klage
> ihrer zerbrochenen Münder. . . .

*The night embraces dying warriors, the wild lament of their shattered
mouths.*

Like Stefan George's poem *Auf stiller stadt lag fern ein blutiger
streif,* Trakl's *Grodek* is one of the few war poems that are both
really poetic and emotionally convincing, fraught with terrible
apprehension and illuminating vision. Free in rhythm and
conceived at first in an elegiac tone, it is whipped up in the
second half to a fearful cry of accusation. None the less, this
wild lament of the fallen is, as a whole, held subdued beneath
the pall of a dark, autumnal melancholy. The poem, is, moreover, distinguished through effective alliteration and preg-
nancy of expression suggesting at times an affinity with
Klopstock and particularly with Hölderlin.

Here, as in other songs, the landscape is symbolized, e.g. *Ein
Winterabend.* In this way, Trakl, in a few broad strokes, often
conjures up spiritual landscapes over which broods an atmosphere of horror; thus in *Der Herbst des Einsamen* :

> . . . Es rauscht das Rohr; anfällt ein knöchern Grauen,
> Wenn schwarz der Tau tropft von den kahlen Weiden.

> *The reed rustles; a bony horror snatches*
> *when black the dew drips from the bare willows.*

This is probably one of his profoundest poems. Slight reminiscences of George ('. . . ein reines Blau . . .') and Hölderlin
('. . . gekeltert ist der Wein . . .') in no way detract from its
originality. The simple delineation of the autumnal images is
characteristic as are above all the use of sound and colour
symbols (Frucht-Fülle, blaudunkel-schwarz), the feminine
rhymes and the haunting reiteration of the word 'leise' in each
verse.[1]

[1] cf. Irene Morris, *Georg Trakl,* German Life and Letters, 1949, II, No. 2.

Trakl's stylistic idiosyncrasies are found in his essentially musical rhythms, in such favourite words as: dunkel, einsam, golden, purpurn, kristallen, dämmernd, versteinert, monden (adj.), Hyazinthe, Verwesung, Weiher, etc., in a predilection for certain colours (cf. *Ein Winterabend* or *Frauensegen*) and again in the following suggestive images: ein Brunnen singt=a fountain sings (*Musik in Mirabell*), des Abends blauer Flügel= the evening's blue wing, Brot und Wein=bread and wine, das hyazinthene Antlitz der Dämmerung=the hyazinthine countenance of twilight, die Lider schwer von Mohn=the lids heavy with poppy (*Unterwegs*). A favourite tree of his is the elderberry (*Sebastian im Traum*):

> Mutter trug das Kindlein im weißen Mond,
> Im Schatten des Nußbaums, uralten Holunders,
> Trunken vom Safte des Mohns, der Klage der Drossel....

Not infrequently a poem is modulated on *one* single or on a couple of tones. A proof of Trakl's true poetic power and insight is that, unlike the expressionistic Schreikünstler, he never rends the delicate web of his poem's atmosphere with a violent explosion but mitigates his most gruesome visions by a mellow ending; cf. his *Helian*:

> O ihr zerbrochenen Augen in schwarzen Mündern,
> Da der Enkel in sanfter Umnachtung
> Einsam dem dunkleren Ende nachsinnt,
> Der stille Gott die blauen Lider über ihn senkt.

> *O you shattered eyes in black mouths, whilst gently benighted*
> *the grandson lonely ponders on the darker end, the silent*
> *God closes the blue lids over his eyes.*

or the end in *Sebastian im Traum*:

> Tasten über die grünen Stufen des Sommers. O wie leise
> Verfiel der Garten in der braunen Stille des Herbstes,
> Duft und Schwermut des alten Holunders,
> Da in Sebastians Schatten die Silberstimme des Engels erstarb.

> *Groping over the green steps of summer. O how gently the garden*
> *decayed in the brown stillness of autumn, scent and melancholy of the old*
> *elderberry when the silver voice of the angel died in Sebastian's shadow.*

Like Hölderlin, Trakl seems to have felt that the poet is the passionate interpreter of sensual life, and that in song man reaches his highest fulfilment and transcends himself. While in his *Elegies* Rilke teaches us that through suffering Death transforms and completes our existence, and Stefan George hails in *Maximin* the personification of an ideal, thus also Trakl, in the short time granted him, rises high above the limits of pure aestheticism and proclaims his faith in poetry as a supreme power over the human heart.

X

Rainer Maria Rilke's Poetic Vision

Darkling I listen; and for many a time
I have been half in love with easeful Death.
KEATS, *Ode to a Nightingale*

I still think Rilke a great poet though I cannot read him any more.
W. H. AUDEN, *Making, Knowing and Judging* (1956).

R M. RILKE (1875-1926) has been enjoying a literary
vogue here and abroad for over a generation. Apart
from Goethe, Hölderlin, and Kafka, Rilke is, in the eyes
of the modern English-speaking intellectuals, perhaps the most
famous modern poet to have written in the German tongue,
although he hated the 'superpower' of the U.S.A. and was
very critical towards England herself. Although it cannot be
refuted that the *man* Rilke cannot vie with the artist Rilke,
and his tragedy seems to be that of Henrik Ibsen's *Master
Builder*, who could not climb as high as he built, as an
artist Rilke is no doubt ruthless and 'formidable'. 'The word
formidable . . . exactly describes Rilke's genius, which no one,
not even Rodin, could enslave for long . . . and against which
matrimonial, paternal, economic, and social claims were
powerless.'[1] Everything, even friendship, loyalty, marriage, is
sacrificed to his work. In a letter to Ludwig Ganghofer (16
April 1897) Rilkes writes: '. . . Not as martyrdom do I regard
art—but as a battle the chosen one has to wage with himself
and his environment. That needs a *whole* man! Not a few weary
leisure hours. . . .' And in a letter to Lou Andreas-Salomé
(11 August 1903) he maintains: 'Art is far too great and too
difficult and too long a thing for *one* life, and those who are of a
very great age are only just beginners in it. . . .' Hokusai,
Rodin, Leonardo, '. . . They always lived in their art and concentrated on the one thing, let all the rest become overgrown'.

[1] E. M. Butler, *Rainer Maria Rilke*, 1941, p. 417.

In this connexion we are reminded of Tolstoy's unedifying household or Rodin's domestic discomfort or of Cézanne, who would not go to his mother's funeral in order not to lose a working day. Finally, in a letter to Jakob Baron Uexküll (9 August 1909) he writes: 'The marvelling with which art flings itself upon things . . . must be so impetuous, so strong, so radiant, that the object has no time to think of its own ugliness or depravity. . . .'

Unfortunately, some hagiographers, particularly his many adoring women friends, have overestimated or distorted Rilke's art and personality. He was no 'Doctor Seraphicus' or 'Serafico', no Saint. But he was also not merely the poet of the Nuance (according to some critics, he knew only the nuance and no substance of realities). On the contrary, Rilke's poetic work has a profound message to tell us in our post-war age of lost values and mass psychology.

In a letter to Countess Aline Dietrichstein, August 1919 (translated by R. F. C. Hull), Rilke says: From the outset the *Man of the Spirit* must needs be the—

> opponent and controverter of all revolutions, it is precisely he who knows how slowly all changes of lasting significance come to completion . . . and how nature in her constructive activities, hardly anywhere brooks a spiritual violence. And yet on the other hand it is this same spiritual man, who by virtue of his insight, *grows impatient* when he sees the faulty and floundering conditions into which human affairs fall . . . how Life . . . is . . . crushed under a mass of irrelevant and effete superstructures: who then would not yearn for a *great storm* to tear down everything obstructive and decadent so as to make room again for the creative, infinitely youthful, infinitely benevolent powers?

Moreover, as to Nature and politics, both are interconnected in Rilke's life and thought. In Nature he found the totality of our existence. After the war Rilke had gone abroad, to Switzerland, in June 1919; he went to a country not immediately scarred by the war and not yet struck down as the rest of Europe by the predominance of ambition amongst power states. Rilke now felt stronger than ever that he could not be on anybody's side. In times of political unrest, he found intimate connexion with Nature again—a tree, a field, the grace of evening. He knew that 'there exists an unutterable bond between the quietly creating spirit and the holy, deep self absorption of Nature'. . . . We are all too often accustomed to excuse our own cruelty by invoking the cruelty in Nature, but, as Rilke says, man 'forgets how innocently even the most terrible things can happen in Nature, she does not look at them, does not hold aloof from them; in the Terrible she is entire, also her fruitfulness is in it, her magnanimity . . . she contains *everything*, she contains horror also'.

This totality in Nature is, according to Rilke, not understood by man who in times of social upheavals or in war becomes a one-sided inhuman being—'a raving madness, a gushing wound or a soulless automaton'. We may condemn Rilke for his selfishness, but we cannot afford to ignore his poetic vision.

Moreover, there is another significant feature, perhaps the most important one in Rilke's work, especially in his later *Duino Elegies* and *Sonnets*; it is faith in art, i.e. in the creative transformation of all 'things' in spite of decay and destruction. For him, the poet (or the artist in general) is the creative transformer who shapes a new reality out of a chaos of accidents, irrelevances, or brutalities. Rilke is no mystic. He believes in the actuality of earthly existence. But his poetic vision transforms it into a new reality which can claim permanence in a frail and transient world. Art is 'to be experienced as a great forgetting or as a greater insight' (letter to Countess Aline Dietrichstein, 1 November 1916), a step to a riper awareness. Rilke preaches neither intoxication nor renunciation: 'All the soarings of my mind begin in my blood.'[1]

His admiration for the *human* values of things which seem to possess a life of their own is well known.

In the famous letter to his Polish translator, Witold von Hulewicz, Rilke says about *'things'*: 'They are *our* possession and *our* friendship, knowing *our* wretchedness and *our* joy, but as they were the familiars of our ancestors. . . . Transform them? Yes, for such is our task; to impress this frail and transient world so sufferingly, so passionately on our hearts that its essence shall rise up again, in us, invisible. We are the bees of the Invisible. . . . We are the transmuters of the earth. . . .'

Transformation and acceptance of life—these are most

---

[1] *To a young girl,* about summer, 1921.

important visions through which Rilke the poet again and again
symbolized matter in his lyrical poetry, but which Rilke the
man could not always live up to. Nevertheless, not only his
art but his own life shows a remarkable power of permanence
and change. He was born in Prague, travelled to the south
and to Russia, lived in Worpswede with a little community of
artists whom he brought to public notice, and later became
a part-time secretary to Rodin in Paris.

There is a long road from Rilke's early lyrical effusions to his
late *Duino Elegies*. He *began* as an impressionist. In his first
poems echo the whispering of the trees, the raging of the storm,
the awakening of spring, and the murmuring of water. Yearning is the essence of Rilke's early poetry:

> This is yearning: to be borne on the wave
> And to have no home in the span of time.
> And these are desires: gentle dialogues
> Between the faint hours and eternity. . . .

But he later rejected such personal emotions: 'Those verses one
writes in youth aren't much.' He knew that he had to wait and
gather sweetness and light all his life, a long one if possible, and
then 'maybe at the end he might write ten good lines. . . .
Poetry isn't merely feelings (these come soon enough); it is
experiences.' In his second sonnet to Orpheus (1st part) Rilke
expresses this symbolically with the words 'Sie schlief die
Welt'. . . . Rilke knew that in order to create, the poet's
emotion must be transfused into form. In a famous passage in
his novel *Malte Laurids Brigge* Rilke elucidates the poet's task:
'every poet must be able to think back the way to old places . . .
to partings long foreseen, to days of childhood . . . to days on
the sea . . . to nights of travel . . . many nights of love, not two
alike . . . one must have sat by the dying . . . but it is not enough
to have memories. One must be able to forget them and have
vast patience until they come again.' The later Rilke rightly
calls his poems experiences. In order to be able to write poetry,
he says, one must visit cities, and must get to know men and
things, must observe gestures, follow the flight of the birds and
know how the flowers grow; a poet must command his imagination. His feelings must be transformed by his creative impulse.
It must be born of an inner necessity. Russia (Tolstoy), Lower

Saxony (Worpswede), France (Rodin and Paul Valéry), Spain (Toledo), Egypt, the landscapes of Switzerland and of Duino on the Adriatic, where he enjoyed the generous hospitality of Princess Marie von Thurn and Taxis-Hohenlohe, whom he had met in 1909 for the first time—these countries, persons and places became not only stimulating sensations, but also important media, experiences, and symbols for his poetic expression.

In spite of the apparent variety of expression, there is a distinct keynote in all his artistic development under the decisive influence of Russia, the European capitals, the War years, and afterward in Duino and Muzot. The keynote is his relentless will to overcome suffering by *accepting* it. As Dante sought fulfilment in Beatrice's love, and Hölderlin in a reconciliation between Greece and Christianity, Nietzsche in the eternal recurrence of existence, so Rilke in the patient acceptance of evil and death until in the end lament transformed itself into ecstatic praise: 'Hiersein ist herrlich. . . . Die Adern voll Dasein . . . wo doch das sichtbare Glück uns erst zu erkennen sich gibt, wenn wir es innen verwandeln. Nirgends, Geliebte, wird Welt sein als innen' = (7th Elegy): 'Life here's glorious! . . . Veins full of existence . . . the most visible joy can only reveal itself to us when we've transformed it, within. Nowhere, beloved, can world exist but *within*.'[1] This clearly indicates how Rilke surrenders to life by re-creating it inwardly.

From Rilke's mouth such a eulogy of our early existence is indeed heroic, it is particularly so in our age of depersonalization, when, as K. Kippenberg says, we use the railway instead of the horse, or when we don't fetch water from the well in which by day the sun and by night the moon are reflected—but unromantically from the water tap, or when, Rilke laments, men as well as women in concert hall and museums and exhibitions behave like whores eager to enjoy and to take, but not to conceive, or when human beings although herded together in a metropolis are haunted by its monotony and utter loneliness, as depicted in his *Malte Laurids Brigge*, that subtle but terrible indictment of our anxious and lascivious civilization.

Rilke is certainly its offspring, and he inherited its morbid

[1] Trans. by J. B. Leishman and Stephen Spender.

tendencies. His mother made things worse by bringing him up wrongly. For five years she foolishly brought him up and treated him as a girl, she made him play with dolls and gave him girls as companions, made him perform little household tasks. His clothes were those of a girl; he even, we are told, had 'the most delicate underclothes'. He grew long curls. Rilke took a long, very long time to recover, if he ever recovered, from the shock when his father suddenly plunged him into the other extreme, i.e. into the harsh discipline of a military academy. In his brilliant essay, *Reluctant Admiration: a Note on Auden and Rilke*, D. J. Enright remarks that 'Rilke occasionally enervated his work through an excessive horror of vulgarity; Auden has frequently damaged his through an excessive horror of seeming refined'.[1]

Journeys, friends and an uncanny single-mindedness beneath an apparently aimless waiting or receptive drifting shaped Rilke's poetic inspiration. Rilke's first supreme experience was his contact with Russia and Tolstoy. In the latter he discovered a unique awareness of life penetrated with death: 'that ugly cup with the broken handle and the meaningless inscription: Faith, Hope, Love, from which a bitterness of undiluted death had to be drunk'.[2] His famous Stunden-Buch (*Book of Hours*) to a great extent was conceived when in 1899-1900 he travelled twice with Lou (who was also Nietzsche's friend) to Russia: on the first visit they met Tolstoy in Moscow and were overpowered by 'the prototype of the eternal Russian'.[3] On the second visit they looked him up in Yasnaya Polyana. Alas, this time Lou and Rilke were not welcome; Countess Tolstoy, in an ill mood, tried to frustrate their plan. The unwelcome and hungry visitors had to wait in the hall for some time. They heard angry voices and crying. When Tolstoy appeared at last they were not invited to a meal, but Tolstoy accompanied them for a walk, offering them a choice between food and the women, or Tolstoy alone and no food, and no women. They chose spiritual instead of material refreshment.

The above *Stunden-Buch*, a collection of poems, also partly

---

[1] *Essays in Criticism*, 1952, pp. 194-5.
[2] *Later Poems*, translated by J. B. Leishman.
[3] Nora Wydenbruck, *Rilke, Man and Poet*.

inspired by Rilke's former visit to Florence and his stay in Worpswede in the lovely house on the moor, is a modern book of devotion. Amid the vast loneliness of the Russian steppes he meditates on human destiny. He loves not the harsh light of day, but the twilight of solitude and death. For him the modern city breeds falsehood, its children are but shadows, and the multitude becomes a herd, but the poet bursts these barriers in his striving towards God.

The images in the *Book of Hours* several times remind us of the language of mystics:

> He loves God like his own son.
>
> His soul is like a woman before God.
>
> God is his heir.

The poet with self-effacing endeavour seeks to fathom the mystery of all things. Alas, he realizes that we are always frustrated, because we always mean *ourselves*—even when we love. We speak of *our* flowers, *our* house, *our* dog, *our* lover and *our* friend, although we cannot possess anything. Every one of us harbours his own death in himself. Progress is an illusion; so is life in the metropolis. Rilke is attracted and repelled by modern cities. They are filled with deception, yet again and again God scatters us among their luring lairs. Man is lonely. But the God of the *Book of Hours* is not transcendental; He promises no world beyond; there is no prophecy; His identity is replaced by poetic symbols: cf. E. C. Mason's thoughtful statement: 'In Wirklichkeit handelt es sich aber nur darum, daß Rilke das Gottsymbol erschöpft und durch andere ersetzt hat . . . Die Ehrfurcht vor sich selber ist der Zopf des Münchhausen.'[1]

With bold imagery, Rilke depicts his God as the neighbour, 'der raunend Verrußte':

> You, neighbour God . . . I always listen. Give but a
> small sign. I am quite near.
> There is but a thin wall between us . . . and my senses,
> which all too soon grow lame, are separated from
> you and homeless. . . .

The God in his *Book of Hours* is no mediator. Rilke dismisses the

[1] E. C. Mason, *Der Zopf des Münchhausen*, Einsiedeln, 1949, pp. 73 and 68.

orthodox idea of Christ the Redeemer. There is no mention of
original sin in the strict sense of the Catholic Church; there
is in Rilke's poetry, therefore, no necessity for atonement. In
the godless metropolis, which is more a hospital or a stony
desert than a town, demons hold sway over human beings.

Rilke's further decisive experiences were Worpswede and
Paris, where he came under the spell of Rodin and Paul
Valéry.

Returning from Russia, Rilke had settled in Worpswede in
the Low German Lüneburg Heath from 1900 to 1901, where in
1901 he married the sculptress Clara Westhoff, a pupil of
Rodin, who had a studio there and belonged to the Worpswede
School of Painters.

It was in the 'Romantic' period of his development that he
met Clara, whom he describes impressively: 'She was wearing
a gown of white batiste without corsets in the Empire style,
girded high under the breasts and falling in long, smooth pleats.
Her fine, dark face was framed by cloudy black hair which
flowed over her cheeks in open ringlets, her coiffure according
with the style of her dress. . . .'

Clara bore him a daughter. Rilke, however, was tempera-
mentally as well as financially incapable of sustaining or even
living a family life. He went to Paris, where he became a part-
time private secretary of Rodin (1902-6). Thus the greatest
modern French sculptor and, next to Stefan George, the greatest
modern German poet came into close contact with each other.
Alas, this relationship was doomed to be a one-sided one, as
Rodin did not understand the German language and was
therefore debarred from appreciating the depth of Rilke's
poetic vision. But for hours Rilke watched the sculptor at his
work, and many of Rilke's *Neue Gedichte* show clear evidence of
the poet's turn towards objectivity.

After about four years Rodin's overpowering and volcanic
personality led to the ungracious dismissal of Rilke, when the
latter had failed to report a letter to him. This was, of course,
only the outward, casual symptom of a deeper reason. Both
later became reconciled again, forgetting the rupture which
had caused their estrangement. Rilke's letter to Rodin at the
time of the break (May 1906) shows unique tact and real

greatness of character. He writes: 'Mon maître . . . I understand that the wise organism of your life must reject immediately what seems harmful to it in order to keep its functions
intact. . . . I am persuaded that there exists no other man of
my own age (in France or elsewhere) equipped like myself—by
temperament and through study—to understand you, to understand your great life and to appreciate it so scrupulously. We
were agreed that in life there is an innate justice which is
accomplished slowly but surely. In that justice I repose all my
hopes; one day it will repair the wrong which you have
thought fit to inflict on one who has no longer either the
means or the right to reveal his heart to you.'[1] He understood
Rodin intimately indeed. Rilke saw that Rodin was solitary
before fame came to him; afterwards he became perhaps still
more solitary. 'For fame is ultimately but the summary of all
misunderstandings that crystallize about a new name.'

'. . . Rodin's message and its significance are little understood by the many men who gathered about him. It would be a
long and weary task to enlighten them; nor is this necessary,
for they assembled about the name, not about the work, a
work that has grown far beyond this name's sound and limitations, and that has become nameless as a plain is nameless or a
sea that has a name but on the map, in books, and to men, but
which is, in reality, but distance, movement and depth. . . .'

Rodin the craftsman and Rodin the man had no doubt profoundly influenced Rilke. Through him Rilke was confirmed
in his belief in work *and* patience—'il faut travailler, rien que
travailler, il faut avoir patience'. And in a letter to Clara
(5 May 1902) analysing Rodin's art principles, he agrees with
them: 'You should not think of wanting to *do* anything, you
should only try to build up your own means of expression so as
to say everything. You should work and have patience. Look
neither to the right nor left. Draw your whole life into this
circle, having *nothing* outside this life. As Rodin has done. . . .
You must choose . . . Either happiness or art'; and Rilke's letter
to Lou Andreas-Salomé (8 August 1903) about Rodin, sees
even deeper, when he now rejects the poetic *dream* but advocates
objectivity: 'The *thing* is definite, the *art-thing* must still be more

---

[1] Trans. by Hull.

definite; removed from all accident, reft away from all obscurity, withdrawn from time and given over to space, it has become enduring, capable of eternity. The model *seems*, the *art object is. . . .*'

Apart from Rodin, Rilke fell under the spell of another great Frenchman, Paul Valéry, some of whose poems he translated. I have referred to Rilke's fame amongst our modern European intellectuals. He was not only a sensitive translator of André Gide, Paul Valéry, Elizabeth Barrett Browning (*Sonnets from the Portuguese*), but his own work found most gifted and eminent interpreters and translators in France (Maurice Betz and J. F. Angelloz, etc.), and in many other European countries. Of course, the jibe is often only too true—'traductore traditore' (translator, a traitor), for we may instance how difficult it is to translate such words as Urleid (douleur originelle), Leidland (pays de la douleur), etc.

Rilke's language is as difficult as that of his revered French friend Paul Valéry, whose *Eupalinos* Rilke translated into German. Both poets have much in common; Paul Valéry (l'homme de verre), like Rilke in his *Duino Elegies*, endeavours to reconcile analysis and ecstasy—'enchaîner une analyse à une ecstase. . . .'. Both admire the unity of science and art in a Leonardo da Vinci; both matured late, Valéry after long years and serious study of mathematics, Rilke after many years and incessant occupation with foreign languages. Of course, there are essential differences between the two: Rilke lacks Valéry's extraordinary plasticity, while Valéry lacks Rilke's gentle power of empathy. Rilke's new development is clearly reflected in his new poems. Thus in his description of man and beast (e.g. in *The Panther*) he endeavours to penetrate to the essence of all being:

> His eye has become so tired from passing the bars that it can take in nothing more. It seems to him as though there were a thousand bars, and behind the thousand bars no world. The supple tread of lithe and strong steps, revolving round and round in smallest circles, is like a dance of strength around a centre in which lives a mighty, but numb, will. Only now and then is the veil of the pupil slightly raised. Then an image enters, quivers through the tensed stillness of the limbs, and ceases to be, on reaching the heart.[1]

[1] My prose translation can hardly do justice to this famous poem.

This and other poems reflect the fundamental developments in Rilke's new artistic vision: art to him is the humblest service, not stimulation from outside, but inner intensity. Art is 'founded absolutely upon law'. Art is an actualization, 'diametrically opposed to music, which transforms the apparent realities of the daily world and still further de-actualizes them into insubstantial, ephemeral appearances', says Rilke. He now creates with intellect and ardour:

> 'No intellect, no ardour is redundant:'
> to make one through the other more abundant
> is what we're for, and some are singled out
> for purest victory in this contention;
> no signal can escape their tried attention,
> their hands are wieldy and their weapons stout.
>
> No sound must be too soft for their detection,
> they must perceive that angle of deflection
> to which the dial-pointer scarcely stirs,
> and must, as might be with their eyelids, utter
> reply to what the butterflies out-flutter,
> and learn to fathom what a flower infers.
>
> No less than others they can be extinguished,
> And yet they must (why else were they distinguished?)
> feel even with catastrophe some kin,
> and, while the rest are helplessly bewailing,
> recapture in the strokes of each assailing
> the rhythm of some stoniness within.
>
> They must be stationed like a shepherd keeping
> his lonely watch: one might suppose him weeping,
> till, coming close, one feels his piercing sight;
> and as for him the speech of stars is clear,
> for them must be as intimately near
> what climbs in still procession through the night.
>
> In slumber also they continue seers:
> from dream and being, from laughter and from tears
> a meaning gathers, which, if they can seize
> and kneel to life and death in adoration,
> another measure for the whole creation
> is given us in those right-angled knees.[1]

It is the poetic vision which counts, but a vision fortified by intellect. At this stage of his artistic development Rilke has reached real greatness.

[1] Trans. by J. B. Leishman.

Now he wants to condense. In his book *Rodin* there are some unique observations which proved R. Kassner's view that Rilke's genius was primarily visual and not musical. Many of his images are strikingly visual: see, for instance, the passage: 'But hands are . . . a delta in which much life from distant sources flows together and is poured into the great stream of action', or Rilke's Baum-symbol: the tree as image of pure existence in the *Sonnets to Orpheus* (Sonnets 1 and 2).

But we can easily see in the above lines, and particularly in the poems, *Panther, Römische Fontäne, Karussell, Kapitäl*, etc., that Rilke cannot do without any associations altogether. But as an artist he tries to sink himself into a given object. Already in his *Book of Hours* he thus rescued his vulnerable soul from chaos or nihilism or irony by the creative love of things.

In his *Letters to a Young Poet* Rilke expresses his inmost thoughts which testify to the maturity which he has now reached as an artist. He rejects irony and subjectivity:

> I wanted to say two further things to you today: *irony!* Do not let yourself be governed by it, especially not in unproductive moments. In productive ones try to make use of it as one more means of seizing life. Used purely, it is itself pure, and one need not be ashamed of it; and when you feel too familiar with it, when you fear the growing intimacy with it, then turn towards great and serious subjects, before which it becomes small and helpless. Seek for the depth of things: there irony never descends—and when you have thus brought it to the edge of greatness, test at the same time whether this mode of perception springs from a necessity of your being. For under the influences of serious things it will either fall away from you (if it is something non-essential), or else it will (if it belongs to you innately) with gathering strength become a serious tool and be ranked among the means by which you will have to form your art.
>
> And the second thing that I wanted to tell you today is this: Only a few of all my books are indispensable to me, and two of these are actually always among my things wherever I am. Even here they are round me: the Bible, and the books of the great Danish writer, Jens Peter Jacobsen . . . to await with deep humility and patience the hour of birth of a new clarity: that is alone what living as an artist means: in understanding as in creation.
>
> There is no measuring by time there, a year there has no meaning, and ten years are nothing. To be an artist means: not to reckon and count: to ripen like the tree which does not force its sap and stands confident in the storms of spring without fear lest

no summer might come after. It does come. But it comes only
to the patient ones, who are there as if eternity lay in front of
them, so unconcernedly still and far. I am learning it daily, learning it through pains to which I am grateful: patience is all! . . .[1]

Rilke now demands sacrifices from the artist who can only
achieve that objectivity by waiting for the inner necessity of his
creative impulse. Rilke thus could not and did not want to
help the young poets who had not yet discovered their own self,
because 'what is prematurely sown does not come up'.[2] Some
of Rilke's best images arise out of this patient waiting for the
hour of change: 'Who talks of victory, to endure is all', he states
in the *Requiem*; and, thinking of the young poet, i.e. the tragic
Graf von Kalckreuth who, overcome by the brutal ugliness
of life, shot himself at the age of twenty, Rilke (in the said
Requiem) condemns subjectivity and asks the poets to transform
their emotions, not to pour them out defencelessly. Instead of
lament he demands with determination its transformation
into the poetic word:

> wie sich der Steinmetz einer Kathedrale
> verbissen umsetzt in den Steines Gleichmut.
>
> *doggedly, as the carver of a cathedral*
> *transfers himself to the stone's constancy.*[3]

In this preparedness and self-denying single-mindedness lies the
promise. Hence Rilke's rejection of suicide:

> Why could you not have waited till the point
> where heaviness grows unbearable: where it turns,
> being now so heavy because so real? Do you see,
> this might perhaps have come with your next moment;
> perhaps that moment was even then adjusting
> its garland before your door when you flung it to.

Instead of throwing one's life away, the poet can, according to
Rilke's message, save his self from a disenchanted 'collective'
and 'factual' world by accepting and transmuting the latter
into a 'realm of poetic symbols'.

The precise 'factual' world of our intellect is certainly not the
true, i.e. *total* world. How often this has been proved in history

[1] Trans. by R. Snell. [2] Cf. also *Letters of R.M.R.*, translated by H. Norton.
[3] Trans. by Leishman.

and particularly in the last two Wars! In spite of all faultless planning, some mysterious and incalculable accident occurs and destroys the seemingly unconquerable edifice. Rilke compares our existence to a game of ball—we throw the ball, which, however, keeps falling back into our hands. He also favours the motif of the mirror, emphasizing thus the difference between appearance and reality—a conflict which inspires him to praise and lament.

The ten *Duino Elegies*, which are not poetry in the accepted sense of the word, but which can truly be called gigantic thought-images, philosophical landscapes, and compelling visions rather than lyrical poetry, revolve round that central idea of appearance and reality, praise and lament.

The first two *Elegies*, written ten years (1912) before the completion of the whole cycle of elegies (1922), confront man with relentless barriers. On earth there is nothing but dissonance and solitariness: we are not secure at home 'within our interpreted world'. Only those whose love has never found consummation know the mysteries of our existence. 'For our heart transcends us' ('Denn das eigene Herz übersteigt uns'): we must free ourselves from the loved one, because there is no tarrying; cf. also Rilke's *Departure of the Prodigal Son* in which the biblical story is given a new interpretation: 'the legend of one who did *not wish* to be loved'.

The third *Elegy* deals with the conflict between pure love and sexual passion—'that hidden guilty river-god of the blood'. . . The fourth *Elegy* sings the praise of the sure instinct and of childlike single-mindedness; alas, we have lost the happy unity of feeling and thinking. The hours of childhood are gone. 'We comprehend flowering and fading simultaneously . . . we, though, while we're intent upon one thing, can feel the cost and conquest of another. Hostility's our first response.'[1]

But by using his will-power, man like the acrobat in the circus (fifth *Elegy*) can set free spiritual forces. So does also the hero. His fleeting span of existence (sixth *Elegy*) is foretold in the stars. We, however, linger here on earth; only the hero is strangely near to the dead.

The poet must renounce such glorious fruition (seventh

[1] Trans. by J. B. Leishman.

Elegy). His heroism lies in his humble acceptance of our existence, yet he has the power of transforming our world through
inwardness, and thus to turn suffering to praise: 'Life is
glorious'—'Hiersein ist herrlich.' . . . 'All veins full of existence'—'Alles. Die Adern voll Dasein.' . . . 'Nowhere, beloved,
can world exist but within.'—'Nirgends, Geliebte, wird Welt
sein als innen.' Man's art can triumph over nature—'Chartres
was great—and music reached still higher and transcended us'.

This elegy of praise is followed once more by one (eighth
Elegy) of lament over man's limitations, because our Destiny
means: 'being opposite, and nothing else, and always opposite'
—'gegenüber sein und nichts als das und immer gegenüber'.
Here all is 'distance'.

But we love and must love our circumscribed individual
existence (ninth *Elegy*). We must affirm this 'once and no more'
of our individuality, which is our happiness, because, as Rilke
says, 'being here means so much. . . . Just *once*, everything, only
for *once*. *Once* and no more. And we, too, *once*. And never again.
But this having been *once*, though only *once*'—this is irrevocable,
it is our deepest concern.

In the last *Elegy*, the elegy on death, the poet's praise of life
is balanced by his affirmation and acceptance of sorrow and
death. These visions of the city of suffering (Leid-Stadt), the
original pain (Urleid), and the spacious landscape of lament
(weite Landschaft der Klage) are unique in our modern
European literature.

Rilke the poet, we see, does not want us to escape from
reality, he accepts life and death as a unity. But the transient
matter must become *invisible in us* through the above power of
transformation. This is the keynote of one of the most important
letters Rilke wrote to his Polish translator, Witold von Hulewicz, about the *Duino Elegies* in November 1925. I have
already referred to this letter when explaining Rilke's conception of 'things' which he creatively transforms. The *Elegies* show
him engaged on this work: 'the work of the perpetual transformation of beloved and tangible things into the invisible
vibration and excitability of our nature . . . we build in this
way not only intensities of a spiritual kind, but, who knows?
new bodies, metals, nebulae and stars. And this activity is

sustained and accelerated by the increasingly rapid disappear-
ance today of so much of the Visible which we cannot replace.
Even for our grandfathers a house, a fountain, a familiar tower,
their very clothes, their coat was infinitely more, infinitely more
intimate; almost every object a vessel in which they found some
thing human or added their morsel of humanity. Now, from
America, empty indifferent things crowd over to us, counterfeit
things, the veriest dummies. A house, in the American sense, an
American apple or one of the vines of that country has nothing
in common with the house, the fruit, the grape into which have
entered the hope and meditation of our forefathers. The lived
and living things, the things that share our thoughts, these are
on the decline and can no more be replaced. *We are perhaps the
last to have known such things.* The responsibility rests with us not
only to keep remembrance of them (that would be but a trifle
and unreliable), but also their human or "laric" value ("laric"
in the sense of household gods). The earth has no alternative
but to become invisible—in us, who with a portion of our being
have a share in the Invisible, or at least the appearance of
sharing; we who can multiply our possessions of the Invisible
during our earthly existence, in us alone there can be accomplished this intimate and continual transmutation of the Visible
into the Invisible . . . just as our own destiny becomes unceas-
ingly more present, and at the same time invisible, in us.' This
call for *inwardness* reveals Rilke's inmost message to us. No doubt,
it has a tragic ring. Before the Angel we human beings are
annihilated, but at the same time we feel that our task is not in
vain. Thus there is a promise of happiness in sorrow. The poetic
image of that joy is enshrined in the smile of the self-sacrificing
artist. Like the acrobat in the Fifth *Elegy* we experience joy
amongst tears:

> . . . Your smile.
> Angel, Oh take it, pluck it, that small flowered herb of healing!
> Shape a vase to preserve it. Set it among those joys
> not yet open to us: in a graceful urn
> praise it, with florally soaring inscription:
> 'Subrisio Saltat.'[1]

[1] *Duino Elegies*, trans. by J. B. Leishman and Stephen Spender.

XI

Stefan George's 'Third Humanism'

Steinur brestur fyri manna tungu
Stones break before the tongue of man.
FAROESE PROVERB

WHEN A HUMAN being has passed away, said H. von
Hofmannsthal, he takes with him a mystery—the
mystery of how it was possible for him to live. In the
case of Stefan George it is the secret of his creative expression.
   George conjured up the power of the word and the grace of
form in our world of material things:

> Kein ding sei wo das wort gebricht.
> *A thing which lacks the word must go.*[1]

Against the illusion of progress George announces his belief in
the totality of the human being who strives for God until he
'grasps' Him.
   'Wir gingen einer entstellten und erkalteten menschheit
entgegen . . . Massen schufen gebot und regel . . .' writes George
in the Preface to *Maximin* (1906). Thus the loneliness of the poet
is necessary and desired:

> Menschlich glück verschwor ich um dein lied
> Fügte mich der not des wandertums . . .
>
> *Scouted trifling pleasure for your song,*
> *Took the yoke of pilgrimage upon me.*[2]

This wandering was not without a goal. A plan lay behind all
his work. In 1934 in his *Erinnerungen an Stefan George*, G. Bondi,
George's publisher and friend, showed that the things of practical life were not foreign to the poet, and that Stefan George
travelled a carefully mapped-out road not as a bourgeois, yet

[1] *Das Neue Reich*, trans. by O. Marx and E. Morwitz, from whose excellent
translation quotations are taken in this chapter.
[2] *Der Stern des Bundes.*

185

not completely as a bohemian. The hasty, somewhat cheap comparison with Goethe is based on mere external qualities.

To separate George's so-called 'Third Humanism' from Goethe's Classicism would be just as much a mistake as the fashion of placing the movements of German Naturalism, Impressionism, and Expressionism chronologically behind one another in the order of development. Moreover, our biological position is basically different from that of the Greeks and of Goethe's time. Every conception—for instance, that of Classicism or Humanism—is simultaneously an historic and aesthetic and psychological phenomenon, demanding in each case the most exact illumination, which cannot be obtained by the notorious 'tuning-fork' technique.

And yet in the sense of G. T. Fechner's *Büchlein vom Leben nach dem Tode* (1836) we may speak of a rebirth of German Hellenism, for a Goethe, a Schiller, a Luther still lived amongst us, in us, 'poured out through the world'. Poets such as Goethe and George have taught us to believe in the spiritual strength of the world. Our present existence is still deeply rooted in ancient culture, in Christianity and medieval history; moreover, George's works are unthinkable without the heritage of Goethe. But George's so-called Third Humanism does not allow any conclusions analogous to the Weimarer Klassik. Above all, the world around us undeniably shows an altered face.

In this connexion George's own utterances about Goethe are very significant—for instance, *Goethe-Tag* (*Der Siebente Ring*) and *Goethes Lezte Nacht in Italien* (*Das Neue Reich*). Both poems provide the key to George's concept of Goethe and at the same time to George's own creative work.

Already externally a sharp contrast between both poets is evident: Goethe rejects any normalization of his verse, whilst George weaves around his poetry the magic monotony of an incantation.

The *Goethe-Tag* is an indictment: On Goethe's birthday, 28 August, crowds pilgrim to Weimar. But George, in the early hours of the morning, pays his visit to Goethe's house in order to pay his homage silently before the arrival of the visitors, who are curious and greedy for sensation. They only desire to see themselves reflected and glorified in Weimar's fame. Before

George, Schopenhauer had already shown up the inane Goethe cult of the so-called cultured mass of people. George himself is no less bitter. If Goethe returned to us, he would pass us by as a king unknown and unrecognized:

> Und wenn Goethe nun aufstünde,
> Wer dann ehrte ihn? er ginge
> Ein könig ungekannt an euch vorbei. . . .

Only the all too human Goethe often finds response in justification of one's own life. Even the image of the 'Olympian' Goethe is a deception. The real Goethe remains a mystery: What, complains George, does the mob know of the struggles of the child in Frankfurt, of the bitter restlessness of the youth, of the suffering of the man behind a happy guise? We are reminded here of the words of Schopenhauer that he in whom genius lives, suffers most; suffering is the spring of creation. But Schopenhauer sees in Goethe the star of salvation, a marvel of nature who became our 'redeemer' and the 'cross-bearer' of humanity, whereas George regards Goethe as one who after a successful struggle somehow rises triumphant over the tide of Fate.

George's pessimistic outcry against modern civilization is not the only one. Paul Ernst, the acrid judge of our 'barbarous' age, placed the end of humanity in the autumns of the lives of Goethe and Hegel, and maintained that since 1830 the spirit of Europe was dead; what has been since that is a realm of imitators: 'The World War of 1914 was the death sentence of Europe.' Paul Ernst was, however, like George, an opponent of O. Spengler's prophecy of general decay, and he even dedicated to youth the first edition of the work he wrote during the War, *Der Zusammenbruch des deutschen Idealismus,* but subsequently gave up his belief in youth as a 'romantic illusion', as only the individual, the really great and solitary being could lead us into a hopeful future.

Similar indications are reflected in George's work—for instance, in the poem *Goethes Lezte Nacht in Italien,* which is at the same time George's self-portrait. It begins with an impressive landscape. Near the southern sea, where the pines stretch up their black wings and a single silver star gleams in the blue

of the night, Goethe is the witness of an eternal oath of loyalty
between two youths. The oath is carried by the fragrant
breeze over the slumbering land and the whispering sea:

> ... der duftige wind
> über das schlummernde land und die raunende see.

It is Goethe's hour of departure. Upon Italian soil he, the
'echteste Erbe' of his race, feels poverty of the innermost soul.
Here he becomes a man for the first time, and he cries out to his
fellow countrymen the words from his heart:

> ... Nicht nur in tropfen. Nein traget auch fürder in strömen
> von eurem blute das edelste jenseit der ferge ....

> *Over the mountains you still shall continue to lavish*
> *Not only drops of your knightliest blood, but a torrent.*
> *This be your share and your task until you are freed ...*

for Fortune had granted them no real son of Gäa, no earthly
prophet. Goethe himself was only her indirect descendant; he
does not dare descend into the abysses of the horrid guardians
to tear from them the magic spell. Yet the sparks of divine
existence did flame up in Goethe. He, too, was touched by
holy awe. It was when still a boy that he spent a Bacchus
festival with wild abandon amongst the garlanded vine-
growers of the Rhine, and when he passed from the 'land of
dreams and music', from the land of ornate German cathedrals
into the land of the sunny south. Now he bears the 'living ray',
the knowledge of the body's beauty and of heavenly law,
back into his misty homeland. But in the distant future the
longing for the South will be satisfied once more in Maximin:
'einem knaben den ihr zum gott erhoben'.

Moreover, in the poem *Goethes Lezte Nacht in Italien*, Stefan
George describes Goethe's meditations at the sight of the youthful pair of heroes in the Southern landscape, full of movement
and light, of roses and marble, sweetness and strength, youth
and maturity, all nobly balanced. George evidently simplifies
his concept of Goethe when he sees him as the representative of
Classicism and mainly as the author of *Iphigenie* and *Tasso*.

If, as in the above poem, Goethe is addressed as the 'grand-
child of the Gäa' (not her son), who has only barely touched
the secret of the earth, then George thinks only of that Goethe

who had freely and deliberately imposed chains on the daemonic forces in and around himself and above all on his titanic
spirit of creation. Whilst the proud certainty of being the elect
still swells the opening lines of Goethe's *Harzreise im Winter*
(1777): 'May my song hover like the vulture on gentle wings,
over heavy morning clouds, looking for its prey':

> Dem Geier gleich
> Der auf schweren Morgenwolken
> Mit sanftem Fittich ruhend,
> Nach Beute schaut,
> Schwebe mein Lied! . . .

the Promethean poet already knows the secret of self-detach-
ment. He who in the years of 'Storm and Stress' had shown little
self-control and who in *Prometheus* had created as a symbol the
self-assurance of genius and in *Ganymed* a symbol of the man's
burning penetration of the universe, had now undergone a
fundamental change. Under the soothing influence of Weimar
and Frau von Stein he taught himself moderation. In the
Harzreise im Winter the scenery is symbolic and is a mirror of
this journey of the soul out of the mist of sentimental enthusiasm into clear self-knowledge. In the song, *An den Mond*, the
gentle atmosphere of evening is freed in the fluid magic of
words. Stress on the inconsistency of existence lies in *Gesang
der Geister über den Wassern*. An ultimate simplicity and deep
longing for peace pervade the words in *Ein Gleiches*. The one-
time unparalleled titan recognizes the *Grenzen der Menschheit*.
He becomes reconciled with his fate and feels himself bound in a
pantheistic union with the divinities; cf. *Das Göttliche*. Even
before the Italian journey he admits in *Ilmenau*:

> Allein wer andre wohl zu leiten strebt,
> Muß fähig sein, viel zu entbehren.

Stefan George thinks similarly when he says: 'Ich bin nur
frei weil ein gesetz mich engt'; yet this idea is conceived in the
sense of freedom within hard rules, as, for instance, we find it
expressed in pictures of the Swiss painter Ferdinand Hodler.

In the *Zueignung*, a poem already externally subject to laws,
Goethe's moral renunciation is stated plainly: 'Erkenne dich,
leb' mit der Welt in Frieden.' Into this period of victorious

humanitarianism falls also the fragment *Die Geheimnisse* with its Christian wisdom of self-control:

> Von der Gewalt die alle Wesen bindet,
> Befreit der Mensch sich, der sich überwindet. . . .

Instead of the Holy Grail, the rose-garlanded cross is set up. But the artistry of Goethe, which in view of such ennobling sentiment threatened to dim, was renewed on the journey to the South where he matured to become a 'Greek'.

This fettered daemon was close to the poet and prophet George, whose selection of Goethe's poetry *Deutsche Dichtung*[1] is highly characteristic. In it the editors guard against not only tasteless, gaudy editions and binding or bad annotation of the poems, but also against gloomy or sentimental, effeminate 'Blütenlesen': 'We selected those poems which seemed to us to contain the deepest glow of life in the finest control.' Goethe's lyrics are thus subjected to a rigid code of selection. Goethe's *Wandrers Sturmlied, Heidenröslein, An Schwager Kronos, Harzreise im Winter*, etc. (yet not the *Magisches Netz*), are sacrificed. Moreover, only three of Goethe's ballads are accepted: *Mignon, Erlkönig* and *Der Gott und die Bajadere*. The abundant gleanings from the *West-Östliche Divan* (nearly a third of Goethe's volume is given over to the '*Divan*'), do not surprise us.

In *Tage und Taten* the strictest control is at the same time called the 'highest freedom'. It is the control which George values in the paintings of Böcklin (in the *Siebente Ring*).

> Du gabst dem schmerz sein mass: die brandung musste
> Vertönen, schrei durch güldne harfe sausen,

> *You staked the bounds of grief, the surge was gentled.*
> *You forced lament to pour from golden lyres.*

In the poem *Hyperion* (*Das Neue Reich*) George places grace as high as the deed and he harmonizes Spartan restrained courage with Ionian sweetness:

> Spartas gebändigten mut
> Ioniens süsse vermählt:

His words about 'Attisches Mass neben Stärke' seem to tally externally with Goethe's conception of the Greeks, but George

[1] With an introduction by Stefan George and Karl Wolfskehl, Vol. II, *Goethe*, Bondi, Berlin.

simplified it rigidly. Moreover, he introduced Hölderlin's longing for a new-born race into his consideration of Goethe.

And yet another difference: whereas Goethe embodies his ideal being in the eternal feminine: cf. *Iphigenie*, *Zueignung*, *Tasso* (Prinzessin), *Wilhelm Meister* (Natalie), *Faust* (Gretchen), George seeks it in the heroic figure of a young man. Moreover, George creates in a more detached manner than Goethe. Whereas the former sees himself, as a young man, in the Pindaric image of the charioteer and allows himself to be swept away by the force of unlimited enthusiasm, George tempers such a pouring out of inward emotion with a cool formality that holds the verse captive like a surrounding wall.

Therefore in George's verse we notice a certain tension and we miss Goethe's miraculous and natural balance in form as well as in life. Every single poem, so the publisher Bondi tells us, is allotted a definite place in George's work. Yet the single lines of his poems are very often interchangeable inside the same poem.

Goethe's mature verse is woven into a harmonious whole. George's is the opposite, particularly in regard to his attitude to nature, for it marks a decided break-away from Goethe and, even more so, from the soul-reflecting art of the German Romantics.

Naturally, the age in which George lived lies on the threshold of our epoch which is often called the existential century of modern civilization. But apart from this, George has his own peculiar development.

A glance into his *Origins* (*Ursprünge*), and into George's uncannily disciplined striving towards a goal will confirm the above statement. In that poem *Ursprünge* in *Der Siebente Ring*, we learn of the inheritance which George, through history, homeland, and inherent spiritual forces, had acquired for his own advantage. The legend-whispering Rhine imprinted itself on his whole being, the river with its wine-covered banks and merry harvest festivities, its memories of Classic culture, the Catholic Church with its pagan ceremonies in the towns of Büdesheim (so near to France and steeped in Roman history) and above all Bingen, where Goethe on 16 October 1814 had once participated in the festival of St. Rochus. Those *Ursprünge* by no means made George a poet; they gave him, however, definite and fateful directions for training of the spirit, which, contrary to Goethe's self-examination in *Eins und Alles* (1821) and *Vermächtnis* (1829), is built up on education for rule and service in a national, masculine community, calling the lonely creative man into publicity. With an almost uncanny singleness of purpose George's art and life grew to a cogent unity, based on what is evidently a law of necessity—a unity in which George, with the feeling of being elected, experienced the world-creative force of Eros and Kairos (opportunity, chance). These mighty forces, Eros and Kairos, became decisive especially in George's case. But they ripened at first only slowly and from the tenderest beginnings:

> Wie in die herbe traube
> Erst mählich duft und farbe dringt.
> Wie aus dem nächtigen laube
> Die lerche scheu ins frühlicht schwingt.[1]

In his first poetical works George's language is forceful and sounds scanty in comparison with a naturalistic redundance. Reason lays cold hands on 'my fever-glowing head'. Yet George's youthful soul is still as 'a lonely house around which a sea of mist pours', but already future heights can be suspected. Eros, without which neither Plato nor Goethe (cf. *Wanderjahre*) were able to think of true education, points him the way to greater wisdom.

The language in the following anthology, *Hymnen, Pilgerfahrten, Algabal* (1890-2), is still harsh, and the heart remains torn between passion and control. The solemn tone and the magic spell of their imagery, the artistic splendour of colour are completely out of tune with George's own times which replaced quality by quantity ('Schon eure zahl ist frevel') and measure by mass. The vision of the emperor-priest Algabal is related to George's own self. As a symbol of an apparently unscrupulous lust for power in an oversatiated world, Algabal is at the same time beyond the personal. His quest for jurisdiction and freedom is without the reconciling element of Goethe's formal balance.

---

[1] *Die Fibel.*

George is the master of a consciously withheld art of inference. How sparing are, for example, the features with which George portrays women, and that in an epoch when the reckless abandonment of the enchanted senses had become the main content of European literature, e.g. in E. Zola's *Nana* (1881), Strindberg's trilogy *Nach Damaskus* (1898-1901), Schönherr's *Weibsteufel* (1914-15), Wedekind's Lulu in *Erdgeist* (1895) and *Büchse der Pandora* (1904), and *Hidalla* (1904), etc. In his *The World as Will and Imagination* (1819) (II, metaphysics of sexual love) Schopenhauer had already realized that the portrayal of sensual love afforded *the* contents of by far the greater part of lyrical poetry, and equally so of the epic. Whilst the sensual fetters of man allow in the above cases no hope of free choice, George, like Nietzsche, is bitterly opposed to the feminine daemon. George's strong and decided will either subdues her or raises her to the position of his gracious mistress.

In the later volumes, the female portrayals become sparse: in the volumes *Der Stern des Bundes* and *Das Neue Reich* woman completely fades out in view of the completion of his high poetic vision. *Die Törichte Pilgerin* of the *Das Neue Reich* bears only vague features. George speaks more about love in the abstract while Goethe infuses the sensuous appearance with symbolic features; George praises love, not the loved one.

As an artist, George is fastidious. Colours are often used selectively to create a formal pattern—for instance, *Ein Angelico*: 'Er nahm das gold von heiligen pokalen'; or *Auf der Terrasse* (Hymnen) with its simple but big and effective outlines. Yet in *Tage und Taten* the representation of Böcklin's *Pietà* is a failure, for the description of the angel 'rigid as one of God's commands' ('Streng wie ein befehl Gottes . . .') refers to his external facial expression, not to formal values. From the point of view of form, the angel is not 'rigid'. The adjective 'streng' could sooner be applicable to the Byzantine angels on Rubleuv's fresco in Moscow, *The Trinity of the Old Testament*. Moreover, we look at the charming Fra Angelico in a light different from that of George, who here strikes a sentimental note which makes him seem a little inconsistent.

In the third volume, *Die Bücher der Hirten-und Preisgedichte, der Sagen und Sänge und der Hängenden Gärten* (1895), the burden of the historical knowledge of our times is moulded into poetic form, in which George includes for us the characteristics of antiquity, of the Middle Ages, and of the East. The Arcadian idylls are clearly inspired by the spirit of antiquity, i.e. the experience of consecration and of cult, the election of the first-born, the beauty of the wrestler, of the singer, the joyful community and preparation for death in a world transfigured by beauty; but again it is a world born of strong tension of will in a time of disintegration of form and other values. George's ideal of noble and serene calmness is only apparently anchored in the classical ideology of Weimar. Norm, measure, harmony, selection, and ideal types founded on proportion are indeed the characteristics, too, of a beautiful form that Vasari once had called the 'buona maniera antica e moderna', and in opposition to which the various styles, Gothic, Baroque, Mannerism and Realism, were considered barbaric. Dufresnoy's 'maiestas gravis et requies decora' and Winckelmann's 'noble simplicity and serene greatness,' 'edle Einfalt und stille Größe', strength-ened this yearning for an ideal beauty. Raffael, Corregio, and Titian were amongst others considered as the precursors of a ideal which, in Stefan George's circle was not only called into being for the establishment of a new modern art, but also for educating a new society.

In his *Sagen und Sänge* George seeks to re-create the images of the spiritual powers in the Middle Ages. As in the case of the *Hirten-und Preisgedichte* and in the *Hängenden Gärten* those images are deprived of their sensuous, historical surrounding and represented as types, e.g. *the* young medieval knight, *the* vigil, *the* Parzival-mood, etc.; all these abstractions are depicted in an un-Goethean manner. Thus, certain meanings are pro-jected into the Middle Ages which are not to be found there at all. Gundolf fails to grasp the significance and formal values of medieval literature when he asserts that in Walther's, Wolfram's, or Gottfried's verse there was a lack of that primordial expression:

Nirgends ein Urton, ein übergesellschaftlicher Schauer.

As to the Parzival-mood, let us compare George's *Die Tat* (The Deed):

Am abend nach den wäldern die vor schrecknis pochen
Ist er nach tod und wunden gierig aufgebrochen.

But in the twilight, starved for death and wounds, he sped
On to the forest, pulsing with the beat of dread,

and George's *Irrende Schar* with Wolfram's *Parzival* III and IX,
or George's anaemic *Tagelied* with Heinrich von Morungen's
passionate dawn-song and Wolfram's repudiation of cunning
(in *Parzival* III): 'He who obtains love by cunning gains a
victory which brings with it shame. However softly the thief
may creep, the dry wood in the copse betrays him.'

For George, drawing his timeless pictures, Nature remains
sufficient in itself and completely independent. The descriptions
of Nature by George are principally states of mind, particularly
in his *Jahr der Seele* (1897). Insight and experience are indeed
not strange to the poet:

Dies leid und diese last: zu bannen
Was nah erst war und mein. . . .

This burden and this grief: To ban
What once I called my own. . . .

But on the whole, his picture of Nature is broken up into a
mosaic pattern and is joined together by magical utterances,
or it is animated anew to a landscape of the soul in an en-
chantingly noble pattern. Characteristic of this method are
George's short sentences, threads of a finely woven material, as,
for example, in the poem *Komm in den totgesagten park und schau*,
where the deep yellow, the pale grey, the roses, asters and
scarlet vine are interwoven with green and are combined
with azure blue to make up an autumn bouquet. It is not a
Romantic way of looking at Nature—neither is it Goethe's way,
for the unity of Nature and man is sacrificed by George. The
connexion between both worlds is not presented by an address
to the moon; cf., for example, his poem *Wir schreiten auf und
ab im reichen flitter* . . . Nature is not activated or romanticized
as in Eichendorff's *Schläft ein Lied in allen Dingen*, nor is it set in
sympathetic motion, as in Goethe's *Mondlied*.

A relentless dualism, often shown as South and North, a
journey to Rome and a monastery, or continence and passion,

also characterizes the *Teppich des Lebens* (1900). George, struggling for the unity of Greece and Golgotha, presents the polarity in the picture of the Greek temple and in the picture of the Church straining towards Heaven. In both these pictures lie the antitheses which are in balanced opposition:

> Im maasse mit der landschaft wuchs dein haus
> Nicht höher als der nahe baum es sinnt. . . .
> In wolkige nebel deuten seine türme. . . .
>
> *The landscape taught you how to build your house:*
> *No higher than the nearby tree allows! . . .*
> *Your towers vanish in a mound of vapour. . . .*

Thus the two worlds: to be and to become, light and darkness, are reconciled. *Der Siebente Ring* (1907) centres on the 'Maximin' experience and both powers of fate: Kairos-Eros. The Maximin or boy-god myth is based on George's belief in the union of the beautiful soul and the beautiful body. But as to Gundolf's interpretation of this Maximin experience, D. J. Enright rightly writes: 'Our objection is that Gundolf is concerned with "Georgeanism" instead of with George's poetry.'[1] In the *Der Stern des Bundes* (1914)[2] he sings of his new vision of life, in which 'Rausch und Helle', exaltation and lucidity, form a unity. The last volume of poems, *Das Neue Reich* (1928), brings the fulfilment of Algabal's dream: 'Ich bin nur frei weil ein gesetz mich engt. . . .' Infinity is enshrined in the finite as the souls of the heroes are in the roaring of the shell which a boy holds to his ears (*An die Kinder des Meeres*).

Stefan George's sense of form differs as we see fundamentally from that of Goethe. The former's verse seems to be built of stone. The frequent use of monosyllabic words slows down the rhythm which very often is stressed by a trochaic metre. George's verse is, moreover, characterized by a peculiar tension which is caused by abbreviated word-forms in adjectival position wedged between article and noun; cf. '. . . das starke bösem ferne zeichen':

> He runs his fingers through his mop of hair,
> And staunchly signs away the Evil One (from: *Vigil of Arms*).

[1] *German Life and Letters*, 1952, p. 182.
[2] Cf. J. M. M. Aler's illuminating study: *Im Spiegel der Form*, Amsterdam, 1947.

*Die Bücher der Hirten-und Preisgedichte, der
Sagen und Sänge und der Hängenden Gärten.*

Such compactness is reminiscent of the *Pandora* by Goethe
who himself speaks of its terse style ('ineinander gekeilt'), e.g.:

Daneben zieht . . . Schmucklustiges
des Vollgewandes wellenhafte Schleppe nach

or

In Flechten glänzend schmiegte sich der Wunderwuchs,
der, freigegeben, schlangengleich die Ferse schlingt. . . .

While the young Goethe seeks to free poetic superfluity in
Pindaric sentences, the mature form of his *Pandora*, as of
George's verse, is consciously compressed and charged with
adjectival participles. Goethe had arrived at the rule by experience. Now he can say with Prometheus: 'Zufall ist mir ver-
haßt. . . .' In George's creative work the extravagant, energetic
youthful genius of a Goethe, without which the latter's Classicism is unthinkable, is missing. Humour saved the creator
of Mephisto, of the 'Jahrmarkt' of Plundersweilen, of the
Auersbach cellar, etc., from petrification.

Plato, Goethe, and George knew the *daemon* as their destiny,
but the word 'daemon' is not synonymous for all three.
Plato means the daemon which (in his own way) everyone
must first fight and conquer through self-discipline. In *Christianity* the inner lawfulness of being is deepened by the belief in
the personal God. But man plunged swiftly from the religious
and sublime feeling of responsibility for his own soul into an
all too human dependency on Church and State. Gradually
the *worldly state* grew stronger: civitas mundi instead of civitas
dei. Machiavelli's worldly self-responsibility developed in the
end into an arrogant cult of the ego. This ego sought its ultimate
justification not before God but before the judgement seat of
the *inner voice*.

Goethe was the first to experience, as no one before him ever
had, the shudder of the irrational, the 'namenlose Gefühle',
which were blessed by the godly spirit. In *Urworte. Orphisch*, a
poem considered Platonic in many ways, Goethe speaks of the
daemon of his life which, with Tyche, Eros, Anagke and Elpis,
determined his creative activity as a superhuman power. Not

only Werther, Götz, Faust, Egmont, whose soliloquy Stefan George turned into verse without important alteration in his last years at school, and the Pindaric odes, but also works of his later years, such as the *West-Östliche Divan*, betray the glowing soul whose fate is symbolized by the figure of the charioteer.

This mystery of the 'epikratein', the victorious guiding in the storm of life, remained with Goethe. No loss of feeling arrived with maturity. Yet Goethe, the Classical master, now sought regularity in the ephemeral apparition without robbing life of profundity. 'Things in themselves' should uplift the soul, no longer may the intoxicated soul form objects, he wrote in his diary to Frau von Stein (24 September 1786).

Above all, the difference between Goethe and George becomes evident in their interpretation of and attitude to Nature. Already in George's *Jahr der Seele* there is an approach to Nature by magic. In his *Urlandschaft* (*Teppich des Lebens*) and *Traurige Tänze* (*Jahr der Seele*), Nature quietly 'serves'. The faun in *Das Neue Reich* knows of her activities: 'Uns tilgend tilgt ihr euch. . . . Nur durch den zauber bleibt das leben wach'. 'Slaying us, you slay yourselves. . . . Only by magic, life is kept awake' (*Der Mensch und der Drud* (*Man and Faun*)). Moreover the remark in the poem *Urlandschaft*: 'Starker arme spur', clearly suggests a struggle with Nature.

Sharply differentiated from 'the Other', the terrifying intangible forces in Nature, are the formal 'park-landscapes' in George's poetry. Nature is subject to his domineering will. The single objects, such as stones, metals, are compelled into an artificial unity. In contrast to Goethe, Stefan George does not seek infinity in Nature, but in man. In his *Templer* (*The Seventh Ring*), the conception of the subjection by man of the enigmatical, horrible 'Other' is most clearly depicted. Nature is here the great nourisher, but she is not a pantheistic divinity as with Goethe; she is an opposing force:

> Und wenn die grosse Nährerin im zorne
> Nicht mehr sich mischend neigt am untern borne.
> . . . So kann nur einer der sie stets befocht
> Und zwang und nie verfuhr nach ihrem rechte
> Die hand ihr pressen, packen ihre flechte. . . .

STEFAN GEORGE'S 'THIRD HUMANISM'

And when in wrath the Mighty Mother scorns
To lean and couple at the lower bourns. . .
Then only one who always strove with her,
Ignored her wishes and denied her will,
Can crush her hand and grip her hair. . . .

The material here is not divine; it is only a means of conveying
the spiritual effect. On the other hand in his *Friend of the
Meadows* the creative force in nature is given a mythical significance (*The Tapestry of Life*):

Er schöpft und giesst mit einem kürbisnapfe
Er beugt sich oft die quecken auszuharken
. . . Und reifend schwellen um ihn die gemarken

He draws the water with a gourd and pours,
He often stoops to pull the quickening grasses,
(Beneath his foot the region spills with flowers)
And ripens to a harvest where he passes

Thus George is here once again quite close to Nature, but still
far removed from the satyr-representation of the Greeks, for
the satyr is, as Nietzsche says, 'the primeval image of man, the
expression of his highest and strongest powers', a symbolic
representation of the racial omnipotence of Nature which the
Greeks are accustomed to regard with an awed amazement.
The satyr was something exalted and divine (Nietzsche, *The
Birth of Tragedy*). George's *Teppich des Lebens* and *Maximin*
experiences extend only into the second stage of human culture,
the three stages being: socratic—artistic—tragic, i.e. into the
artistic which wears the role of dignity for the sake of self-
preservation. But the core of Grecian life was touched, the
appearance of its pleasing serenity, rendered to a colourless,
formless state by the all too weak imitators of the Weimar Class-
ics, was again broken through, and the mask ripped away from
the mystery of 'Being'. In the same way as the rigid strophes are
formed, so too is George's whole being. Goethe's own development, which grew out of Nature and was not afraid of temporary failures and relapses, presents an essentially different
picture. With Goethe, Nature itself is the fiery, forceful strength,
creative, ever transitory as Faust's Earth Spirit.

The so-called 'Nature hymn' (which, even if it does perhaps
not originate from Goethe, proclaims Goethe's 'Storm and

o   199

Stress' feeling as well as his Classicism) reveals this difference
between the two poets. With Goethe, Nature is the eternal
mother of everything, the artist of many forms, not the formless
'Other' one. George only rarely finds reconciliation with the
earth, as, for example, in *Der Siebente Ring*: 'Wie dank ich sonne
dir ob jeden dings', *Gebete III*. Nature, on the whole, remains for
him especially threatening. The intoxicated outburst of Goethe
in his *Mailied*, 'Wie herrlich leuchtet mir die Natur', is unthinkable in George's poetry. Goethe pours his overflowing
heart into Nature, though he does not give himself up to her
unreservedly. At the same time, unlike George, he does not
remain calm and strangely detached in face of her.

To Goethe, God does not work through Nature (as was
Herder's opinion), but God is the world itself. Yet Goethe
looked upon god-like Nature with the eye of an artist, and he
drew his philosophy (cf. *Dichtung und Wahrheit* and *Wiederfinden*)
from a picture of Nature inspired by Spinoza, which was after
all not fundamentally different from Herder's and not far from
Schelling's pantheistic *Weltseele*. At the end of the eighth book
of *Dichtung und Wahrheit* it becomes clearly pronounced that
creation is nothing but a falling off and return to the source.
It is the representation of egoism and of love, of the in-and
out-taking of breath, division and union of Monads,—ideas
which we meet again in Goethe's *Wiederfinden* and the poems on
cosmogony under the title of *Gott und die Welt*:

> Kein Wesen kann zu Nichts zerfallen,
> Das Ewige regt sich fort in allen. . . .

Goethe has an antipathy against approaching Nature by
magic, as is already seen in the story of his boyhood in Frankfurt (cf. Book I of *Dichtung und Wahrheit*). He approaches
Nature with loving feeling and reverence for that which is
above us, *in* us and *beneath* us, cf. *Wilhelm Meisters Wanderjahre*,
II, 1.

We have in the past frequently touched on Stefan George's
conception of beauty. He saw in Goethe the symbol of the
concrete 'godly norm'. The most wise with 'flowing beards' also
perceive the happy tidings and 'the soberest minds and the
most stiff-necked' bow before the secret of the golden mean.

In the final verse of *Goethes Lezte Nacht in Italien* George lets the departing poet utter a promise, that in his own fatherland also, the 'golden mean together with strength' shall become reality, for 'Miracle has fulfilled itself in marble and roses'.

Thus George sees the ideal realized in the future of his own people,[1] an ideal which Winckelmann had once found in controlled expression, in the blending and balancing of contrary forces, an ideal which lives on through the whole Classical theory of art, as for instance in Herder's *Nemesis*, in W. von Humboldt's *Skizze über die Griechen*, in Schiller's *Kalliasbriefe*, *Anmut und Würde*, *Briefe über die ästhetische Erziehung*, in Fr. Schlegel's *Über die Grenzen des Schönen*, and above everything in Goethe's essay *Winckelmann* (1805), wherein Winckelmann himself is praised as a re-embodiment of Antiquity.

[1] Cf. the suggestive studies by C. M. Bowra: *The Heritage of Symbolism*, 1943; V. Lange: *Modern German Literature 1870–1940*, 1945; R. Minder: *Allemagnes et Allemands*, 1948; and E. K. Bennett: *Stefan George*, 1954.

XII

Gerhart Hauptmann (1862-1946)

L'ULTIMO DEI GIGANTI

IN HIS *Aufzeichnungen* (1922), Gerhart Hauptmann claimed the drama to be the noblest form of art. In contrast to the German Romanticists who praise the novel, especially Goethe's *Wilhelm Meister*, as the highest achievement of art, he upholds that life and thought are drama. Today we are far too inclined to visualize Gerhart Hauptmann's works mainly through the eyes of the social critic or the politician. The poet wanders along freer paths, his art embraces the heights and depths of life. Redemption of sinful man by the uniting force of love and the transformation of the philosophy 'I am' into that of 'We are' is Gerhart Hauptmann's gospel. But both in art and life he realizes that two beings can never merge absolutely one with another. The struggle between ego and world, man and society is the keynote of his dramas. Moreover, his characteristically Silesian mysticism seeks to fathom the mysteries of the dualistic soul and penetrate into the secret regions of the unconscious.

At an address, delivered at the opening of the Heidelberg Festival in 1928, Gerhart Hauptmann compared the German drama with a tree he saw at New Abbey in Gallowayshire. Growing from the ruins, it plunges its boughs into the soil in order to reap nourishment. The branches take root, a new tree shoots up and lives a life of its own. So, too, the German drama rises anew from the wreck of its past. The dramas of Lessing, Schiller, Goethe, and H. von Kleist are the first shoots which since the days of Hans Sachs and Andreas Gryphius once more grow from German soil and the very heart of the people. The cinema, 'reared in the hotbed' of effective bureaus, often cannot arouse our deepest emotions, and it is these which Gerhart Hauptmann seeks to awaken in his audience.

Naturalism influenced him first. What he saw, heard and suffered was rendered by him into drama. As a child of the waning nineteenth century, he looked upon life as a product of milieu and inevitable historical development, influenced by man's striving for power and the daemonic forces of hunger and sex. Thus literature at that time was deeply rooted in the same materialistic conception which characterizes also the political and philosophical outlook of writers, who believe man to be the slave of economic structure, only ruled by natural and mob instinct. These tendencies are particularly reflected in Gerhart Hauptmann's earlier works.

As an author of the naturalistic school, the world is to him not a setting for the heroic deeds of great personalities, but a chaos of passions. Sympathy with erring mankind inspired his poetic vision. The sight of misery stirred his inmost being when he journeyed to the South, and his *Promethidenlos* (1885), an unsuccessful imitation of Byron's *Childe Harold's Pilgrimage*, reflects the harrowed state of his mind. Here also we meet with the underlying idea of Hauptmann's philosophy: 'World woe is the root of man's yearning for heaven.' And again and again social problems, such as the disastrous effects caused by poverty, drink, heredity, and the relations of individual to mass form the keynote of his plays.

Gloomy pessimism overshadows the first dramas which were heralded in by *Vor Sonnenaufgang* (1889), which in 1932 received its counterpart in the drama of *Vor Sonnenuntergang*. The former was produced on the stage of the 'Freie Bühne' under the directorship of Otto Brahm in Berlin. It is a play of milieu biassed with strong social propaganda, just as in Zola's *L'Assommoir* drink is pointed to as the main cause of moral degeneration. The effect of this drama was that Naturalism became the fashion in Germany and led to the popularity of the foreign leaders of this school, such as Tolstoy, Zola, Ibsen, Strindberg, and Björnson.

Yet Gerhart Hauptmann is not the originator of Naturalistic technique, but had borrowed it from Arno Holz, the leader of so-called 'consequent Naturalism'. Monologue, systematic dialogue, and effective endings to the individual acts are now renounced in favour of verisimilitude. The absolute of good and evil find no place in a world where all is the result of circumstance.

In the dramas, *Das Friedensfest* (1890) and *Einsame Menschen* (1891), we may discover an echo of Ibsen. In the former, man's spirit is broken by the curse of inheritance. With the *Weber* (1892) Gerhart Hauptmann perfects the art of Naturalistic technique. The rebellion of the Silesian weavers in 1844 forms the background of the play. The stamp of misery lies not alone on the individual, but on the mass. The form of the play also follows the characteristically Naturalistic ideal. It is not built up according to the law of the Classic play, but on a far more complex system of a series of crises. The song of weavers acts as the driving power throughout the drama. Gerhart Hauptmann dedicated this drama to his father. His grandfather was a weaver, who, as one of the characters in the play, could have spoken those words at the end of the third act: 'A jeder Mensch hat halt'ne Sehnsucht!' The social revolt of the starving Silesian weavers had already been treated by Heine in his poem:

> Im düstren Auge keine Träne,
> Sie sitzen am Webstuhl und fletschen die Zähne.

The play, *Hanneles Himmelfahrt* (1893) which was awarded the Grillparzer Prize, inaugurated a new phase in the author's development. From out the dark hovels of poverty we are led into celestial spheres of light. The scene of the first part is laid in a workhouse, where the child Hannele, who to escape the cruelties of her drunken father had tried to drown herself, lies tossing in fevered dreams. Amongst the phantoms of her visions is that of her beloved teacher, who, in the shape of our Saviour, leads her out of the state of human degradation into regions of heavenly bliss. The wonders she beholds are painted in colours reminiscent of Böcklin's dream landscapes. Here Gerhart Hauptmann for the first time turns his back on Naturalism.

A period of personal and creative disillusionment followed. Critics and public threw scorn upon the great tragedy, *Florian Geyer* (1896), which, with Schiller's dramatic verve, presents to us a picture of the social revolt at the time of the Reformation.

In vain Florian Geyer endeavours to pierce the heart of German dissension, only to fall wounded to death.

The success of the *Versunkene Glocke* (1896), in which the world of fairy intermingles with religious thought and marriage problems, freed Gerhart Hauptmann of melancholy doubts as to his creative power. The hero of this drama is a bellfounder whose wife cannot follow his visionary flights of imagination. He forsakes her and flees into the mountains, where he, like Shelley, dreams of a kingdom of love and freedom. Like Ibsen's Brand, he finds new strength in pantheistic adoration of Nature and plans the foundation of a new universal Church. The bells which he now intends to create shall herald in our future realm of joy, where after the long wintry night, spring will blossom beneath the feet of god Baldur.

Here we hear an echo of the Chorus in Shelley's lyrical drama, *Hellas* (1821):

> The world's great age begins anew,
>   The golden years return,
> The earth doth like a snake renew
>   Her winter weeds outworn.
> Heaven smiles, and faiths and empires gleam
> Like wrecks of a dissolving dream.
>
> . . . . . .
>
> Oh, cease! must hate and death return?
>   Cease! must men kill and die?
> Cease! drain not to its dregs the urn
>   Of bitter prophecy.
> The world is weary of the past,
> Oh, might it die or rest at last!

Hellas ends on a melancholy note. In the case of Heinrich, the bellfounder, his dreams are shattered by his own weakness.

Gerhart Hauptmann has often been blamed on account of the feeble character of his heroes. Here, however, it is rather his desire to fuse *Weltanschauung*, fairy motives, and realism to a unity, which could provoke criticism. In spite of its insistence on ideas, and its broad Silesian dialect, this play has won world renown because of its lyric charm and the figure Rautendelein, that Undine-like creature who is born of an essentially German Romantic conception of Nature.

The poetic harvest of the succeeding years seems inexhaustible. In 1896 appeared *Elga*, a dramatization of Grillparzer's story, *Das Kloster von Sendomir*. In his drama, *Der arme Heinrich* (1902), he turns to the Middle Ages for inspiration. The Classic mind of Goethe was repelled by the pathological character of Hartmann von Aue's epic, not so the Naturalistic trait in Gerhart Hauptmann, who, with the knowledge of modern psychiatry at his disposal, draws a persuasive picture of the girl Ottegebe, who in her love shrinks before no sacrifice.

Nevertheless, the modern reader is rather inclined to take the miraculous recovery of the knight Heinrich as a symbol of his spiritual redemption. Renunciation of worldly pleasures is here expressed as the noblest revelation of life's pain, and he who had hated the inimical world surrenders his pride and believes once more in the good of humanity. *Rose Bernd* (1903) signifies after *Die Weber* another high-water mark of Gerhart Hauptmann's power of realistic representation, but in the much-discussed *Und Pippa tanzt* (1906) his dramatic form is symbolical. This truly Romantic *Glashüttendrama* characterizes the struggle of four men for the possession of beauty. The first typifies the primordial force of Nature, the second an enlightened industrial magnate, the third the German 'Michel' whose head is ever in the clouds, the fourth the resignation of old age. All four strive in vain.

Only here and in a few other works is Hauptmann what we should call a 'metaphysical' poet. On the whole he does not re-create the world in symbols of his own vision, but records the impressions made on his sympathetic spirit in his passage through life.[1] In the poem *Wie eine Windesharfe sei deine Seele, Dichter* this sentiment is re-echoed.

Gerhart Hauptmann's universal fame increased. In 1905 the honorary degree of D.Litt. was conferred upon him by the University of Oxford, and in 1912 he was awarded the Nobel Prize. In Germany too, even after 1933, he was considered the foremost poet of his nation. The *Festspiel* (1913), written in commemoration of the war of liberation, had given rise to much misunderstanding because from his high vantage-place the

[1] Cf. also C. F. W. Behl, *Gerhart Hauptmann. His life and work*, trans. by H. Taubert, Würzburg, 1956.

author dangles his characters like puppets from a string. But he who doubts his patriotism may be reassured by the two lines which he wrote in his own copy of the *Festspiel*:

> Keiner hat einen so hohen Stand,
> Daß nicht höher stände sein Vaterland,

and in his sonnet *Ritter, Tod und Teufel* (1921), which is reminiscent of Albrecht Dürer's engraving, he appeals to the German people to unite: not towards power, but humanity, should mankind be directed. In his later dramas which inclined to obscurity of thought and style, this gospel is specially stressed. His play, *Before Sunset (Vor Sonnenuntergang)*, appeared in the year of the Goethe Centenary, 1932, when Hauptmann was seventy years of age. The favourite theme of the conflict between father and son (which appears in the *Bogen des Odysseus* and in the dramas about artists, *Michael Kramer, Kollege Krampton, Peter Brauer*) is here treated in a manner which bears resemblance to the tragic fate of King Lear. The powerful acting of Werner Krauss as Old Claussen caused a sensation amongst a politically divided audience at a London performance of *Before Sunset* in the Shaftesbury Theatre in 1933.

Death alone frees the hero from the burden of life. Here the poet ends on a melancholy note. Nevertheless, his work is not altogether pessimistic, for he hails man as a heroic sufferer and ultimate victor: 'Du bist Dulder, bist Überwinder' he writes in one of his poems.

Gerhart Hauptmann is also a distinguished prose-writer. In the *Griechischer Frühling* (1908) he presents a series of impressionistic travel sketches. His short story, *Der Apostel* (1890), forms the preliminary study to his first masterpiece in the narrative style, *Der Narr in Christo Emanuel Quint* (1912). Quint, a Silesian joiner, is regarded as the Saviour by the poor. Lacking strength to dispel their illusion, and carried away by their enthusiasm, he himself comes to believe in his divine mission. He is afterwards forsaken by his followers and in a snowstorm meets with a hapless end.

Modern psychologists have come to the conclusion that the character of Quint provides a convincing case of insanity of self-exaltation, i.e. megalomania. But in reality Gerhart

Hauptmann has portrayed no pathological phenomenon, nor did he intend to tell the story of Jesus Christ in disguise; rather he creates in the figure of Quint an embodiment of humanity which is trodden underfoot by unfeeling cruelty. We are best able to realize the full meaning of this Utopian novel if we read Quint's interpretation of 'Our Father'. Through prayer, not through the book, Emanuel finds God in himself. It connects him with the Universe and mankind:

> Es kam ihm vor, als ob er damit in sich eine heilige Quelle anschlüge, ein reines, heiliges Streben erweckte, einen neuen tätigen, heiligen Geist; und inwendig in uns war ja das Reich. Es sollte sich durch den Geist ja in uns errichten. . . . Es brach eine schmerzhafte Liebe und Sehnsucht zu Menschen in ihm auf. . . .

Prayer is the holy source at which man's spirit may drink, but the aspiring soul is dragged into the dust by man's vanity and egotism. Here we are led to think of that unforgettable scene in Dostoevsky's *The Brothers Karamazov*, in which the chief inquisitor visits the imprisoned Jesus in His cell. In Max Kretzer's novel, *Gesicht Christi*, and in Ricarda Huch's *Der wiedererstandene Christus* similar thoughts are expressed.

The shortcomings of modern civilization are also branded by Gerhart Hauptmann in his novel *Atlantis* (1912), which describes a shipwreck. The catastrophe is skilfully attached to the adventures of the hero.

Gerhart Hauptmann, the poet of suffering, presented us in the last year of the First World War with a eulogy of Nature and love in his great novel, *Der Ketzer von Soana* (1918). The theme is reminiscent of Zola's *La faute de l'Abbé Mouret*. A Catholic priest Francesco rejects his former life. The influence of Nature breaks the barriers of his ascetic mind, spring arousing in the young priest the inebriation of passion. Not Logos, but Eros becomes his gospel, and after making his way into the mountains in order to convert heretical shepherds, he is himself overcome by the mysteries of Nature and love for the shepherd's daughter. To him she is Madonna and Eve, Heaven and earth, body and soul, not only the fulfilment of sexual desire, as many have tried to misinterpret her. 'Sie stieg aus der Tiefe der Welt empor und stieg an dem Staunenden vorbei—und sie steigt und steigt in die Ewigkeit, als die, in deren gnadenlose Hände Himmel und Hölle überantwortet sind.' In the beating of her heart he hears re-echoed the pulse of the universe.

Amongst the later novels, that of *Die Insel der großen Mutter oder das Wunder von Île des Dames* (1924) deserves notice. The development and decay of a matriarchal state are described here. The story of these women, shipwrecked on an island, is dreamlike, but the psychological and social problems propounded, the inquiry into the factors necessary for the constitution of a successful Amazon state, still remain of interest to the reader. Not the invasion of men, but the fact that the women gradually cease to believe in the dogma of the miraculous propagation leads to the fall of the State. Johann Jakob Bachofen's and Leo Frobenius's conceptions of matriarchy form an analogy to some of the ideas expressed here. Moreover, the theme had attracted German writers already beforehand, e.g. The Anacreontic poet, J. N. Götz, wrote an elegiac poem, *Die Mädcheninsel*, and K. Immermann is the author of the comic poem, *Das Land der Weiber*.

The harvest of Gerhart Hauptmann's lyrics is surprisingly small if one omits those interspersed amongst his dramas and novels. As regards rhythm, he allows himself great poetic licence. He often cares more for emotion than form. Personal sentiment asserts itself to such a degree that he rarely raises it into the sphere of the universal. This is especially true of his epic *Anna* (1921), where matter and form are not transfused to a unity, and the hexameters are treated with a freedom far removed from the Classic style.

The same also applies to that great epic poem in hexameters, *Till Eulenspiegel* (1928), in which he discusses philosophical questions of the time. The ethos of his writings is here stressed yet once more. It is the community, not the individual that counts. Love pierces the mask which man is forced to wear in his struggle with daily existence. Man returns to the bosom of Nature to play a part in the creation of life. Till Eulenspiegel's last (XVIII) adventure leads us into the 'Saviour's Inn', in which he meets a strange shepherd (Christ) who alone knows the secret of life:

... Auch du, Till, stirbst der Zeit. Wer allein in ihr lebt, lebte
   niemals:
und wer tot ist, vermag auch in ihr, der Zeit, nicht zu sterben. ...

*... Also you, Till, will die to time. He who lives for it only, has never
lived: And he who is dead, cannot die in it.*

The conflict between the individual and the world ends in the
resignation of the former.

In this, some of Gerhart Hauptmann's works bear a certain
resemblance to the works of the Russian writer Chekov. The
pessimistic tone struck by Gerhart Hauptmann is the heritage
of the nineteenth century, but it is balanced by his often defiant
attitude representing the new generation which seeks the
combatant in the battle of ideas. Where, as in *Und Pippa tanzt,
Der Narr in Christo Emanuel Quint*, and *Der Ketzer von Soana*,
Gerhart Hauptmann calls forth the vision of humanity he may
surely be called a champion of our age. G. Hauptmann's other
epic poem, *Der große Traum*, which appeared for the first
time in his *Gesamtausgabe letzter Hand* (1942), shows him deeply
involved in memories of the past and obscure dream visions
about the future of mankind:

... Den Namen 'Mensch', hier möcht' ich ihn verstecken,
doch ihn zu nennen, ist verfluchte Pflicht. ... (*XXII*).

and the last of G. Hauptmann's posthumous verses of *The
Great Dream* raises Nothingness to the mysterious All:

... Ein Mann, ein Nichts. Und dieses Nichts war fort.
Das Nichts ist alles. Alles ist das Nichts.
Das Nichts die Leere und das Nichts der Hort.

Das Nichts: das Ein und Alles des Gesichts.

It is no coincidence that the American authority, W. J. Heuser,
sees in G. Hauptmann's interest in the inner world of bold
intuition some convincing contact with Novalis.

Gerhart Hauptmann's love of Goethe, on whom he modelled
his life (e.g. his journeys) as well as work (e.g. his love of Greece,
autobiography, etc.), is beyond doubt. G. Hauptmann, who in
the Diebskomödie, *Der Biberpelz* (1893), had created one of the
few successful German comedies, is essentially a playwright,
perhaps Germany's greatest in our time. In his best plays his

power of dramatic presentation and plastic character studies
is unchallenged nowadays. He felt an affinity not only to
Goethe, but also to Shakespeare, who dominated him throughout his life. He made variations on Shakespearean subject-
matter and dramatic devices, e.g. in *Schluck und Jau* (1900), a
play in a play, in *Indipohdi* (1920), and in *Hamlet in Wittenberg*
(1935). Unlike Otto Ludwig, the author of the *Shakespeare-Studien*
(1871), he did not feel crushed by Shakespeare's force of creation, but inspired and rejuvenated. According to a highly
understanding study by E. Alker, *Das Werk Gerhart Haupt-
manns in neuer Sicht* (1947), G. Hauptmann's artistic development after the First World War, can, on the one hand, be
summarized as 'Surrealism'; this term, all too often abused and
misunderstood, here means an art which penetrates a world of
double meanings, of magic reality, or as E. Alker calls it:
'Überwirklichkeitskunst, Doppelbödigkeit, Hintergründigkeit
der Welt . . .'. On the other hand, G. Hauptmann's latter
works are steeped in Classic themes, e.g. not only *Die Goldene
Harfe* (1933) and *Die Tochter der Kathedrale* (1939) with its
Cathar heresy and medieval background, but particularly the
Greek subject-matter in his powerful Atriden-tetralogie,
Iphigenie in Delphi (1941), *Iphigenie in Aulis* (1943), *Agamemmnons
Tod* (1947), *Elektra* (1947), which grew out of the sombre background of the Second World War and its aftermath. In contrast to the *Bogen des Odysseus* (1914), these dramas which
K. H. Ruppel called the most gigantic German tragedies
written since the days of H. von Kleist, turn to a concept of an
archaic Greek world seen through the eyes of J. J. Bachofen,
E. Rohde, F. Nietzsche, and J. Burckhardt, which is far removed from Goethe's and Winckelmann's ideal of noble
simplicity and serene greatness. G. Hauptmann began this
tetralogy at the age of seventy-eight, and completed it when he
was well over eighty.

Magnus Garbe, one of his starkest tragedies, appeared not
until 1942, four years before his death, and had its première
in Düsseldorf not until 1956, ten years after his death. But
Gerhart Hauptmann had already, before or about the First
World War, planned the sombre subject of persecution and
mass-anxiety for his tragedy. The latter—an echo of it can be

discovered in *The Great Dream*—deals with a bestial outburst of cruelty at the time of the Inquisition, which annihilates two noble and innocent people, Felicia and her husband, a Bürgermeister of a free German town. The background is sixteenth-century religious unrest, but the theme of the tragedy is clearly ours: modern man caught in the vortex of irrational fear and satanic torture. Evil seems triumphant. Magnus Garbe's last cry of despair is: 'Es ist kein Gott, es ist nur der Teufel.' Though Felicia's tragic suffering reminds one of Ophelia's madness and above all of Gretchen's violent end, the inescapability of Felicia and Magnus Garbe's fate is presented with crushing, dramatic power by the author who can indeed be called 'l'ultimo dei giganti'.

XIII

German Poetry After 1945

Every man carries with him through life a mirror;
as unique and impossible to get rid of as his shadow.
W. H. AUDEN, 'Hic and Ille', in *Encounter*, IV, 1956.

APART FROM THE lamentably weak 'opposition lyrics' in
Paul E. H. Lüth's anthology *Der Anfang*, there appeared
in Hanover, in 1946, a thoroughly representative collection of the newest German poems edited by Friedrich Rasche
under the title *Gedicht in unserer Zeit*.

This selection, and above all the publications of verse by
Hagelstange, Holthusen, Krolow, and in most recent years
by Schwedhelm, Höllerer (cf. his *Transit*) and Jesse Thoor's
Sonette und Lieder (ed. by A. Marnau), etc., testify to the fact
that an important inner movement is once again struggling
for expression in Germany. The living springs of German
lyricism seem to be inexhaustible. The continuance of a
strong tradition is sufficiently proved by the naïvety of Hermann Claudius, the forceful free-rhythmic verse of Klopstock,
Goethe, Hölderlin, Novalis and Heine, as much by the rare
tension and immediacy of the young Goethe, as by the daemonic maturity of the old Goethe and of Mörike. Finally one
might mention the magical incantation of Stefan George's
Sänge and the depth of Rilke's *Elegies*.

The tradition has clearly never been broken, e.g. Baroque
characteristics and a Classic heritage again come to the fore in
Germany's most modern lyric poetry. Once more we discover
the nothingness of all existence when confronted with death;
the theme of the unity of life and death, but at the same time a
recognition of pure spirit and faith in the goodness of creation;
despair of life in spite of overpowering apocalyptic visions; the
'comforted despair' which recalls the antithesis of Baroque
verse; shattering self-accusation, though there are exceptions

213

as in the all-too-emphasized 'Thou' of the poet Hagelstange's detachment in the sonnets, *Venezianisches Credo*; the desire for the harsh formal discipline of the sonnet which acts as the anchor of salvation for poets such as Hans E. Holthusen (born 1913) in *Hier in der Zeit*.

Moreover, though there is a tendency towards 'free' rhythmic poetry, we also find a characteristic predilection for Classical forms, together with a return to the theme of the worth of man and to the inheritance of Goethe and Hölderlin, in short to a new humanitarianism which through sensitive translations from Classical poetry finds its most passionate advocate in Thassilo von Scheffer (+ 1951).

In this connexion H. Buddensieg's *Hymns to the gods of Greece*, with its discussion of the important types of 'free rhythm' and of the all-too-hackneyed forms of the newest lyrical expression is extremely valuable. The author of those hymns demands Goethean change and rebirth. He devotes his poetry to those who, despite the barbarism of an age of technical science, remained human. According to him, a study of ancient values helps us, because if today Aeschylus no longer appeals to us 'it is not worth living in this world'. As in the days of Goethe, Schiller, Hölderlin and Novalis, the poet is praised as the interpreter and prophet of a mythical world in which only a brotherly intimacy with death gives to life depth and fullness. If the poet can once more conjure up the names: Mother Earth, Air, Sea, Fire, before our souls, it is no deification of existence in Stefan George's sense. Man must submit himself 'humbly to the will of the gods'. Then our timebound word will fall away like an empty shell, for it is unconsecrated and worthless.

All greatness must be objective. Aeschylus's *Persians*, or Sophocles's *Ajax*, or Euripides's *Trojan Women* are closer to our time than many plays that our present age has to offer. It is a question of basic humanity as it is in Goethe's *Faust*, for erotic, nervous, sensitive 'reportage' acts merely for the day, and the feeling of the emptiness and arrogance of analytical comprehension can only end in anarchy. Therefore the great lyric poet only *appears* to be estranged from the world. His work is of *this* and *all* time. The really profound poet's work is individual as well as universal, i.e. applicable to all ages and to all men. He achieves this by combining Apollo and Dionysos, clarity and visionary ecstasy. But another characteristic feature of the most recent German lyrical poetry is its inwardness. In its intense feeling, poetry has emerged as a force opposing false pathos and the threatening total uniformity and utilitarianism of life.

Karl Krolow (born 1915), now living at Göttingen, has written a *Foreword* to the above anthology of Friedrich Rasche. This presents almost all the important features characteristic of the most modern German writers, penetrating to the core of the problems in post-war Germany and maintaining that amidst the barrenness of a world politically and morally bankrupt the countryside should be won back again for poetry, that the rivers, trees, fields, flowers, the stars themselves should speak once more through poetry. Thus the intimate relations between Nature and mankind, between God and man, should once more be kindled or awakened.

Moreover, the tendency towards 'intellectual' poetry, towards vague mysticism and a guilt-laden consciousness should yield to a new mode of poetic form, which is beyond time but not timeless. The poet's deepest concern should be the creation of lyric poetry expressive of *our* present age and *our* generation. The most modern lyric, Krolow likewise asserts, should be deeply religious, without being limited in creed. Finally an earnest sense of form should be revealed: the sonnet has different functions from those of the elegy, the simple song different ones from those of the ode. The best poems in the 'Rasche Anthology' certainly show a definite feeling for form.

The editor of this anthology, Friedrich Rasche himself, feels deeply the atmosphere of the *Götterdämmerung* that overshadows us, yet he nevertheless has faith in life. Existence is a levelling out of grief and comfort. Again and again Rasche struggles to a firm centre in the storm of historical chaos. He rejects the Christian conception of resurrection, but he remains sensitive to nature. Thus his work is an affirmation of the desperate need of our life and of the 'sweetness of the universe', as in his *Schicksalslied*: 'Nirgends daheim und immer zuhaus'. K. Krolow decries the 'world of beautiful machine guns'. He, too, does not avoid the question of guilt; he does not veil or make the word or deed seem more beautiful than it is:

> Ich bin das Land, das im Gerichte steht,
> Und allen Ländern bin ich das Gericht.

But the basic motif is solitude amidst terrifying Nature. Silence is to him like a thunderclap. Nature becomes daemonic, the spirit of the time is rejected. His *Lobgesang* is a hymn in praise of the imperishable universe. Karl Krolow is not alone in his endeavour to preserve old values and build up new ones in post-war Germany. We can certainly not speak of a complete break with the older generation.

In a critical essay, well worth the reading, and entitled *Who dares compose a poem today?* the poet W. Lehmann (born 1882) scorns the dilettantism of many recent verses which revolve continuously round the theme of factories and barracks. Moreover, he ridicules the foolish imitators of Rilke, and the enthusiasts of the hackneyed image of the pumpkin, symbol of massive existence, and above all the empty versifers of platitudes and of vulgar mixtures of images and abstractions. But he nevertheless says 'Yes' to the present—to existence. He seeks a way out of the conflict between the realists' surface play of manners, and the ecstatic flights of the idealists.

Elisabeth Langgässer (1899-1950) is, in many ways, spiritually related to W. Lehmann. Her work reflects the poet's shrinking from civilization and return to nature. The blooming of wild flowers over a stony waste of bombed houses is a joyous consolation for the homeless and hope for the rebirth of the year. Thus the primeval love for the cycles of the years, the acceptance of Goethe's belief in 'change and permanence' and especially in all-embracing Nature, explains itself:

> I become both man and woman, all-embracing nature, released
> from the spell, root and scent.

Perhaps quite unknowingly, Jacob Böhme's theory of our origin here becomes a song: 'My origin is the breath'—the breath enters into all names, but the name withers like the seed —'The world streams in, I breathe it back,' as it does in Goethe's 'diastole and systole'. Thus the rose ceaselessly opens, blooms, bears fruit and changes. In the beginning is the end, in the end the beginning. Here we are reminded of T. S. Eliot's similar theme.

The unity of all life is presented in Elisabeth Langgässer's poetry as a unity of the present and the past: the ancient world and the middle ages, and man's intimate relationship with the realm of the lower and higher worlds, with Merlin, Ariel, Klingsor, Rapunzel and Frau Holle. It is a poetry in which the animals and plants of children's fairy tales are friendly to the yellow-hammer, the lark, the dove, the swan, the siskin, the hoopoe, and also to the hare, the lizard, the stag, the bee and the snail. The Norn 'Verdandi' under the ash spins the thread of fate and her magic words cast a spell on seeds and fruits.

In an essay written in August 1948 on W. Lehmann, Elisabeth Langgässer points to the two most characteristic forms of the German lyric: 'naïve' expression and 'artistic' expression. But Elisabeth Langgässer like W. Lehmann himself takes a *third* road, which leads directly from the Romanticism of Novalis and Runge to Clemens Brentano and Droste-Hülshoff. She too draws upon fairy-tales, the magic of Nature, and the old German proverb. Her world with its elves, its woods and its birds nesting among trees is a very intimate world. It is a dream world, which deliberately devotes itself to the lyrical creation of magic and incantation.

Unfortunately, Elisabeth Langgässer's poetry is so heavily laden with names from mythology, fairy-tales, the Middle Ages, Early History and botany, that the reader can hardly grasp the sense without a dictionary. Her nature kingdom is like Klingsor's 'Magic Garden' in which the names of plants occur in overwhelming number: mistletoe, foxglove, etc., especially the symbolical 'wonder of the roses'. North and South are one. Modern European imagination joins with that of Antiquity: Persephone with Amfortas, Parzival with Avalon, Morgana with Maria, as in the poem *Schneeschmelze am Dom*. And we meet Demeter, Frau Holle and the Norns; Arethusa, Joringel and Jorinde, Ossian and Orpheus, and last but not least the Nymph Kore, Hermes and even Unke the toad. In thus making plants and animals into a new mythology Elisabeth Langgässer is akin to W. Lehmann. This poetry clearly points to a common source and origin, to Clemens Brentano's *Romanzen vom Rosenkranz* and Droste-Hülshoff's *Heidebilder*, etc.

Whilst Lehmann and Langgässer tend towards a mythical interpretation of nature, the joy of summer being brought out through associations with the saga of Helen and Paris, Hans Egon Holthusen's verse voices the religious fervour amongst the Germans in a time of tribulation. The very title of his book of poems, *Hier in der Zeit* (1949), is characteristic of their actuality. In the poem *Tabula rasa* he calls upon mankind to make a new start in a world of destruction and suffering:

> Ein Ende machen. Einen Anfang setzen,
> Den unerhörten, der uns schreckt und schwächt.
> Noch einmal will das menschliche Geschlecht
> Mit Blut und Tränen diese Erde netzen.
> Wir sind nicht mehr wir selbst. Wir sind in Scharen.
> Wir sind der Bergsturz, der Vulkan, die Macht.
> Der ungetüme Wille der Cäsaren
> Wirft uns in großen Haufen in die Schlacht. . . .

The poet, like Hölderlin in his *Song of Fate*, laments the iron necessity of our human existence. We are hurtled into time— our beginning is a blind fate; so is our end: 'Wir alle sind wie Stürzende.'

Time is our death. Earth-bound man becomes his own enemy when he divides time into peace and war. Here on earth fulfilment is denied to us, even in love. We are imprisoned by the 'barbaric order of our blood'. Beauty is merely a mysterious poison, because 'the sweet concert of our limbs' results only in the despair of the lovers. Under the yoke of the ecstatic moment man and woman are hurled into each other. Yet in love there can be no harmony. We blindly lose ourselves in an 'empty paradise'. Sleep alone can extinguish our sense and re-establish the primeval equilibrium. Such is the theme of the poem *Nocturno*.

When Holthusen speaks of the guilt of the body he seems to hark back to the Manichaean concept of evil. It is our human intellect, the perpetual wound of the Universe, which sharpens the conflict.

Nor does he shirk the question of war-guilt. According to him we all are guilty: 'Schuldig wir alle'—but Germany, lying in the heart of Europe, became 'a crater of evil'. In spite of this note of despair, Holthusen affirms life, though a curse seems to lie upon it. He realizes how terrible the individual as well as the nations can be; he maintains that man is already vanquished at birth: 'Jeder Geborne ist ein Besiegter.'

Yet Nature is unconquerable and God's mercy unending: 'Das Bad deiner Liebe . . . Weltmeer deines Erbarmens.' These two consolations help to reconcile man with time and death. The third comfort is the message of compassion, for we are all brothers in God:

> Aus Millionen erschlagener Russen den Bruder erwählen . . .

Thus Holthusen's lament becomes an affirmation of life whose joy is deeper than sorrow as in Nietzsche's Zarathustra song: 'Lust tiefer noch als Herzeleid.' Man's tortured nights and God's grace balance each other. The poet's God is, like Kierkegaard's God, 'fearful', a primordial rock on which our hands are rent, and bleed. Here and elsewhere we feel a certain affinity with Rilke's and Hölderlin's thought and imagery, which, however, by no means detracts from Holthusen's originality.

His *Eight Variations on Time and Death*, published in *Merkur*, 1949, and later in his *Labyrintische Jahre* (1952), resume the theme of the futility and monotony of our human existence: Time means Death—Love seeks Death—We try to seal time with kisses, but in vain. Our body, the coarse aggressiveness of sex, is destined to disintegrate and decay. Above all we are consumed by history:

> Geschichte, furchtbar und ganz wie umsonst.

Human laws and treaties are 'withered into sound'—Truth is a water-mark beneath the motley imprint of Time. The reference to the Germany of 1939-45 is transparent when Holthusen speaks of Caesar, 'standing erect in the car, an idol of the masses' and describes the last days of Berlin's agony and the Dictator's end in the Reichskanzlei.

Not until our pride is brought low can we seek God's grace;

not until we rid ourselves of time and of the flesh, can we reach
the true realization of our inner selves:

Nun und nimmermehr, hier, in der Zeit und im Fleisch.

In the *Ballade vom verschütteten Leben* (1952) by Rudolf
Hagelstange, born 1912, the tragic fate of six German soldiers
is raised to the symbol of the threatened existence of our time.
The theme is set clearly and vividly before us. On 17 June 1951
it was reported from Warsaw that Polish workmen whilst
clearing away an underground shelter, discovered two men,
one of whom fell dead after walking a few steps; they were the
last two of six German soldiers, who, as far back as the beginning of 1945, had been cut off from the outside world, by an
explosion in a gigantic underground store-house of provisions.
Report revealed that shortly afterwards two of the trapped
men committed suicide in the Bunker and two of the remaining
four fell ill and died.

The motif: 'All is dust. There are only steps.' . . . 'Now,
O man, you are dust and you will return to dust. . . .'

—Memento, homo, quia pulvis es, et in pulverem reverteris—

is the keynote of this ballad of night and despair. But the new
'saga of the dust' is at the same time the old saga of the eternal
light. At the end the following promise is revealed to us:
'That they finally witness out of a thousand dark silences a
single shining child.' This sudden conclusion comes to us as a
surprise, for the whole poem is overshadowed by a spirit of
despair and frustration. We are here reminded of E. Holthusen's Manichaean variations on Time and Death in the above
Acht Variationen über Zeit und Tod.

The above six victims have been effectively sought out by the
author, according to name and character. The number six
itself has significance: six war years, six years of captivity in an
apparently golden cage, which then covered the six soldiers in
night and dust.

Each single fate has symbolic meaning: for instance Benja-
min's death is that of an anchorless dreamer; Christopher's
death is that of a steadfastly believing Christian, and the death
of the sergeant Wenig is that of a repenting sinner:

. . . Then he went—the others lay down to sleep—,
He loaded his service-pistol and paid
What was left to him. It was only a little—,
Yet the whole 'Wenig' (Little). And he had
No more than this. . . .

Thus this 'Schlaraffenfalle' is by no means an accidental occurrence, a fatal trap in a golden cellar—it is our own relentless destiny. From time to time the author feels urged, perhaps to the detriment of the artistic impression of the ballad, to emphasize that symbolism: . . . They knew they were shut in and buried ('We do not know it yet . . .'); or the passage about the eyes in the tenth and final section of the poem: We imagine we can empty a sea with two thimbles . . . 'Yet—, we do not see. Light sees out of us. . . . The bright stays bright, and the blind one remains blind.'

Unfortunately, the poem lacks a unifying tone and form. There is a mixture of exalted language, ornate imagery and wise thoughts which somehow spoils the artistic effect as a whole. A greater control of form would, to our mind, have improved this unequal long-verse form with its forceful rhythmic lines and loose construction. But there is no doubt that beneath the apparently casual 'reportage' of facts there lies in this ballad, especially if one reads it again and again, a well-prepared and often powerfully expressed artistic vision. It is perhaps one of the most striking poems published by a poet of the younger generation[1] in post-war Germany.

[1] Cf. also the informative study of the immediate post-war stage in German poetry by L. Forster: *German Poetry 1944–48*, Cambridge, 1949.

XIV

Reconciliation

BERNT VON HEISELER'S 'VERSÖHNUNG'

THE NAME OF von Heiseler has already become famous through the German-Russian writer Henry von Heiseler (+1928), who is known as the translator of Pushkin, Tolstoy, Browning, Yeats, etc., and above all as a contributor to George's *Blätter für die Kunst*. His son is Bernt von Heiseler (born in Brannenburg am Inn on 14 June 1907) whose first public success was the story *Apollonia*, reprinted later in *Reclam*. His reputation as a creative writer became even more widely known through the Swiss journal *Corona* which he helped to edit from 1943. He is also the author of plays: amongst them the *Hohenstaufen-Trilogie* (1945) and *Der Bogen des Philoktet* (1947), of essays in criticism and, above all, of the novel *Versöhnung* which has established his fame beyond doubt as one of the chief writers of present-day Germany.

Versöhnung (1953) is not only an outstanding work of art, but one of the most significant documents of the time, mirrored in the destiny of three generations of the Degener family. A vast panorama is unrolled in the course of the story: the near fulfilment of the Barbarossa yearning for the Imperial millennium, a sudden outbreak of violence, an equally sudden collapse of ancient and treasured values, followed by an epoch of fear, hatred and sacrifice. The most recent past springs to mind in all its terrifying immediateness. The Röhm-Putsch, the assassination of Dolfuss, Hindenburg's death, Neville Chamberlain's frustrated efforts for peace, the Narvik expedition, the mysterious death of Generaloberst Fritsch, Dunkirk, Rudolf Hess's hazardous flight to England, Hitler's Russian campaign, Field-Marshal Paulus's heroic stand in Stalingrad who according to Hitler 'gave in on the threshold of immortality', the allied insistence on 'unconditional surrender', Count Stauffenberg's unsuccessful attempt on the Führer's life, Germany's downfall and the victors' revenge . . . all that is presented in *Reconciliation* as personal and universal fate.

In contrast to the two 'generation' novels of Galsworthy and Thomas Mann, *The Forsyte Saga* and *Buddenbrooks*, von Heiselers' *Versöhnung* is, as the title itself suggests, built up on purely ethical and religious foundations. The author is concerned with the problem of existence, he creates out of his own experience, for he lived, a German writer, amongst the Germans, in his country's darkest hour. He describes how exulting expectation gradually weakens at the growing awareness of the impossibility of any solution. He embellishes nothing, but neither does he condemn out of hand. The presentation of the question of 'guilt' is singularly noble and honest. It is also a tribute to the author's delicate, artistic feeling that in this 880-page novel he does not once lose his grip on his characters.

It is in the Christmas sermon of Georg Degener, the parson, that the author reveals his own innermost thoughts and feelings. 'We have no right to the kind and gentle message of Christmas unless we first contemplate without bias the evil in our own life. Man's very existence means to live in misery . . . driven through his own guilt from his true home, which is with God.' Not just the one or the other of us is guilty; we are all guilty. But we are also under God's protection. Thus *Versöhnung* is an indictment, but consolation too. In his volume of poems, *Spiegel im dunklen Wort*, von Heiseler expresses something very similar; the holy Earth lives by the sufferings of her children:

> Denn unser Leiden regt den Grund der Welt,
> Der sonst erstorben ruhte, und es müssen
> Die untern Quellen hinauf. So will es Gott,
> Daß eins das andre wecke. . . .

For the words of Saint John are offered in a motto to the novel: 'And he is the propitiation for our sins, and not for ours only, but also for the sins of the whole world.' The picture of the crucified Messiah in the hall at Grünschwaig, the house of Degener's grandparents, remains for Hanna and everyone a symbol of the intensity of that propitiation. Yet the author is an artist (not a preacher) and he creates the symbolic meaning with delicate tenderness: 'He hung there, almost unnoticed, in mysterious semi-darkness, and one might easily pass by without seeing Him. But He was there, and from Him Hanna returned to men, inwardly free and calm.' In that conversation between Jakob and Delia concerning their child, held at night and overshadowed by anxiety it is the poet himself who is speaking when he makes Delia say: 'You must realize that this child's life is not our own property, not ours nor even the child's. No life in this world is its own, not even that of our people, of which you so bitterly complain.'

A 'Reconciliation' which does not mean either complacency or callousness but arises from deep faith and love: this is the poet's message. 'Reconciliation is possible. It happens every day. . . . It is the earthly symbol of God's love.' It is out of such certainty concerning Divine justice that Delia confesses to her Polish hosts: 'It is only just that every deed should reap its reward.' Might or Right? Which shall prevail? The real enemy is neither German nor Pole, but he who uses force against his neighbour, for thereby he sins against himself and harms the cause of his own people. The author's uncompromising and repeated indictment of 'racial-biological nonsense' and of the persecution of the Jews bears eloquent testimony to his moral integrity. He honestly eschews every aspect of fanaticism and herd-instinct whilst seeking for the reasons which led to the emergence of the German dictatorship.

Thus does the author merge the fate of his characters in a unique pattern of light and shade. He knows that pain must be involved in the doings of mankind. In this vein Cordelia (the name is surely symbolic) writes to Ninette from Rome: 'To be drawn into the whole, into life . . . is the all important thing. We must not exist for ourselves, neither are we able to.' Human happiness is not attained by chance, but through the concord of hearts. Seen from such a viewpoint our passions and troubles seem no more than the play of shadows and no less comical that that of Pyramus and Thisbe with the wall and moon. It is of highly artistic and symbolic significance that von Heiseler begins his novel with the play performed by the grandchildren in the Degeners' home. Illusion and reality, happiness and mourning mingle together and point to future destinies.

EPILOGUE I

The European Scene

SOME TRENDS IN PRESENT DAY LITERARY CRITICISM

CRITICS AND SCHOLARS of literature have to face a real difficulty. In seminars and essays students produce highly subjective impressions, reactions and evaluations, and they often express the view, either explicitly or implicitly, that even their most distinguished teachers are able to produce nothing but subjective opinions. But if history of literature is only an expression of personal likes and dislikes it is certainly not worth studying or even writing unless the author is a genius. Moreover, readers very much rely on authority, and sometimes on authority and rank *only*. On this matter many an amusing story could be and has been told (see pp. 230–1).

We ask ourselves: must and can literature (and in its narrower sense, poetry) provide the standards of value? And again we ask ourselves: are such critical standards derived from literature alone, i.e. without a whole set of preconceived principles which are not literary but moral or social, traditional, conventional, political, etc.? To answer these questions is a prerequisite to all that follows, because everything depends on how we stand towards such problems. All modern trends of literary criticism reflect our attitudes to such views.

Everyone of us must honestly seek a set of standards. The best critics have always tried to derive them from literature. Yet a purely analytical method or technique cannot suffice. Analysis is not and cannot be the final word. After all, literature is a human expression, it is 'human activity'. We must, however, be careful. In our opinion, the work always comes first, although the story of the poet's life and trials is not irrelevant. Criticism must be rooted in the analysis of the work itself, and it must not become a kind of vain self-reflection, or

225

a confession of political and religious creeds; above all, it must not be a private heaven of a few who can boast of a 'unique emotion' which others cannot share.

Moreover, we are not only children of a tradition but we also live in the world of today. No human being can have the 'angelic' view, i.e. see the whole of our human activities in a simultaneous unity. Mozart and Rilke, spoke of, and longed for, this 'angelic' view of an artist's work: for instance, a symphony seen as one whole. Yet our human efforts, our critical analysis particularly, however scrupulous, must remain limited and fragmentary. Therefore the author may be forgiven if his own ruminations fall short of the reader's expectations. Moreover, no attempt is made to achieve completeness in this survey of new approaches and methods.

One more difficulty: A scholar's private sensibility dies with him. But his method and ideas can be handed on to future generations. Again we ask ourselves: which method are we to use? S. Hyman in his discerning *Armed Vision* refers to the many-levelled criticism of T. S. Eliot's *Waste Land.* There is the *Freudian* view: the poem is a symbol of artistic sterility; the *biographical* approach: it is a symbol of T. S. Eliot's pre-conversion state; the *social* aspect: it is a symbol of the frustration and decay of the bourgeois class; the *Marxist* view: symbol of destruction of capitalism; finally, perhaps, in *Jungian* terms: it is a symbol of death and rebirth. Moreover, S. Hyman is right in suggesting that the poets themselves are not always their own best critics. It is true that Ezra Pound says: 'pay no attention to the criticism of men who have never themselves written a notable work . . . if you wanted to know something about an automobile, would you go to a man who had made one and driven it, or to a man who had merely heard about it?' But we also know about Goethe's attitude to H. von Kleist, Schiller's to G. A. Bürger. In extreme cases Jekyll and Hyde are indeed uncannily united in one person.

On the matter of method, the critics are very often irreconcilably divided; e.g. H. Taine stressed the three principles of criticism: time, race, milieu. These criteria very much remind one of Herder's Zeit, Volk, Umgebung. Such a 'positivistic' approach to literature was, as we all know, harshly criticized, particularly towards the end of the last century. The 'ideal critic' would be an impossible combination of the most eminent and original critics who have lived so far. The 'actual critic' must have his own individual yet integrated method. For a critic it must be rather disturbing to have to bear such great responsibility in regard to critical judgement: 'He is, alone and on the authority of his own knowledge, taste and intelligence, the sole guardian of art and its magic portals. A collective or symposium criticism would have the virtue not only of establishing a multiplicity of readings and meanings, but also of giving them all a hearing, and in the last analysis of establishing some true and valid ones. . . . From the interplay of many minds, even many errors, truth arises.'[1]

I

T. S. Eliot's *The Sacred Wood* (1920) is a document of the time. Much of the so-called 'new' criticism stems from it. The author advocates integrity of literature. At the same time he is aware that poetry has something to do with morals and with religion and even with politics. This very much reminds one of Herder's view in his *Briefe zur Beförderung der Humanität* (1793-7) in which he says: 'Poesie ist eine öffentliche Angelegenheit'. Therefore it is not surprising that Herder loves the poetry of Luther, Gleim (*Preussische Kriegslieder von einem Grenadier*, 1758, after the Chevy Chase), E. von Kleist and Klopstock.

T. S. Eliot sees the poet in his time and tradition when he says that a 'historical sense compels a man to write not merely with his own generation in his bones, but with a feeling that the whole of the literature of Europe from Homer and within it the

---

[1] S. Hyman, loc. cit.; cf. also R. S. Crane, *The Languages of Criticism and the Structure of Poetry* (1953): 'The multiplicity of critical languages is . . . something not to be deplored but rather rejoiced in.' My MS. had already gone to print when Miss Helen Gardner's three Riddell Memorial Lectures, *The Limits of Literary Criticism*, were published by the Oxford University Press (1956). In these reflections on the interpretation of poetry and scripture Miss Helen Gardner rightly states: 'One obvious defect of the concentration on the approach to meaning through form and pattern is blindness to the notion that meaning also inheres in style' (p. 56). Analysis can leave out essential values, as we have shown in the chapter on 'Substance and Symbol'. Every serious critic will admit his limitations in his honest attempt to fathom the work in question by analysis *and* interpretation. The way to any real understanding must and can, however, only lead *through* the work itself.

whole of the literature of his own country has a simultaneous existence, and composes a simultaneous order . . . no poet, no artist of any art has his complete meaning alone'.

Of course too much learning might kill the poetic inspiration: 'Some can absorb knowledge, the more tardy must sweat for it. Shakespeare acquired more essential history from Plutarch than most men could from the whole British Museum. . . .'

T. S. Eliot sees the progress of an artist in a continual self-sacrifice and in a continual *extinction of personality*. He demands *tradition* and he rejects the search for novelty; instead of new emotions he seeks the *ordinary ones*; the process of writing is, according to him, conscious and deliberate: 'The bad poet is usually unconscious where he ought to be conscious, and conscious where he ought to be unconscious . . . poetry is not a turning loose of emotion but an escape from emotion; it is not an expression of personality but an escape from personality.' Therefore he does not seek 'sincere' emotion nor merely 'technical' excellence but the expression of *significant emotion which is impersonal* and 'which has its life in the poem and not in the history of the poet'.

There is another aspect to the question which is expressed in literature by figures such as the two Scrooges in Dickens's *Christmas Carol*, Dr. Faustus in Thomas Mann's novel, Wieland der Schmied, and above all the story of Philoctetes. Edmund Wilson in his book *The Wound and the Bow* interprets this story as that of a 'victim of a malodorous disease which renders him abhorrent to society', but makes him master of a super-human art. The bow is useless without Philoctetes; both belong together. According to Edmund Wilson, the creative activity is released because of this physical illness; thus superior strength and human disability are inseparable. In this connexion I need hardly refer to Walter Muschg's brilliant work *Tragische Literaturgeschichte* (1948). He treats not so much of literature but of the misery of our human existence, in particular of the creative writer whose life, in the Greek sense, is tragic, and who has a knowledge of the impending doom. Muschg refers to writers who committed suicide: H. v. Kleist, Nerval, etc., and to those who went mad: Hölderlin, C. F. Meyer, Nietzsche, and to those who took artificial stimulants: Poe, E. T. A.

Hoffman, Verlaine, thus showing literature and tragedy relentlessly linked together. Georg Büchner said: 'Wir haben der
Schmerzen . . . zu wenig . . .' and similarly Grillparzer: 'Ich
brauche eine große Krankheit oder ein großes Unglück. . . .'

The fact is that nowadays writers *and* non-writers suffer
from a psychological 'wound'. We call it neurosis. Is art mainly
a product of suffering? Are all the artists neurotic? The
interpretation of the story of Philoctetes is not absolutely convincing, as S. Hyman points out. The hero has his bow *before*
he suffers the wound: the latter is really 'unrelated to the power
of the bow.' Moreover, according to Professor C. G. Jung, the
artist is *not* a neurotic, as S. Freud at one time thought he was,
but a collective man, 'the carrier and former of the unconsciously active soul of mankind'. And as to the actual creative
process, art is a mystery of whose origin and inner workings
we really know nothing or, at the most, very little indeed.

We seem to have wandered some distance from T. S. Eliot's
Sacred Wood but the problems touched upon here are already
anticipated in T. S. Eliot's criticism, even if not explicitly
mentioned. His judgements are intimately connected with the
whole set of themes which are not literary at all.

2

The book, *Principles of Literary Criticism* (1924), by I. A.
Richards is to some extent a sharp attack on the book, *Art*, by
Clive Bell, who says: 'To appreciate a work of art we need
bring with us nothing from life, no knowledge of its ideas and
affairs, no familiarity with its emotions.' An aesthetic experience
is therefore an experience *sui generis*, and criticism is a kind of
'private heaven for aesthetes'. I. A. Richards rejects such an
implication of the existence of an abstract beauty which is
ineffable, unanalysable. Consequently, he condemns 'l'art pour
l'art'. Like T. S. Eliot, he sees art and morals in close inter-
relationship. He refers to Matthew Arnold's 'poetry . . . a
criticism of life', and also to Shelley's statement: 'the basis of
morality is laid not by preachers but by poets', and to Tolstoy
who denies the value of all human endeavours with the
exception of those which are valuable to all men. In his

Philosophy of Rhetoric (1936), I. A. Richards deals with the working of words and the inter-animation of words. No word has a meaning of its own, independent of its use: 'Bricks, for all practical purposes, hardly mind what other things they are put with. Meanings mind intensely—more indeed than any other sorts of things.' Therefore: 'no word can be judged as to whether it is good or bad, correct or incorrect, beautiful or ugly, or anything else that matters to a writer, *in isolation.* . . . Gross uses of *beautiful* might make the word itself a thing suited only to gross uses. . . . The mere putting together of two things to see what will happen—is a contemporary fashionable aberration.' I. A. Richards bans the word 'beautiful' from criticism, and he shows up many pseudo-statements about good, beautiful and true. He advocates the organic unity of the human personality and a continuity of experience, e.g. man as poet, reader, family man, social being and so on. Poems according to him as well as to T. S. Eliot are experiences which do not differ essentially from a standard ordinary experience; and they are 'communicable'. Such a view is directly opposed to that of Clive Bell.

I. A. Richards in his *Practical Criticism* tried to found a laboratory technique in literary criticism. He wants to improve the reading and appreciation of literature, calling for intelligent and sensitive reading. For years he tried out his method which is a simple one. He gives us examples in his *Practical Criticism.* He handed printed sheets of poems, without mentioning the names of their authors and with modernized spelling, to his students at Cambridge who were asked to read them carefully and comment on them. These comments, called 'protocols' were collected after a week and discussed in class. There was no compulsion to write the protocols, but 60 per cent. sent them in regularly. Great precautions were taken to ensure anonymity. These protocols, we hear, revealed 'the most shocking picture of the general reading ever presented'. First of all, the students were accustomed to lean on authoritative judgements. As soon as this 'help' was taken away from them they were like invalids without crutches. Secondly, without any guiding authority upon whom to lean, almost all the accepted assessments of literary values were reversed. But 'the really terrifying thing' was the realization that the protocol writers were '*not* typical readers of poetry, but particularly superior readers: prospective teachers, writers, even poets reading under almost ideal conditions'. Of course, there were some difficulties: no authority mentioned, no guidances as to old spelling or the provenance of the work in question.

The indecisions as to what a word or expression means are analysed in William Empson's *Seven Types of Ambiguity* (1930): 'a word in a speech which falls outside the expected vocabulary will cause an uneasy stir in all but the soundest sleepers; many sermons rely with a painful frankness upon this'. . . . This study of double meanings is followed by Empson's still more detailed verbal analysis, called *The Structure of Complex Words*, which will occupy the attention of scholars fascinated by the so-called poetic keywords in Shakespeare's dramas.

3

F. W. Bateson, in his recent study, *English Poetry* (1950), goes a long way with I. A. Richards. But he also goes much further, when he interprets Gray's *Elegy written in a Country Churchyard* (1751) as a 'tract for the times'. He stresses the primacy of meaning. 'The contribution that each word, image, or rhythm makes to the poem must be primarily explicable in rational terms. . . . Poetry differs from prose and everyday speech mainly because it says so much more in the same number of words. But it is a difference of degree not of kind. In analysing and paraphrasing a poem we are not transposing it into a wholly different medium.'

Poems, however, such as W. Blake's *O rose thou art sick* . . . or Goethe's *Auf dem See*, or Hölderlin's *Hälfte des Lebens* seem to have been created in a language of their own, which primarily is not only meaning but at the same time also symbolic sound and imagery. The irrational quality of incantation is equally significant. As we shall see, F. W. Bateson later endeavours to reconcile both views.

The subject-matter of poetry is, according to F. W. Bateson's book on *English Poetry*, not things but a synthesis of conflicting moods and attitudes. These must be 'opposite' or 'discordant'. Whenever such fundamental conflicts of human and social

attitudes are absent, poetry, according to him, is empty.
Consistently, the author in this connexion stresses less the verbal
magic and more the semantic synthesis (which is a normal
function of thought) in a poem. Things, though apparently
disconnected, and even contradictory, are seen in an inner
inter-relationship. Poetry is defined as 'human nature in its
social relations'. All poems are therefore in the last analysis
public poems. The reading of poetry and the writing of poetry
are both social duties, and the poet is a functional member of
society. But we have already referred to the six notions, singled
out by R. de Souza from Abbé's doctrine.[1] A more recent,
and a more decisive discussion of the whole subject is to be
found in Thierry Maulnier's introduction to his anthology,
Introduction à la poésie française (1939).

There is no doubt that several of the above essential points
can also be accepted by F. W. Bateson who tries to understand
and interpret the inner form of a work of art with special
reference to the pattern of social relationship of which it is both
an effect (sociologically) and a cause (aesthetically). Thus he
attempts to catch its human significance in between the two
poles or attitudes. F. W. Bateson can most aptly call himself
a cultural middleman who keeps up with both Medusa and
Perseus, or perhaps better, with Medusa, Perseus, and Perseus's
mirror; cf. pp. 38ff. here.

The key to a real understanding of F. W. Bateson's views lies
in his suggestive manifesto: *The Function of Criticism at the Present
Time* (*Essays in Criticism*, Vol. III, January 1953), in which the
author neither reduces literature to 'cultural anthropology'
nor confines it to textual interpretation. Whilst the author of
English Poetry, in our opinion, over-stresses the exploration
of literature's social roots he here happily combines all four
levels of criticism in his deliberations on the four stages of
criticism: the verbal, the literary, the intellectual, and the
social stages. The assumption is, of course, that the critic as well
as the reader are responsible beings who do not surrender to
the glamour of a 'bright idea', and who try to understand
literature as an expression of 'life frozen into immobility at its

---

[1] Cf. *La Poésie Pure*, par Henri Bremond, de l'Académie Française, avec *Un
Débat sur la Poésie*, par Robert de Souza (1926).

points of highest consciousness and integration'. The emphasis lies neither on verbal analysis, stylistic details and structural patterns nor on social, ideological background studies, but the author demands an 'equilibrium between literary meaning in the ordinary sense and the social contexts in which meaning alone acquires value'. Thus responsible literary criticism should result in the 'reconstruction of a human situation that is demonstrably implicit in the particular literary work under discussion'.

Such a view as expressed by F. W. Bateson's above-mentioned book, will rely neither solely on the infallibility of the so-called 'practical criticism' nor on sweeping biographical, historical and sociological interpretations, but it will always endeavour, in the sense of its distinguished forerunner (Matthew Arnold), to combine all the above stages in a balanced critical assessment of the work of art in question. Similar thoughts are also expressed in *The Broken Cistern* by the eminent scholar and writer, Bonamy Dobrée. His book consists of the Clark Lectures, 1952-3, which he gave under the significant title: 'Public Themes in English Poetry.' To him poetry is 'the product of the creative imagination, but also the vehicle for communicating what would seem to be the basic and permanent emotions through which the mass of humanity lives out its life'. The very lack of public, i.e. impersonal themes such as stoicism, scientism, patriotism accounts, according to Bonamy Dobrée, for one of the reasons why poetry is so little read today.

4

In his *Essays in Criticism*, F. W. Bateson accuses the dauntless chief Editor of *Scrutiny*, F. R. Leavis, of reducing literary history to criticism. Leavis rightly says that he knows of 'no literary history that does not make a show of criticism. . . . Any history that deals in influence is committed to criticism,' and in *New Bearings in English Poetry* (1932) he gives new directions to literary criticism: 'English poetry in future must develop, if at all, along some other line than that running from the Romantics through Tennyson, Swinburne, *A Shropshire Lad*, and Rupert Brooke.' T. S. Eliot's *Prufrock* (1917) is, according to

F. R. Leavis, an important event in the history of English poetry.
Here is a characteristic intermingling of irony, memory, and
desire in the present barrenness, and it is a poetry which is
complicated, because 'not only poetry, but literature and art in
general are becoming more specialized. The process is implicit in the process of modern civilization. . . '. Again, as in
the case of I. A. Richards, *words* are the basis of criticism.
F. R. Leavis wants a precise discrimination over words; moreover, the use of 'negative emotion' is stressed.

By negative emotions the 'Scrutiny' criticism understands
'emotions engendered by the clash of personality and the
hostility of circumstances', i.e. satires, invectives, e.g. Swift's
The Lady's Dressing Room. In the selections from *The Calendar
of Modern Letters 1925-7*, called *Towards Standards of Criticism*
(chosen and introduced by F. R. Leavis) the use of negative
emotions is dealt with by Edgell Rickword: 'A poem must
at some point or another, release, enable to flow back to the
level of active life, the emotions caught up from life and pent
in the aesthetic reservoir. . . . The modern poet is to his audience an author, not a man. It is interested in his more generalized emotions, not in his relation with the life and people
around him. Yet to himself the poet should be in the first
place, a man, not an author. . . . At the present he is inhibited
by a set of emotions (those we call negative emotions) because
of a prejudice against them. . . .'

Scrutiny, as its brilliant exponent, F. R. Leavis, himself had
made known in his 'manifesto', was no mere supplement for
literary criticism, but adapted itself to the movement of the whole
of our modern civilization; although it was mainly based on anti-
Marxist views, the magazine did not disclaim the dependence
of the human spirit on economic conditions, but it rested
essentially on the belief of the autonomy of art and the preservation of the century-long tradition of its inheritance: *Scrutiny* was
generally formed on liberal lines free from fashion and did not
fall victim of the Determinism of the 'thirties nor the Existentialism of the 'forties.

The criticisms are penetrating and constructive. It speaks for
itself that, since 1932, *Scrutiny* has stood in the foreground of
intellectual analysis. Although it unfortunately came to an

end in October 1953 it has made history in the world of letters. In his 'Valedictory' (last issue of *Scrutiny*, October 1953) the Editor, F. R. Leavis, could proudly put this statement on record: '*Scrutiny* lasted for more than twenty years, and has not had to stop for any lack of a supporting public.' A year later (October 1954) in 'La Revue des Lettres Modernes' A. Charles Tomlinson ('*La Critique en Angleterre depuis la Guerre*', pp. 19ff.) published a most lucid and succint appreciation of *Scrutiny* and literary criticism in general.

This new interpretation of the poetical power of expression rests in its beginnings on certain standards of criticism which go back to the 'twenties and 'thirties, for example T. S. Eliot's *The Sacred Wood* (1920), J. Middleton Murry's *The Problem of Style* (1922), I. A. Richards's *Principles of Literary Criticism* (1924); indirectly, through T. S. Eliot, Remy de Gourment's conception of style ('le style est une specialization de la sensibilité') is also in sympathy with them. What *Scrutiny* understands by 'standards of criticism' is elucidated in F. R. Leavis's Foreword to the *Calendar of Modern Letters 1925-7* (1933), the direct predecessor of that new literary interpretation. Its main concern is the analysis of words, images and word gestures. He who does not understand poetry, will, according to him, not understand the novel and drama, because he lacks an essential qualification—the understanding of word values which must be rooted in life.

5

Amongst the Danish studies on the problems of reality and symbol, Erik Lunding's *Strömungen und Strebungen der modernen Literaturwissenschaft* (Aarhus, 1952), is a remarkable achievement in literary criticism. In the foreground of this book, which excels in its pleasantly concise analysis and keenly intellectual perception, lies the study of German literary history and analysis. The following are emphasized as the two main methods of research: (*a*) Geistesgeschichte and Stil- und Gattungsgeschichte; (*b*) Wortkunstinterpretation. Unfortunately, all too often either literature or analysis suffers, the one by overstressing scientific ideas and constructions, the other by overstressing subjective impressions. In this connexion the author speaks forcefully of the struggle of logic with myth, and he looks for the synthesis between Stoff- und Sinnhuberei, and a combination between Anglo-Saxon sense of realism and Herder's philosophical universalism.

The author successfully singles out a concrete example, i.e. the analysis and interpretation of A. Stifter's work, and he points to the dangers of the too-frequently eclectic method of research, e.g. the work of Alfred Winterstein, who interprets Stifter's paintings as a sublimation of 'Analeroticism', carries psychoanalysis to absurdity; according to Winterstein 'daemonisch' means 'psychopathisch'. Walther Rehm in his study of A. Stifter's *Nachsommer* is revealed as master of the art of creating moods and as preserver of our Western values. Hermann Kunisch in *Adalbert Stifter* lucidly interprets A. Stifter as the poet of mankind. Curt Hohoff masters the intangible element of impressionistic art. Moriz Enzinger's positivistic research deals with A. Stifter's early *Studienjahre* and investigates the latter's textbooks and school reports, etc. Marianne Ludwig's interpretation of A. Stifter's motifs and symbols is a valuable contribution to our Stifter research. Other works, in contrast, are basically philosophical and political propaganda or a disguised biography which stops short before the actual analysis of the work. The morphological method of literary analysis hovers between the spirit and real life, occasionally at the cost of form- and word-analysis.

Günther Müller and Horst Oppel are brought forward as representatives of the morphological approach, but E. Lunding goes different ways whilst H. Oppel, to whose original research we all are much indebted, is deeply concerned with Gestaltanalyse. Horst Oppel, the distinguished author of the *Literaturwissenschaft in der Gegenwart* (1939), *Morphologische Literaturwissenschaft* (1947) and the most recent new contribution to Wolfgang Stammler's *Deutsche Philologie im Aufriß* (second edition, 1956): *Methodenlehre der Literaturwissenschaft*, interprets literature in accordance with Goethe's concept of the term 'Gestalt', i.e. as an expression of organic creation in poetry. A work of art has, accordingly, its own compelling laws of unity, its own life as regards use of language, metre, rhythm, imagery, etc. Horst Oppel's ingenious research above all endeavours to free criticism of its frequent pitfalls: mechanical formalism and impressionistic aestheticism.

Erik Lunding in his above work disapproves of G. Müller's predilection for 'vegetation similes' (seed, bloom, fruit, etc.) which, he declares, are typical contaminations of spiritual with natural organisms. As an example of a biologically directed interpretation of literature, F. J. Billeskow Jansen's *Esthétique de l'oeuvre d'art littéraire* (1948) is cited, in which the stages of animal development: egg, larva, cocoon, butterfly—are transposed into terms of human art. Such a 'morphological' approach in literary criticism is called fundamentally an escape from historiography, but E. Lunding's research is not in essential disagreement with the best results of morphological studies. Moreover, if the study of the influence of generations is recognized in its importance, it must, according to him, not get tangled up in the web of abstract numbers of statistics. The author fights for a new and intimate welding of the history of intellectual ideas, style and species, especially with regard to the late Middle Ages, Gottsched, 'Storm und Stress' and 'Poetic Realism'; for each work of art, although a unity in itself, has depth and breadth which go beyond its own bounds. He therefore rejects the blind analysis of pure formal patterns; he equally decries any slavish dependence on ideological themes, especially in the case of poetry which does not contain in itself any assumption of a higher intellectual subject-matter, e.g. E. Mörike's *Auf eine Lampe*. (It would be misleading to interpret this poem in terms of Heidegger's formulae and E. Staiger's far-fetched arguments, cf. p. 248.)

The ideal of E. Lunding's research lies in a combination of form and idea. We must, according to him, reconcile the histories of language, word, style and spiritual development.

Erik Lunding's book, *Wege zur Kunstinterpretation*, also *Acta Jutlandica* (Aarhus, 1953), continues the preceding thoughts, and enlarges upon them by means of illustrative examples. The author proceeds from the realization that the terminology of style is, in general, international. In the foreground of his research is the problem of reality and symbol, above all the 'intrinsic approach, the inner form'. This means: the only way to the understanding of a work of art lies through its inward form. In literary criticism we must start from the centre of growth. (This is also the ideal method of the true morphological approach, of which H. Oppel is one of the most renowned exponents.)

At this point the value and the futility of psychoanalytical and sociological research (particularly with regard to Minnesang and Baroque literature) are assessed. It is repeatedly stressed—as already in the previous book—that although we are to concentrate on the work of art, we must at the same time delve into history, for by denying the historical aspect false verdicts occur: for example, Hans Sachs may not be reproached for a lack of elegance, nor the German Baroque poets for a lack of restraint, nor should literary research encroach too much on the grounds of comparative mythology.

Here the writer turns not so much to the study of German literature as to that of Russian, American, French and Italian writers. He is concerned with the study of that 'inner form' which is so often found lacking in literary criticism, for the latter often has its origins only in the inquisitiveness of the mere seeker after knowledge, and is burdened by impressions which are in the nature of a history of culture, or, when gathered together, is an assortment of biographical-historical-geographical data, instead of an organically functioning unity.

In the passage on 'Interpretation' the author puts forward the undeniable fact that, in Germany, it is only after the Second World War that the art of analysis and interpretation has come into full fashion.

6

As regards the study of imagery, W. H. Clemen's *The Development of Shakespeare's Imagery* (1951) (in German, *Shakespeares Bilder*, 1936) is one of the most distinguished German contributions to modern Shakespeare research. The J. G. Phil. states: 'Clemen investigates for the first time the bearing of Shakespeare's Imagery on the many-fold aspects of his dramatic art (or theme, structure, characterization, diction) . . .' the character of *Richard II* is expressed through imagery. The king 'who characteristically thinks in images, sees himself as a sun, as an actor, as a bucket, who sinks in a well while the opposite bucket (Bolingbroke) rises, and thereby reveals himself as one who spends his energies in words rather than deeds. . . . Through images Shakespeare creates a unity of atmosphere and mood that binds together the separate elements into an organic whole in which all the parts are inter-related and mutually attuned. This is a new dramatic unity comparable in effect to the Classic unity of time, place and action. . . . The images are not isolated.' W. H. Clemen's method is entirely different from Caroline Spurgeon's *Imagery And What It Tells Us* (1935), e.g. her statistics about *Nature*: flowers, trees, fruit; *Weather*: cold, storm, cloud, etc. *Sea and Ships, Stars, Moon, Shadows, Animals*: dogs, birds, bees, flies, spiders, reptiles, fish, *Human Daily Life*: learning, arts, etc. C. Spurgeon gives us a classification and static list of images in Shakespeare's plays. She enumerates facts about his life, his sense of sight, hearing, his likes, his dislikes, his acute sense of smell, his dislike of perfume (Coriolanus), but W. H. Clemen studies their relationship between imagery and the situation, which gave rise to it. He shows how the imagery fixed the character of a person, or atmosphere of a play or the dramatic action. The images, according to him, prepare the audience for coming events; they suggest, anticipate and emphasize dramatic action, and ambiguity plays an enormous part in it: cf. 'Our day is gone': is it Cassius's day, is it a real day, or a whole period of life?

In Shakespeare's greatest tragedies the image is the central point, die Urzelle in the organism of a work of art, and is not to be divorced from its context or the life of a poem, e.g. Hölderlin's image *Chaos* (meaning 'das Offene') or the image of the *bucket* and the *untended garden* in Shakespeare's *Richard II*, or the image of the clothed (hypocritical) dagger and the naked babe, the 'uncontrollable mystery on the bestial floor'.

Thus W. H. Clemen shows how Shakespeare in his maturer plays uses imagery as an integral part of his creative work: 'It is the dramatic issues (*not* so much the playwright's individual sympathies) which decide as to the nature and use of the imagery. The latter takes on the function of dramatic unity, of a centrally organizing force which in effect has justly been compared to the so-called classical unities of place, time and action'; cf. the three groups of images: *sex, war, love* through which

Othello's character is revealed. His uncompromising love knows but 'either—or'—II, I.

> '. . . O my soul's joy! . . .
> . . . If it were now to die,
> 'Twere now to be most happy . . .

or cf. the passionate outburst in III, III, 453, the wild despair in the farewell speech, III, III, 348, and his confession in the same act (III, III, 92):

> . . . and when I love thee not,
> Chaos is come again. . . .

He is wounded to the core of his very existence as soon as the security of his feeling and love for Desdemona seems to be shattered (IV, II, 46ff.): 'Had it pleas'd heaven to try me with affliction. . . .'

In *King Lear* the images bring the power of Nature, Heaven, and Cosmos into action. Lear is indeed very rich in imagery—'der bilderreichste Shakespeare Held'. In contrast to W. H. Clemen, William Empson applies a different method in his *Structure of Complex Words*. According to him, the literary metaphors are essentially *cognitive* (not *emotive*). He concentrates his study on *keywords*: 'sense' in *Measure for Measure*; 'honest' in *Othello*; 'folly' in *King Lear*, etc., and is thus also able to throw new light on great works of literature.

7

E. R. Curtius's book *European Literature and the Latin Middle Ages* (1948, German; 1953, English) is 'unique in sweep and scope'. The author, who died in 1956, has a sharp eye for significant facts. He is forever tracing images, phrases, things, words back to their origins, to their archetypes. Thus, the central theme of a book is the development of the so-called 'topoi'. E. R. Curtius stands for strict philological method. He investigates poetry in relation to philosophy and theology, above all, he approaches literature through the technique of philological exactitude. Philology is to him not an end in itself, but it explains the medieval basis of Western thought. He sees the Middle Ages as a coherent whole, as a continuity from antiquity up to our Modern Age. He says: 'he who would study European literature has only to familiarize himself with the method and subjects of Classical medieval Latin and modern philology'. He combines specialization with universalism.

On the occasion of the Goethe Bicentenary in 1949 at Aspen, Colorado, he spoke of this relationship between specialization and universalism. In the above book he shows how special forms of medieval Latin literature took their origin in antiquity, how they were transformed in the Middle Ages, and how they are living on in present-day European literature.

European literary criticism had already, before the book appeared, undergone a radical change of method. Essays, criticism, books, and discussion showed signs of a trend towards new and changed orientation. The Fifth Literary Congress, *F.I.L.L.M.* (*Fédération Internationale des Langues et Littératures Modernes*) of 27-31 March 1951, was a manifestation of that reorientation in literary criticism as regards national histories and super-national interpretation. At Eastertide, the town of Florence with its Strozzi and Pitti palaces, Renaissance sculptures and museums, served, for this Fifth Congress, as a gathering-place of learned guests from Europe, Africa, India, and the U.S.A. The festive inauguration took place in the Palazzo Vecchio, where the Medici had long ago displayed their lavish magnificence. The discussions and lectures dealt with the subject of the interrelationship between art and literature, with special reference to structure, formal patterns, and indeed providing the survey of a vast intellectual space, from the Middle Ages up to the present time.

Those stimulating lectures and debates covered a wide but unified field of interests: methods, interrelationships between theatre and plastic art, Antique and Baroque elements in Shakespeare's works, the sonnets of Michelangelo, Goethe's *Italian Journey*, a comparison of Goethe, Ruskin and Taine; Wölfflin's *Principles of Art Criticism* as applied to literary criticism, imagery, literary, types and motifs, Romanticism and Neo-Romanticism, and C. F. Meyer's indebtedness to plastic art, Symbolism, Botticelli's and Gozzoli's and Fra Angelico's influences on Rilke, etc. Social evenings, excursions to Fiesole and Siena added splendour to the Fifth Congress of *F.I.L.L.M.*, which was inspired not only by a desire to bring together prominent scholars of different intellectual outlook, but also of different nationalities representing almost the whole of Europe.[1]

It goes without saying that this is of course not new ground. There were already distinguished powers at work a long time before that Fifth Congress and even before the First one in Budapest (1930), which emphasized the super-national approach to questions of literary research and the unity of Western thought as opposed to the constricting self-sufficiency of each individual nation. Yet the change of attitude is particularly strongly expressed for the first time in the very recent literary researches. However, in many well-meant instances we find ourselves still a long way from really comparative studies.

Consequently the so-called *Handbook of World Literature*, by Hanns W. Eppelsheimer (2 vols., Frankfurt, 1937, 1947), appears to us a bibliography forcibly thrown together. The author introduces each chapter with a few sentences which all too often lead the unguarded reader astray, by their short 'explanation' and by their generalizations, e.g. with reference to the Chinese lyric (the great R. Wilhelm mentioned in the book has apparently hardly been seriously read), or again with reference to the medieval exemplum, the 'Frau Welt' theme, the 'devil's literature', etc. Finally, where is the important English literature on Hölderlin?

Unfortunately, such books fail to reveal Western unity of expression. It is not yet done by quotations from the texts of different European writings: The works to be compared whether from Romance, Germanic, or English literature, etc., must be judged from the point of view of timeless, formal values. Moreover, literary history and literary criticism do not exclude each other because a sound critical analysis can, to a certain extent, only be achieved within the given facts of space and time. Yet many studies of comparison between literature and society have little in common with literary criticism, but belong to the so-called sociological background studies of literature.

The term 'Vergleichende Literaturgeschichte' is still

[1] The Sixth Triennial Congress of *F.I.L.L.M.* took place at Oxford 1954, when the author of this book expounded some of the above ideas in his Paper: *Scientific analysis and interpretation in modern German literary criticism* (Oxford 1955), 'Literature and Science.'

frequently misinterpreted. According to the Stammler-Merker *Reallexikon* (the second revised and enlarged edition is being edited by the Professors W. Kohlschmidt and W. Mohr), certain germs of comparative literature studies are already to be found in ancient criticism and were developed further by Renaissance poetry with its cosmopolitan tendencies. Goethe's thoughts on 'Weltliteratur' gave a powerful fillip to research, as also did Hegel's consideration of poetry as an entity.

The comparative method was advocated in L. W. Menzel's *Deutsche Literatur*. In 1886 M. Koch founded the *Zeitschrift für vgl. Literaturgeschichte*, in 1903 appeared the American *Journal of Comparative Literature*, and in Paris in 1921 the French *Révue de littérature comparée*. In most recent times, E. R. Curtius and Erich Auerbach among others may be singled out as forerunners and pioneers in research in comparative literature. But that which so often sails under the flag of 'World Literature' is mostly 'Western' writing.

Ernst Robert Curtius, in his *Europäische Literatur und Lateinisches Mittelalter*, considers European literature, not as the sum of national literature, but as a unity, an interconnected system of expression, which can be traced from ancient times, through the Middle Ages, and into the eighteenth century and beyond— for instance, the tradition of 'topics', metaphoric language, allegory, especially speeches of consolation, eulogies ('Lobtopik'), nature symbols, idealized landscapes, etc.

In place of 'Geistesgeschichte', E. R. Curtius presents us with a fascinating system of literary formulas and patterns. He endeavours to project the whole poetic substance on to a single theme, or, as he himself says, like a lens, he seeks to gather rays of light out of thousands of years.

Such literary research revolutionizes much of its traditional method. Thus the French canon, 'la domination du goût français', proves to be too narrow, because Europe consists (according to E. R. Curtius) of *two* cultural spheres: the Antique Mediterranean and the Modern Occidental, and European literature comprises a period of about 2,500 years. Therefore literary criticism entails more than a knowledge of the development from the Middle Ages up to our age. The continuous growing of Western literature from Antiquity must be of greater importance to scholars than the study of certain influences and themes.

In the centre of E. R. Curtius's thought stands, as already mentioned, Antiquity. The continuity of the literary 'constants': the *Topoi* and *Tropoi*, etc., is thereby unfolded before us with the refreshing joy of conqueror and discoverer. It is certain that the *Song of Roland* (it exhibits stylistic elements which show a knowledge of Vergil and late antique Vergilian interpretation), the courtly novel in verse, the allegoric-didactic poetry, Shakespeare (based on Plutarch and Seneca), Racine (Euripides), Goethe, and now J. Joyce (*Odyssey*), T. S. Eliot (Dante, Aeschylus), Baudelaire (Latin hymns), Stefan George (Nonnos), and others indicate the way in which the ancient and modern writers are bound up with one another.

But besides this, other almost equally powerful streams are in motion: Persia and India (cf. *Tristan*, Romanticism, Schopenhauer), China (cf. G. Mahler), Celtic impulses, etc. All this seems to be overshadowed by the powers of Antiquity. Perhaps not rightly so. There is, unfortunately, no room here to go into the matter further.

The chief attraction of E. R. Curtius's vigorous and successful argumentation lies perhaps in his unique research into the so-called 'Topoi'. These are 'loci communes', a string of arguments, which are applicable to the most varied cases. The term 'Topoi', however, seems unfortunate to us because of its strong similarity with the term 'Tropoi', for it easily leads to confusion. These 'Topoi' were originally 'aids for the construing of speeches'; they were already an important source of supply for the train of thought: 'Fundgruben für den Gedankengang' (argumentorum sedes). Curtius points to ancient store-houses of 'Topoi'; he brings an abundance of examples, e.g. the eulogy (praise of the ancestors and their deeds), speech of condolence, affected modesty, moreover Exordialtopik, Schlußtopik, The Mad World (Torentopik), the boy (Achilles) and the old man, old woman and young girl, the 'old-young' super-human woman, the dedication (Topik, etc.). Of course, not *all* 'Topoi' can be traced back to Antique rhetoric.

Amongst the Topoi he mentions the poetic topics concerning the beauty of nature: the ideal landscape with its typical equipment, e.g. grove, pleasance (locus amoenus), exotic fauna and flora, etc., dreamlands, and the dream ages, the earthly paradise and golden age. Such conceptual patterns are traced back to their origins, and investigated in medieval and later poetry. The author shows that medieval poetry was far too lacking in independence to give a living development to *nature topics* which it had received from Antiquity. Medieval poetry does not, on the whole, invoke nature (as Aeschylus', Sophocles', and Homer's do); 'it enumerates its component parts'. Invocation of nature we also find in the Bible, *Matthew* 27, 51, *Psalms* 96, 11-12. As said above, in medieval poetry there is no new development to this topic.

In contrast to the poetic topics the *Tropoi* are figures of speech, metaphoric expressions or 'turns'. In his *Notes and Essays* about the primordial elements in Oriental poetry (see his reference to the camel and the horse), Goethe himself has given us the most important insight into the workings of such figures of speech; see also Goethe's *Maxims and Meditations*.

According to E. R. Curtius, the term 'Tropik' is equivalent to that of 'Metaphorik', but 'Tropik' and 'Topik' cannot be strictly separated, cf. Greis and Mädchen. The author surveys rich sources of material: sea-journey metaphors ('Dichten' = vela dare), personifying metaphors ('Schrecken' = the son of Ares), food metaphors (the Christian teaching as coena), metaphors of parts of the body (eyes of the soul, knees of the heart = genua cordis), stage-metaphors (Calderon's *Welttheater*), book-metaphors (the book of nature, the stars as letters), the monkey (simius becomes simia as a symbol of illusion and delusion). Thus, at individual points of conflagration in the temporally fixed material the timeless image is realized and an inestimably valuable storage of literary forms is unfolded before the researcher with an European attitude of mind.

Although E. R. Curtius sees the whole Middle Ages in its continuity from Antiquity to our modern age, there is no question that the *formal* element is in the foreground, and he clearly rejects the excesses of Geistesgeschichte. Forms are, according to him, 'configurations or systems of configurations in which the incorporeal things of the mind can manifest themselves, and become apprehensible'. Dante, for instance, orders the blessed in circles of life and crosses of life. The author collects such literary and formal patterns and tries to discover their traces in present day literature, e.g. Stefan George, Baudelaire, etc. Thus he proves the continuity of the above literary constants which live on in the memory of European writing.

8

Erich Auerbach in his *Mimesis* (*The representation of reality in Western literature*) (Bern, 1946), seeks, in a similar way, the uniting element in European writing. He breaks with the traditional method of literary criticism when he deals with the problem of mixed style in European literature from Homer to Schiller and even to our present age (Virginia Woolf's *Lighthouse*) and with that of pure style, which allows of no intermingling of tragedy and comedy.

Already the Christian Realism of the Middle Ages had rejected the 'Classical' pre-eminence, and nowadays modern Realism has done the same. It seems to us, however, that, using such a method, in the end everything (including Persian, Indian, and Arabic) could be housed under *one* roof, if only the 'general denominator' were sufficiently wide.

Naturally, one cannot expect here a systematic, all-embracing study of European Realism; such an attempt would already have come to grief in the masses of material alone. But the inner unity is scarcely achieved, for the single themes, however subtly and lucidly analysed, could just as well be taken from European as from *non*-European writings. The period of time which has been chosen spans about three thousand years, but the gaps are too big to ascribe to the work the compelling unity of leading thoughts which the author wants to point out in connexion with fundamental motifs:

(1) Homer: *Odyssey*, 19th canto, the return of Odysseus is compared with the scene: Abraham and Isaac in the Bible (*Genesis*). (2) Fortunata: description of the symposium by Petronius (arbiter elegantiarum) in the house of the rich upstart, Trimalchio; (3) *The Song of Roland*; (4) Chrestien's *Yvain*; (5) *Adam and Eve*, An Old French Mystery Play; (6) Rabelais, Shakespeare (*Henry IV*), Moliére (*Tartuffe*),

Schiller (*Kabale and Liebe*), Stendhal (*Le Rouge et le Noir*), Zola and European parallels; Virginia Woolf; Proust; James Joyce, etc.

The work is most stimulating, perhaps a landmark, but no comprehensive and systematic assessment of the development of European Realism.

Wolfgang Kayser's *Das sprachliche Kunstwerk* (1948) is a very good introduction into literary criticism. According to W. Kayser, the poet's work always comes first in literary criticism. He calls it an organic unity: 'ein in sich geschlossenes sprachliches Gefüge'—'Das einzelne Werk aber ist der eigentliche Gegenstand der Wissenschaft von der Dichtung. . . . Das sprachliche Kunstwerk lebt als solches und in sich selbst.' But his statement that 'a new phase' in the history of literary criticism has begun does not seem to hold good, particularly in view of the epoch-making and already well-established research by O. Walzel, F. Strich, etc. All these have turned away from literary history towards analysis of poetry and interpretation of texts. W. Kayser's work is, however, of great significance. Content and form are seen as inseparable elements of expression, the history of literature is not reduced to literary criticism, but both are equally important.

The principles of method are clearly expounded: (*a*) a work of art is a world in itself, it has its own meaning; (*b*) it is the expression of a creative mind; (*c*) it is, at the same time, the manifestation of a special epoch and race; (*d*) last, not least, it is a historical document. Thus, Taine's three criteria, time, race, and milieu, are reinstated, but not absolutely. Whilst in the nineteenth-century German research the stress lay on literary history and not so much on the study of words and imagery, etc., literary history and a critical interpretation (analysis and evaluation) are now closely interlinked. The work of art is seen and interpreted as an independent whole. The poet is not immanent in his creative work, but no critic or writer can deny his individuality, generation, and provenance. Yet again and again the fundamental principle of the work itself as the central theme of literary criticism is reasserted.

In W. Kayser's essay on literary analysis and valuation:

Literarische Wertung und Interpretation (in *Der deutsche Unterricht*, 1952), thoughts already implied in the above book find further elucidation: for instance, the reliability of certain criteria hitherto accepted is challenged: (*a*) the time factor: a work which has survived fifty years and thus stood the test of almost two generations cannot always claim an infallible value, e.g. Ganghofer; (*b*) there is the question of the effect the work has on other writers, e.g. Opitz's fame is greater than his creative achievement, particularly in comparison with Fleming and Gryphius; (*c*) the historical function of a work or writer can also lead to misjudgements—for instance, Bohse's and other fashionable writers' influence on Wieland; (*d*) the question of authenticity and originality, e.g. Homer's *Iliad* is not the work of *one* man, Gottfried's *Tristan* is dependent on Thomas, Shakespeare's witches scene in *Macbeth* is probably partly by Middleton: in the case of Gottfried's *Tristan*, which closely follows Thomas's story, its originality consists in the artistic style, grace, and musical beauty of the Middle High German romance; (*e*) then there is the question of *actuality* and *genuinness*: they, too, are no absolute criteria. For instance, Iffland's *Ambition and Crime* (*Verbrecher aus Ehrsucht*) is perhaps closer to the actual conditions of life at that time than Goethe's *Iphigenie*.

Finally, W. Kayser (like F. R. Leavis, L. C. Knights, etc.) stresses the *unity* of a work of art which need not mean harmony, but a unity containing intense conflicts. He calls it 'Einstimmigkeit', not 'Unstimmigkeit'. Interpretation and evaluation are with W. Kayser (as in the case of F. R. Leavis and in fact all responsible critics) inseparable. Analysis means also criticism, because we are to find out what the work of art and its author do want and should want.

W. Kayser's presentation is distinguished by clarity and simplicity and stands in harsh contrast to the writings of the 'Existentialists'. M. Heidegger is often given a key position in literary research (e.g. E. Staiger's unacceptably pretentious chapter in *Kunst der Interpretation*), but some expressions—'Stiftung', a term for conceiving poetry, or 'Geworfenheit', a term for man's precarious existence in our doomed civilization—are like 'a rephrasing of an old truth' (*P.M.L.A.*, H. Jaeger, Sept. 1952).

In contemporary German studies in this country and in the U.S.A. the very obvious turn from literary history to literary appreciation, from the search for milieus, background studies, and the spheres of influences ad infinitum to the exact analysis of style, found a welcome echo in the tradition-bound English school of research, e.g. in the Inaugural Lecture, *Literary Interpretation in Germany* (Cambridge University Press, 1952) of Professor W. H. Bruford. During the course of his lecture he points to a very similar development in literary research in Russia after the Revolution of 1917. There, in the year 1918, a formalist movement was formed by Viktor Shklovsky and Viktor Vinogradov, etc., which arose from linguistic and literary form-studies on the basis of foreign, influential movements (represented especially by Sievers, Scripture, Walzel).

The former new movement was borne by the conviction that the literary personality differed throughout from the everyday individuality of a writer. Thus the biographical, historical-sociological and philosophical methods of research were rejected. But with the tightening up of the régime, there occurred another change in Russian literary criticism, which now placed ideological values above the purely artistic, as was done, for example, by L. I. Timofeev in 1948.

The Czechoslovakian school of formalism came via London to the U.S.A., and particularly so through the comprehensive work about literary theory, interpretation, and methodology by Austin Warren and René Wellek (London, 1949), in which, by detailed observation, not only prosody, the analysis of poetry, and criticism were offered, but also literary history. According to W. H. Bruford's estimation, American researchers have already since 1927 turned away from literary history towards analysis of poetry and interpretation of texts.

As a matter of fact, the above-mentioned book by Warren and Wellek, *Theory of Literature*, even if not in every detail, reminds us of O. Walzel's *Gehalt und Gestalt* (1923), B. Tomashevsky's *Teoriya literatury* (1925, sixth edition, 1931), J. Petersen's *Die Wissenschaft von der Dichtung* (1939), and of the post-war works: W. Kayser's *Das sprachliche Kunstwerk* (1948). P. Böckmann's *Formgeschichte der deutschen Literatur*, I, 1949, and W. Stammler's *Deutsche Philologie im Aufriß* (unter Mitarbeit

249

zahlreicher namhafter Fachgelehrter, 1952 ff.), 2nd enlarged and revised edition just appearing.

At first sight the Bibliography and Notes which take up almost a hundred pages of Warren and Wellek's study almost overpower us, and yet a good number of additions could easily be suggested in order to fill up considerable gaps. However, the authors' book is distinguished by their carefully discriminating method, especially in the chapters about literature and psychology, or in the analysis of poetic expression and imagery. The latter is by no means considered an essential requirement of every poem: 'There are good completely imageless poems'; against this see above, pp. 23ff.

If special attention is given to the so-called 'morphological' research in literature, which bring analogies into criticism and interpretation of poetry from Goethe-research and modern biology, then for many English students the well-established Scherer-method shines out again in its former glory, without the newly-won findings losing in value. These are rooted in the following considerations: every work of art has its *own* laws and contains the key to its explanations within *itself*; it is an *organism* in which the inner and outer form fit together into a *unity*. This is not so new as it sounds. We meet such thoughts in Novalis and others, but also in most recent criticisms, e.g. in T. S. Eliot, who, however, discards the Romantic conception of poetry as 'emotion recollected in tranquillity' (Wordsworth).

In the first two volumes of René Wellek's planned four-volume *History of Modern Criticism 1750-1950* (1955) a bold attempt has been made to offer a comparative study of European literary theories.

9

In 1946 Fritz Strich published *Goethe und die Weltliteratur*, dealing with Goethe's European message for Germany and Italy, France, England, Poland, Russia, etc. The origins of that basic work lie in F. Strich's preparatory studies, *Natur und Geist in der deutschen Dichtung* (in *Die Ernte*, 1926) and *Welt-literatur und vgl. Literaturgeschichte* (in Ermatinger's *Philosophie der Literaturwissenschaft*, 1930).

For F. Strich, poetry essentially knows no national

boundaries, for style reaches out beyond time and place like the movements: Romanesque-Gothic, Classic-Baroque, which are ageless. On the other hand, F. Strich does not overlook the national character of every literature (cf. the *German* Renaissance in contrast to the *Italian*) and the characteristic feature of each people, that receives its own supreme hour from the hand of Fate. The root of creative power lies deeply concealed in the heart of the poet's race, but the crown towers up into the eternal realm of humanity.

F. Strich justifiably calls a world's literature only that which has really transcended the horizon of its own nation and is treasured in other countries. Europe is not yet the world by a long way. The works that are all too bound up with time and fashion, e.g. much of modern Impressionism and Expressionism, do not belong to world literature (if to literature at all). The universally acceptable Classic literature has naturally a much easier way into world literature than Gothic or Baroque or Romantic works. How slowly authors of unique originality such as Hölderlin (practically not until the Hölderlin Centenary of 1943) and particularly H. von Kleist found recognition amongst a wider circle of intellectuals abroad!

The forces which nowadays more ruthlessly than ever seem too hostile to the world of poetry, are different from those in Goethe's or Hölderlin's time in as far as they overstress the supremacy of Science over Humane Studies in a measure hitherto unknown in European thought. The great interpreters of our century do not (as before) seem to be the poets, but the scientists and scholars, such as F. Gundolf, W. R. Worringer, O. Spengler, and the political administrators. The state, 'the coldest of all monsters' (Nietzsche), however, can improve only the surface of one's existence, not existence itself. Therefore A. Malraux (in his *Lettres aux Anglais*, 1941) calls upon the social and political reformers to reform themselves and to humanize the future State. Certainly our life is threatened by the steady process of depersonalization. F. Strich's distinguished successor in Berne University, Werner Kohlschmidt, takes up the theme of the cleavage between faith and civilization in his book of searching essays, which bears the significant title: "The Cleft World", *Die entzweite Welt*, 1953.

EPILOGUE II

The Poet and His Age

MAN'S MORTAL CLEAVAGE. THE MASS AGE

ALREADY BEFORE Martin Buber and Arthur Koestler, many modern writers had realized, especially under the influence of the happenings of the French Revolution and the July Revolution of 1830, that the tragedy of revolutionaries is that they achieve the opposite of that for which the most enlightened people sacrifice their lives.

Robespierre was Danton's hangman for the sake of the cause of revolution. In a rule of terror, fanaticism became rampant. Without idealizing his characters, Georg Büchner in *Dantons Tod* portrayed human combats and spiritual greatness in the fight for freedom in a world of satanic pain. But even in the year of the outbreak of the French Revolution and the publication of William Blake's *Songs of Innocence*, Schiller could in *The Artists* address man with these proud words:

> You, the most accomplished son of time, free through reason, strong through laws. . . .

Schiller, in contrast to Büchner, still saw in history the hard justice of the world and, at the end of a struggle, that of God's order on earth. In *Wallenstein* he sets the hero on the border of crime, for every man who concerns himself with deeds alone, often only too easily ensnares himself, in spite of noble motives, in fateful decisions and loses his moral conscience.

Goethe sought for the law in man's existence, in which he acknowledged a balance between that which lasts and that which changes. In the tragedies of Lessing, Goethe, Schiller and H. von Kleist the events of our lives take place in a sphere of accepted order in the world. But with Büchner, Grabbe, and Hebbel, the situation has changed; cf. also pp. 147ff.

Above all, Büchner's characters are, as we have seen, either ghosts or caricatures, or living dead or exceptions who are annihilated by the mechanism of political affairs. The guillotine appears to be the best surgeon for such suffering in a world of fools which Nietzsche later declared 'a godless world' and in which the question of guilt seems worthless gossip, for all life is suffering.

Schopenhauer's concept of 'our senseless existence' and the feeling of our inability to escape from it all is the malady of our own time; cf. also D. S. Savage: *The Withered Branch* (London, 1950) in which the disintegration of the consciousness of modern man is the main theme.

The intellect as the enlightening source of healing has lost much of its power to convince, if it is not spent altogether, for Plato's opinion has proved true once again: the animal impulses in man cannot be controlled by reason alone, but only by the introduction of noble feelings or strivings.

Together with the rejection of the Christian-Augustinian faith in the godly way of the world, there goes a change of opinion about the origin of Evil. The latter is no longer considered, as in Thomas, as a 'privatio boni', but for many, as with Schopenhauer, it is now something totally positive. Whilst the Christian Church attributes the guilt and the evil to sinful Man, and Goethe in his *Faust* makes it serve as a personal opposing power to Goodness, Evil itself, particularly in the literature of the last years of the nineteenth century, moves into the position of the evil Mephisto. So especially in the sombre display of human bestiality, as F. M. Dostoevsky paints it in the *Brothers Karamazov* (1880): 'An animal, even a so-called beast, can never be so cruel as a human-being, never so refined, so artistically cruel . . .' See also the world-known conversation of the Great Inquisitor with Christ, in which the ripening of freedom of body and soul is denied to Man, for Man can simply not carry the 'yoke of freedom'; he needs miracles, above all leadership and authority: 'Man is, and will remain slave' to whom the 'terrible gift of freedom' must only cause endless torments. In the chapter about the 'small Satan', the devilish Lisa, that very power of Evil reveals itself in demoniac sensuality, overweening pride, and human avarice.

253

Ivan represents love, which we human beings have received from Christ, as a 'miracle', an impossibility on earth, for Christ is God, and we are not. Dostoevsky recognizes with horror how much the satiated bourgeois is enslaved. In his Autobiography he breaks out into the despairing question: 'And why are there so many lackeys among the bourgeoisie?'

In *Raskolnikov* or *Guilt and Expiation* (*Schuld und Sühne*), the ill Raskolnikov, in feverish dreams, sees himself haunted as if by a disease: to him the world appears as a madhouse.

But just as, in the time of the 'aesthetic' view of life and the artist, Schiller once threw forth the memorable words, 'Violence annihilates Man', so Dostoevsky challenges our conscience to save our personality from destruction because every man, 'whatever he is and however deeply he has been degraded', demands respect for his dignity as a human being.

Today many worthy ideals of long standing, and even the terms 'Virtue', 'freedom', 'individuality', and 'happiness' have been transformed. In the same way one now regards the question of 'responsibility' from a different viewpoint, for if our existence is senseless, who can then pass sentence on the cynic? According to Dostoevsky, however, we still move in a sphere which has saved for itself the belief in the complete unity of all men, or at least the belief in life alone.

In Jean-Paul Sartre's novels, *Les chemins de la liberté*, and *L'âge de raison et le sursis*, we are on the ground of political anarchy, which has no outlet for the individual. The individual players and counter-players feel themselves senselessly pushed against each other or attracted to each other. Their only hope is to live young: 'I find that one ought not to live longer than thirty years; after this one becomes an "old mark" . . . after thirty years one is a dead man . . .' (*The Age of Reason*).

The element of political impersonality penetrates more and more into the novels and meanings of our time. The discussions are directed to, and in the mentality of, the masses. In the everyday hustle and bustle little time and energy remain to assert oneself against the many ensnaring demands of the public. Instead of quality quantity takes the lead, instead of 'the voice of individuals the claim of the masses, as is manifested in the modern mania for advertisement and sport records, in the

254

possessiveness of the spectators, in the inane curiosity of the philistine when confronted by wireless and television, cinema, and newspaper.

D. Bonhoeffer condemns that 'curiosity' and lack of concealment with these memorable words in *Ethics*:

> I believe that under the guise of 'honesty' something is here presented as being 'natural' which is really fundamentally a symptom of sin; it is really exactly like talking in public about sexual matters. The point is precisely that 'truthfulness' does not mean the disclosure of everything that exists. God Himself made clothes for man (Genesis 3,21); and this means that *in statu corruptionis* many things in man are to remain concealed, and that if it is too late to eradicate evil, it is at least to be kept hidden. Exposure is cynical; and even if the cynic appears to himself to be specially honest, or if he sets himself up to be a fanatical devotee of truth, he nevertheless fails to achieve the truth which is of decisive importance, namely, the truth that since the Fall there has been a need also for concealment and secrecy. For me the greatness of Stifter lies in the fact that he refrains from intruding upon the inner life of man; he respects its secret and looks at men, so to speak, only quite discreetly, always from without and not at all from within.

That merely curious intrusion into the mystery of life is a feature of our mass age. Moreover, the crowd serves as the shield of nameless deeds and emotions and can thus become a terror. Behind the force of numbers are hidden burdens of weakness or guilt. The coward only gathers courage when he knows that he does not stand alone and when he sees Big Brother keeping watch for him.

Who may speak of personal guilt when the roots of all our decisions seem to rest on economic principles and medical evidence? But neither the technical clinical triumphs nor the political experiments of modern power states can heal the collective hysteria with which C. G. Jung deals in the *Axion* (1951), for in both we are easily robbed of our inner freedom: 'wherever rationalistic materialism holds sway, the states become more like lunatic asylums than prisons'.

C. G. Jung places the responsibility for mass-neurosis upon the mortal cleavage of the human mind into the conscious and unconscious. The separation into a yang and yin, into a left and right, smashes the totality of every being. Yet Christ and sin, worthiness and unworthiness, cannot exist separately outside our being, but this duality thrives *within* us. The soul is made up of evil as well as of good. According to C. G. Jung's conception, God is not the Other Being, and we have within ourselves a reflexion of God's ways.

It is no mere coincidence that W. H. Auden has given the title *Age of Anxiety* to our period of collectivism. We might also call it the 'age of Existentialism', an epoch of Kierkegaard-ian solitude and Nietzschean atheism. With the dropping of the atom bomb on Hiroshima in August 1945 a new era opens. The fear of ever possible and threatening self-destruction and even of the end of European civilization and perhaps the whole of the human race, lurks like a deadly poison in the background of our efforts and dreams. That fear is anchored *inwardly* in us: through the consciousness of a feeling of despair, for which the most enlightened surgeon of the human soul can offer us no solution.

The knowledge of the futility of all labour and the possibility of the complete reversal of the universe into chaos in an apocalyptic sun-conflagration and moon-fall, such as is already prophesied to us in the sombre Old High German poem of the *Muspilli*, paralyses the wings of many modern authors. The Germanic myth of the deterioration of the cosmic order has an equally magnificent parallel in the Indian conception of the process of destruction, described by H. Zimmer in his *Myths and Symbols in Indian Art and Civilization*. 'The bonds of sympathy and love have dissolved; narrow egotism rules. Indistinguishable ninnies conglomerate to form a kind of sticky, unpalatable dough . . . the universe is ripe for dissolution. The cycle has complete itself. One day of Brahmā has elapsed. . . .'[1]

How can the artist survive nowadays? In Gottfried Benn's *Ptolemäer* (1949) our worn-out civilization is acridly criticized. Accordingly, history is depicted as a ground of mass exterm-ination, and the spirit of the West as a spirit of revolt, uprooting and unnaturalness. Life is shown as 'a spittoon into which the whole world spat . . . People today reckon neither with the past nor the future . . . The artist is the only person who gets

[1] Edited by J. Campbell (Pantheon Books, 1946), Chapter 3, *The Waters of Non-Existence*.

to the root of things, and who can make his own decisions about them.' Man, therefore, sees his justification only in the creation of existence by the artist. Thus G. Benn's 'aesthetic outlook' is a denial of Schiller's and Goethe's, who believe in the harmonious unfolding of the whole person in his development.

In G. Benn's view of the world the space for the writer has become very narrow. It banishes him to a depopulated region which—in a gruesome vision—one hundred and sixty years after Schiller's ode on *The Artists*, has been put before us by George Orwell in *1984*. According to Orwell (Eric Arthur Blair, 1903-1950) the State is a landscape of horror in which Big Brother, as propagandist and dictator, looks with his televisor right into the most intimate corners of home and heart just like a god, ever watching and probing. The individual has been dragged down, de-humanized, has lost all dignity and become an automaton. He lives haunted by humiliations, evil dreams and intrigues. In a world of this kind, Big Brother no longer needs a death warrant, for he can strip a human of his personality; he can fit him into a wire doll in his technically faultless state machine, or liquidate him within it. Every thought of independence is nipped in the bud; in fact, independent existence is in itself a crime. Here we recall Pascal's pronouncement: 'the acknowledgement of human misery without the acknowledgement of God must produce despair in man', and Thomas Mann's outburst against our barbarous age: 'Das letzte Halbjahrhundert sah eine Regression des Menschlichen, einen Kulturschwund der unheimlichsten Art. . . .' (Versuch über Schiller: Zum 150. Todestage des Dichters—seinem Andenken in Liebe gewidmet), 1955.

George Orwell's 'Utopia' belongs, like H. G. Wells's *Dr. Moreau*, to the most penetrating 'visions of the future' of our whole epoch. Here there is no oppressive piling-up of satire, as in Bernard Wolfe's *Limbo '90*, where are portrayed men of the year 1990, whose elite consists of 'Quadroamps' who amputate all their four limbs and substitute greater suppleness and power for them through plastic apparatus.

Is there still a spark of justification left for the poetic work? If W. B. Yeats before the First World War could say that the artist took on him the role of priest: artists are 'about to take upon their shoulders the burdens that have fallen from the shoulders of the priests,' it is now no longer a question of the priority between theology and art, but of the influence which science has on all aspects of our strivings and our daily problems.

Nevertheless, Yeats's statement, as much as Shelley's defence of the poets as the 'unacknowledged legislators of the world', still holds good. This cry is born from a passionate knowledge of the whole man, a cry similar to Hölderlin's judgement in *Hyperion* of the Germans as a people of specialists, craftsmen and thinkers: '. . . is it not like a battlefield, where hands and arms and limbs lie mangled on top of each other, while the life-blood flows away in the sand? . . .'

Whoever believes in the human race at all and in the validity and unity of the creative personality as against the crippled specialists of our day and the power-maniacs, will take Grillparzer's memorial at Beethoven's grave (autumn 1827) to heart:

> . . . If there is still a sense of unity amongst us in this shattered world, let us assemble at his grave. Before us there have been poets and heroes, singers and visionaries, towards whom stricken mankind can turn to realize their origin and goal. . . .

Index

Abraham a Santa Clara, 89
Aeschylus, 214, 244f.
aitheda, 63, 67
Albigenses, 48ff.
Aler, J. M. M., 196
Alker, E., 211
Andreas-Salomé, L., 169ff.
Angelloz, J. F., 178
Anzengruber, L., 92
Apocalypse, 35, 84
Ariosto, L., 47
Aristotle, 2, 17
Arnold, M., 229, 233
Atkins, S., 96, 99
Auden, W. H., 9, 12, 22f., 29, 169, 213, 256
Auerbach, E., 246f.
Aurelius, Marcus, 83
Averroes, Ibn Roshd-, 53f.
Avicenna, Ibn Sina-, 52f.

Bachofen, J. J., 209, 211
Bamberg statues, 44f., 59f.
Bateson, W. F., 16f, 231ff.
Baudelaire, C. P., 120, 165, 244f.
Becher, J., 165
Bédier, J., 66f.
Beethoven, 90ff., 258
Benn, G., 9, 40f., 165, 256f.
Bennett, E. K., 201
Bernard of Clairvaux, St., 55
Bernart de Ventadour, 52, 60
Béroul (*Tristran*), 62, 67ff.
Betz, M., 178
Blake, W., 8, 18f., 29, 121, 231, 252
Bluth, K. T., 141
Bodkin, M., 30
Böckmann, P., 249
Böhme, J., 35, 141, 216
Bondi, G., 185, 190
Bonhoeffer, D., 43, 255
Borchert, W., 154, 162
Bosch, H., 11
Bowra, C. M., 5, 201
Bowring, E. A., 32
Brentano, C., 217f.
Browning, Elizabeth Barrett, 94, 178
Brueghel, P., 11
Bruford, W. H., 249
Buddensieg, H., 214
Büchner, G., 147ff, 229, 252f.
Burckhardt, J., 211

Butler, E. M., 113, 169
Byron, Lord G. G., 34, 98, 203

Capellanus, A., 54f., 77
Carmina Burana, 54
Castiglione, B., 47
Catharism, 48ff.
Catullus, 135f.
Celtis, K., 88
Chèvrefeuille, 64
Chlumberg, H. v., 162
Chrestien de Troyes, 57, 60ff., 246
Cicero, 47, 81, 147
Clare, J., 22
Clark, K., 162
Claudius, H., 213
Claudius, M., 20, 40
Clemen, W. H., 24f., 238ff.
Closs, Hannah, 46, 51, 66, 82, 134
Crane, R. S., 227
Cukasaptati, 64
Curtius, E. R., 47, 240f., 243

Dante, 26, 40, 45, 57f., 96f., 137, 173, 244f.
D'Arcy, M. C., 102, 138
Dehmel, R., 165
Denomy, A. J., 52
Diarmaid and Grainne, 63, 67, 79f.
Dietmar v. Eist, 86
Dietrichstein, Countess Aline, 170f.
Disney, W., 11
Dobrée, Bonamy, 233
Dostoevsky, F. M., 164, 208, 253f.
Droste-Hülshoff, A. v., 36, 217f.
Dru, A., 164
Duhamel, G., 99
Dunlop, G., 148ff.

Edda, 1, 85
Eichendorff, J. Freiherr v., 10, 20, 40, 195
Eilhart v. Oberge, 60ff.
Eleanor of Poitiers, Queen, 55ff.
Eliot, T. S., 9, 12, 18, 22f., 35f., 44, 99f., 217, 226ff., 244
Empson, W., 18, 231, 240
Enright, D. J., 174, 196
Ernst, P., 187
Euripides, 214, 244

Faust, 31, 98f., 107ff., 153f., 214, 252

259

Fechner, G. T., 186
Fichte, J. G., 142ff.
Fin' amors, 48ff.
Forster, L., 221
Freud, S., 43f., 226f.
Frobenius, L., 209

Ganghofer, L., 169, 248
Gardner, Helen, 227
George, Stefan, 7, 20ff., 37, 44, 120f.,
    138, 166f., 185ff., 213f., 244f.
Gestalt, Organische, 31, 236
Gide, A., 15, 94, 99, 178
Goethe, J. W. v., 3ff., 8ff., 26, 30ff., 44,
    88ff., 93ff., 113f., 132, 134ff., 145f.,
    169f., 186ff., 202f., 213ff., 226, 231,
    236, 244, 252f.
Golther, W., 61, 66
Gottfried v. Strassburg, 20, 24, 46,
    57ff., 72ff., 194, 248
Grabbe, C. D., 147, 152ff., 252
Gray, T., 16, 231
Gregory, Lady Augusta, 2
Grillparzer, F., 13, 29, 83, 90ff., 154,
    206, 229, 258
Grosz, G., 11
Gundolf, F., 24, 100, 193, 196, 251
Gutzkow, K., 152

Hagelstange, R., 213f., 220f.
Hamburger, M., 113
Hartmann v. Aue, 48, 58, 82
Hauptmann, G., 92, 202ff.
Haussmann, W. H., 5
Hazm, Ibn, 52f.
Hebbel, F., 4, 36, 40, 149ff., 156
Hegel, G. W. F., 187, 243
Heidegger, M., 102, 237, 248
Heine, H., 8, 152f., 213
Heinrich v. Melk, 84f.
Heinrich v. Morungen, 45ff., 54, 57f.,
    195
Heiseler, Bernt v., 222ff.
Henn, T. R., 148
Herder, J. G., 124, 138, 200f., 226f.
Heuser, W. J., 210
Heym, G., 164ff.
Heynicke, K., 164
Hiebel, F., 141
Hodler, F., 189
Hölderlin, J. C. F., 3f., 19, 24ff., 34, 41,
    44, 101, 113ff., 134ff., 150f., 165ff.,
    191, 213ff., 228f., 239f., 251, 258
Hofmannsthal, Hugo v., 92f., 165, 185
Hohoff, C., 236
Holthusen, H. E., 18, 213f., 218ff.
Holz, A., 7, 92, 203
Homer, 227, 245ff.
Horace, 6, 81

Housman, A. E., 9
Hóvamól, 1
Huch, R., 14, 208
Hugo v. Montfort, 35
Hugo v. Trimberg, 87
Hulewicz, Witold v., 171, 183
Hull, R. C. F., 170, 177
Humboldt, Wilhelm v., 201
Huxley, A., 96, 108f.
Hyman, S., 226ff.

Ibsen, H., 149, 169, 203f.
Imrama, 62ff., 67
Inge, Dean, 99

Jacobi, F. H., 147
Jaeger, H., 248
Jalál-Uddîn-Rûmî, 134
Jaspers, K., 100, 104
Johann v. Saaz, 88
John, St., 117, 133
Jung, C. G., 226, 229, 255f.

Kafka, F., 104, 169
Kant, E., 31, 99, 123
Kassner, R., 180
Kayser, W., 247ff.
Keats, J., 15ff., 23, 36, 135, 169
Kierkegaard, S. A., 96ff., 150, 219, 256
Kleist, Heinrich v., 4, 44, 122, 149ff.,
    202, 211, 226f., 251f.
Klopstock, F. G., 6, 13, 120, 127, 166,
    213, 227
Knights, L. C., 248
Kohlschmidt, W., 243, 251
Krolow, K., 213ff.
Kürenberger, Der, 86
Kunisch, H., 236
Kurz, H., 76

Lange, V., 201
Langgässer, E., 11, 216ff.
Leavis, F. R., 9, 21, 233ff.
Lehmann, W., 216ff.
Leishman, J. B., 10ff. and *passim*, 14,
    113, 173f., 179ff.
Lenau, N., 26, 40
Lersch, H., 21
Lessing, G. E., 152ff., 202, 252
Leuthold, H., 13f.
Lewes, G. H., 98
Lewis, C. S., 96
Liliencron, D. v., 36, 40
Loomis, R. S., 57, 62ff., 66f., 71
Lunding, E., 235ff.
Luther, M., 227

MacNeice, L., 9, 15, 23, 27, 110
Malraux, A., 251

Manichaeism, 49ff., 218
Mann, T., 11, 13, 100, 223, 228, 257
Marie de France, 59
Maritain, J., 1
Marx, O., 125, 185
Mason, E. C., 175
Master Thief, 65
Mauriac, F., 96, 99
Maximilian I, Emperor, 88
May, K., 155
Melville, H., 29
Menschheits-Dämmerung, 164
Meyer, C. F., 7, 38ff., 228, 241
Michelangelo, 2, 8f., 96, 135, 241
Minder, R., 201
Minnesang, 43ff., 78ff., 85, 238
Mörike, E., 5, 15, 19, 27, 36, 213, 237
More, T., 47
Morgan, E. M., 82
Morris, Irene, 166
Morwitz, E., 125, 185
Mozart, 75, 89, 226
Müller, G., 236f.
Murry, J. Middleton, 17, 235
Muschg, W., 228
Muspilli, 84, 256

Naisi and Deirdre, 63, 79
Naumburg statues, 44f., 59f.
Neidhart v. Reuenthal, 87
Nelli, R., 50
Newstead, H., 65
Nibelungen, 85, 95
Nietzsche, F., 4, 8, 12ff., 40, 76, 92, 96,
    100f., 121, 149ff., 173, 193, 199, 211,
    219, 228, 251f., 256
Norton, H., 181
Novalis, 8, 35, 42, 76, 113, 122, 134ff.,
    213f., 217
Nykl, A. R., 52

Oppel, H., 236f.
Orwell, G., 257
Ortega y Gasset, 30
Ovid, 51ff., 81

Pancatantra, 64
Parry, J. J., 55
Paul, Jean, 6, 147
Paul, St., 5
Peacock, R., 113
Pfeiffer, A., 148
Pindar, 115, 125f., 130
Piontek, H., 17
Piquet, F., 77
Pius II, Pope (Enea Sylvio de' Picco-
    lomini), 88
Plato, 2, 47, 52ff., 125, 192, 197
Prawer, S. S., 118

Prokosch, F., 113
Prometheus, 43, 103, 189, 197
Proust, M., 137, 247

Quincey, T. de, 100

Ranke, F., 61f., 67, 99
Rasche, F., 213ff.
Read, H., 20, 23
Rehm, W., 236
Richards, I. A., 17, 229ff., 234f.
Richey, M. F., 57
Rickword, E., 234
Rilke, R. M., 4, 9ff., 34f., 41, 44, 92ff.,
    165f., 169ff., 178, 213, 216f, 226, 241
Roché, D., 50
Rodin, A., 27, 93, 169ff.
Rohde, E., 211
Rosegger, P., 92
Rudolf v. Ems, 72f, 81

Saar, F. v., 25, 92
Sachs, H., 69, 202, 238
Sartre, J.-P., 254
Savage, D. S., 33, 253
Schelling, F. W. J. v., 125, 141f., 149,
    200
Schiller, F., 3ff., 8, 20, 26ff., 44, 89, 99,
    104ff., 113f., 123ff., 134ff., 151ff.,
    186, 201ff., 214, 226, 246f., 252ff.
Schlaf, J., 25, 165
Schlegel, A. W., 4, 25, 143, 146
Schlegel, F., 4, 135, 143, 201
Schleiermacher, F., 113, 144
Schönherr, K., 92, 193
Schoepperle, G., 62f., 66f., 8of.
Schopenhauer, A., 4, 6, 76, 91, 106,
    139, 149, 187, 193, 244, 252
Schwedhelm, K., 213
Schwind, M. v., 15
Scott, W., 71, 98
Scrutiny, see F. R. Leavis
Sedlmayr, H., 11
Sencourt, R., 2
Seneca, L. A., 81, 244
Shakespeare, W., 9, 24f., 36, 45, 90, 93,
    96f., 148, 211, 238f., 244f., 248
Shelley, P. B., 2ff., 9, 26, 44, 98, 122,
    135, 205, 229, 258
Simrock, K., 76
Snell, R., 181
Sophocles, 13, 130, 214, 245
Souza, R. de, 19, 232
Spender, S., 184
Spengler, O., 187, 251
Spurgeon, C., 24, 239
Stammler, W., 236, 243, 249
Stern, J. P., 18
Stifter, A., 91, 107, 236, 252

Storm, T., 28, 37f.
Stoudt, J. J., 34
Strich, F., 247, 250f.
Strindberg, A., 193, 203
Swinburne, A. C., 9, 80, 233

Taine, H., 226f., 241, 247
Tannhäuser, 87
Thomas (*Tristan*), 60ff., 248, 252
Thoor, J., 213
Tieck, L., 136, 143, 150
Tolstoy, L., 170f., 174f., 203, 222, 229
Tomlinson, A. C., 235
Trakl, G., 23, 135, 164ff.
Tristan und Îsolt, 57ff.
Tymms, R., 134f.

Uhland, L., 26, 40, 55
Ulrich v. Lichtenstein, 87

Valéry, P., 5ff., 8f., 44, 94, 173f., 178
Vergil, 81, 244
Vischer, T., 3

Wagner, R., 5, 11, 25, 30, 43, 45, 76, 82, 87, 101, 139f.
Waldenses, 49
Walther von der Vogelweide, 45ff., 57, 86f., 91, 95, 194

Walzel, O., 14, 247ff.
Warner, R., 29
Warren, A., 249f.
Waters of Non-Existence, The, 256
Wedekind, F., 193
Weinheber, J., 40, 95
Wellek, R., 249f.
Wells, H. G., 257
Werfel, F., 11, 44, 95, 165
Wernher v. Gartenaere, 87
Wessobrunner Prayer, 84
West, C. B., 70
Wieland, C. M., 99, 248
Wiese, Benno v., 153, 157
Willoughby, L. A., 30
Wilson, E., 13, 228
Wilson, K., 20
Winckelmann, J. J., 107, 194, 201, 211
Wolfe, B., 257
Wolfram v. Eschenbach, 24, 46, 57f., 74f., 110, 194f.
Wydenbruck, N., 174

Yeats, W. B., 222, 257f.
Young, E., 35, 140

Zeydel, E. H., 73
Zimmer, H., 256
Zola, E., 193, 203, 208